DECEIVED

THE ASSAULT

OF

REVISIONIST

HISTORY

Also by Keith Hoar

Edge of Madness

DECEIVED

THE ASSAULT

OF

REVISIONIST

HISTORY

Keith A. Hoar
B.S.BA;   M. Min.

Second Edition

Keith Hoar

Published by Zhetosoft Publications

All Scripture quotations are from the Authorized King James Version of the Bible.

Jacket design by Keith Hoar

ISBN(13): 978-0-9994590-3-4 (paperback)
ISBN(10): 0-9994590-3-1 (paperback)

Acknowledgments

It would be impossible to thank all those who knowingly or unknowingly had a part in making this book possible. If I fail to acknowledge anyone it is simply a failure on my part and in no way is it a measure of the value of his or her contribution.

The first edition of this book began, in part, as a Master's Thesis submitted to Louisiana Baptist Theological Seminary as the final requirement for the degree – Master of Ministry. The second edition title has been changed to more accurately reflect the revised premise of the book.

First I would like to thank Pastor Troy Dorrell for his valuable assistance during the early development of the original idea for this book and for his scholarly comments on several early drafts. His scholarship and helpful suggestions proved to be immensely valuable.

I would like to specifically mention: veteran missionary C. Barton Carter for his review of the final draft of the first three chapters of this book and for his many valuable comments; Tom Peeler, Lt. Col. USMC retired, for his friendship and for his early draft review and enlightening comments and suggestions; and Sherrie Davidson for her excellent efforts in providing corrections in grammar and punctuation. A very special thank you to Hal Capshaw for the loan of an intriguing book that was instrumental in the development of the idea for this book and for his insightful comments and suggestions on the final draft version of this book.

I must also thank my loving wife, Kathie, who read many draft versions of this book and provided many, many helpful comments and suggestions that have greatly improved its readability. But especially for her unwavering support, encouragement, and love.

Above all, I must thank Almighty God for His infinite grace and mercy. Without His inspiration and His instilling within me an insatiable hunger for truth, this book simply would not exist.

Keith Hoar

Preface to the Second Edition

In order to reach a larger and more diverse audience, the title of the second edition has been changed to better reflect the vital premise of the book.

In addition to the title change, additional material has been added and some content has been moved closer to the front of the book to make it more visible. A publishing company that performed an assessment on the first edition manuscript said, "Some of the material you've presented is surprising and compelling. Something 'new' for most readers, I would expect!" In addition, some language and expressions have been changed to better express the thought intended where necessary.

This second edition is offered with the hope that students of American political and church history will honestly face the alarming fact that in the late twentieth century and in the early twenty-first century the *true facts* of America's history are either being ignored, minimized, or in some instances, deliberately altered to suit the ideological biases of those that in this book will be called *historical revisionists*.

It is the firm conviction of many, this author included, that an enormous and sinister battle is underway that threatens to destroy the Christian heritage of this great country. A battle that, sadly, is currently being lost.

In this second edition, additional, recent material has been added that shines the light of truth upon the abyss where America now finds itself.

May God enlighten all that read the words of this book to the great and terrifying danger that threatens to eradicate America's Christian heritage from the pages of history, and by His Grace may the knowledge of the *true facts* of America's Christian heritage increase.

Holton, Kansas   Keith A. Hoar

Keith Hoar

Table of Contents

List of Tables

Keith Hoar

"The death of democracy is not likely to be an assassination from ambush. It will be a slow extinction from apathy, indifference, and undernourishment."

Robert M. Hutchins
Great Books of the Western World,
Vol. I, 1952, pg. 80

"I am well aware of the Toil and Blood and Treasure that it will cost Us to maintain this Declaration, and support and defend these States. Yet through all the Gloom I can see Rays of ravishing Light and Glory. I can see that the End is worth more than all the Means."

John Adams letter to Abigail Adams
on the passing of the Declaration of
Independence, July, 3, 1776

Keith Hoar

Chapter One: Erosion of a Dream

If liberty means anything at all, it means the right to tell people what they do not want to hear.

George Orwell

Erosion

Freedom is never more than one generation away from extinction. We didn't pass it to our children in the bloodstream. It must be fought for, protected, and handed on for them to do the same, or one day we will spend our sunset years telling our children and our children's children what it was once like in the United States where men were free.

Ronald Reagan
Address to the annual meeting of the
Phoenix Chamber of Commerce - March 30, 1961

# of a Dream

Something Went Terribly Wrong

"America! America! God shed His grace on thee." So goes the middle of the first verse of the once-adored song "America The Beautiful". Until somewhere around the middle of the twentieth century, those stirring words would evoke a sense of pride and thankfulness in most Americans. Whether it was pride in their country, or gratitude for the things they possessed, or their hope for a bright and promising future, the outlook of the majority of the citizens in America was profoundly optimistic.

America *was* a better place to live. Even in the face of some serious setbacks and numerous wars, there had been improvement in most Americans' lives. Improvement that they could point to in their own lifetimes. Intellectually, technologically, financially, and medically; all facets of American life were being revolutionized. One single sentiment stretched all across America. That sentiment was optimism.

In 1968, on the opening page of his book, *Redeemer Nation*, Ernest Lee Tuveson wrote that three centuries earlier in America (circa 1668) a hope he called 'Christian optimism' sprang up in the colonies. It was an optimism that revealed hope about the future of humanity and of human society.[1] However, two years before the publication of Mr. Tuveson's book there was an address given on BBC that spoke of a 'Christian pessimism' that began to arise during the middle of the 1960s.

From the end of World War II until the mid-1960s there *was* an American Dream and it *was* coming true for thousands of Americans.

Then, quite suddenly, something seemed to go terribly wrong. An American president was assassinated. America was dragged into a military, police action (aka war) that threatened to fracture the country. America's youth, disillusioned and angry, began to

---

[1] Ernest Lee Tuveson, *Redeemer Nation*, (Chicago & London, University of Chicago Press, 1974), 1.

revolt on a scale never seen before. They rebelled against any and all levels of authority, plunging into the mindless void of free love, mind-altering drugs, and psychedelic rock music. As America's youth become more and more discontented and disengaged, they began praising brutal, socialistic dictators. Angry crowds of rioting youths parroted the communistic slogans being chanted by violent radicals.

The most devastating breakdown of all was America's loss of its moral compass. The family, the fabric of America, was blowing apart at the seams. The American family, began deteriorating at an alarming rate. All over America, divorce was becoming the norm. Sexual promiscuity was not just on the rise, it was rampant. The government and the public education system, failing to grasp the severity of the problem, did nothing more than stick a band-aid on the symptoms. In actuality, the government exacerbated the problem by accommodating America's escalating sexual promiscuity through legalized abortion, permissive sex education, and access to better birth control methods. Some states and school districts went so far as to provide *free* condoms to students. Not just to high school students but, unbelievably, to middle school students. America was in serious trouble!

What happened to the *American Dream*? Just a few short years earlier, the mood had been so much different. America was confident. America was proud. America was filled with optimism and hope for the future. Then, everywhere you looked there was

despair, anger, rage, and revolt. The people blamed the schools and the politicians. The schools and the politicians blamed the people. There was much wringing of hands and demanding more and better solutions, but nothing was accomplished. What happened in the span of a few short years? Why did America's optimism so rapidly turn to despair, anger, rage, and revolt? What suddenly went so terribly wrong?

Where there had once been confidence and determination there was now uncertainty and a feeling of helplessness. Rather than attempting to identify the *real* problem, conservatives blamed the liberals, liberals blamed the conservatives, parents blamed the schools, the schools blamed the parents, and the young people blamed *everyone* over thirty. Literally, everyone blamed everyone else. There was finger pointing and blame all around. Soon the finger pointing turned into apathy and capitulation.

Most Americans, quickly tiring of the steady stream of depressing newscasts, simply gave up and quit asking what happened. They shook their heads, and said, "It's a sign of the times." Hoping it would all just *go away*, they went back to their lives and gave little thought to what was happening to their once proud America!

The title indicates this book is about the assault of '*Revisionist History*'. That is true. There is a lengthy discussion of the untruths being propagated by the '*historical revisionists*' regarding the discovery, development, and display of America's Christian heritage in Chapters Five and Six. Then in Chapter Seven there is a discussion of the dismantling of America's Christian heritage.

Before detailing some of the untruths being disseminated, it is crucial to reflect on and *understand* the current chaos in which America finds itself. The final chapters will reveal how individuals (the revisionists) have chipped away at the Christian motives that drove the colonists, early settlers, and Founders to risk life and fortune to found this great country. A thorough understanding of the turmoil, disorder, and the looming threat America faces, will give the facts in the final chapters much more impact. As you consider how the distortion of the facts of history has caused many, especially impressionable youths, to question the motives of the explorers that discovered America and even America's Founders, it will become quite clear how evil men, whose express intention is to destroy America and its system of capitalism, have accomplished many of their stated goals. Hopefully, as you read those final chapters with the current situation in mind, you will be able to say, "I understand '*what happened*'. I see how America has reached the state it is in."

Some recently uncovered explanations for the current pessimism, anger, rebellion, and apathy, and the evidence supporting those explanations, will be presented in the final chapters. But first, some alarming information and facts that many individuals would rather not hear.

What They Do Not Want To Hear

George Orwell's quote that appears on this chapter's opening page bears repeating here: "If liberty means anything at all, it means the right to tell people what they do not want to hear."[2] The concept affirmed in that quote is critically important as this book begins to set out the facts that will answer the question asked earlier, "What happened?" To many, the facts behind 'what happened', as detailed on the following pages, will be shocking, outrageous, and, worst of all, unwelcome and unwanted.

Drawing from research in economics, psychology, and sociology, Carnegie Mellon University's George Loewenstein, Russell Golman, and David Hagmann authored a lengthy paper titled *Information Avoidance*, illustrating how people deliberately avoid information that threatens their happiness and/or sense of wellbeing. Referring to that article, David Hagmann, a Ph.D. student in the Department of Social and Decision Sciences, said, "Bombarding people with information that challenges their cherished beliefs — the usual strategy that people employ in attempts at persuasion — is more likely to engender defensive avoidance than receptive processing."[3]

The 'cherished beliefs' that Mr. Hagmann spoke of could also be defined as 'cultural biases'. When considering a person's beliefs, not all beliefs are equally important. There may be no particular emotional attachment to certain beliefs. However, other beliefs may carry significant emotional importance and, therefore, are held very dear, making it quite painful to alter or abandon them. Those beliefs would be considered 'cherished beliefs'. There are many reasons why certain beliefs would carry special

---

[2] George Orwell, https://www.orwellfoundation.com/the-orwell-foundation /orwell/essays-and-other-works/the-freedom-of-the-press/ (Accessed 6/11/2018)
[3] David Hagmann, Carnegie Mellon University , *Information Avoidance: How People Select Their Own Reality,* https://www.cmu.edu/news/stories/ archives/2017/march/information-avoidance.html (Accessed 6/12/2018)

emotional importance to an individual. Those reasons are numerous and varied and are beyond the scope of this book.

The crucial point to understand here is that most beliefs, especially the 'cherished beliefs', are seldom, if ever, isolated. The 'cherished beliefs' either support or challenge the validity of other beliefs, and they, in turn, may be supported or challenged by other beliefs. If an individual were forced to doubt, alter, or give up a 'cherished belief', in the face of strong evidence against that belief, the emotional impact of such a shifting of beliefs could be severe and life altering. Rather than deal with the emotional stress, the individual faced with such a distasteful situation may choose to minimize, sidestep, or totally ignore the unwanted information even though it is *valid information*. The *valid information* referred to here is that information which is *true* and *corroborated*.

The article *Information Avoidance* states, "A straightforward implication is that valid information should never be actively  avoided, except for situations in which ignorance confers a strategic advantage."[4] The concept of *information avoidance* is not a matter of simply not looking at the information. There are many tactics people use to avoid information they find distasteful or threatening. For example, people may form inconsistent or flawed conclusions from the information due to their firmly held biases ('cherished beliefs'). They may divert their attention away from, conveniently forget, simply ignore, or outright refuse to hear information that would challenge their beliefs.

A dangerous condition arises when valid information is *actively avoided* because of a perceived strategic advantage. As with 'cherished beliefs', the rationale behind the perceived advantages are greatly varied and beyond the scope of this book. The key issue is that *valid information*, otherwise known as *facts* or the *truth*, is deliberately ignored.

In his book titled, *Proper Studies*, the English critic and novelist Aldous Huxley said, "Each person will choose the

---

[4] Golman, Russell, David Hagmann, and George Loewenstein, *Information Avoidance*, Journal of Economic Literature, Vol. 55, No. 1 2017, 96.

rationalization which suits his prevailing or passing mood."[5] That perfectly expresses the act of someone deliberately ignoring facts because of their 'mood' or 'cherished belief'. What would drive someone to deliberately ignore facts? For this book, that would take place when someone was confronted with *valid information* that challenged a strongly held belief. As this section's title suggests, the information that will likely challenge one or more of an individual's 'cherished beliefs' is something 'they do not want to hear'. A few pages later in his book, Mr. Huxley wrote, "Facts do not cease to exist because they are ignored."[6]

The truthfulness of Mr. Huxley's statement is obvious and inescapable. Facts are facts. Truth is truth. Truth is simply *'telling it like it is'*. Truth is the way things *really* are or were. Any other perception or view or opinion is wrong no matter what the motivation or perceived 'strategic advantage' may be.

The only way to avoid the truth of history is to ignore it, to misrepresent it, or to alter it. The everyday individual on the street will likely be guilty of the first. He or she will simply ignore the facts by turning a blind eye to them. The 'historians' who wish to report history the way they 'wish it was', a history that does not challenge any of their ideological biases or 'cherished beliefs', will be guilty of misrepresenting, altering, or *revising* history. Hence, they have been assigned the label *'historical revisionists'*.

Be aware: The information that follows will most assuredly be 'what they do not want to hear'! Perhaps, dear reader, what follows may also be 'what you do not want to hear'. If that is the case, resist the urge to simply dismiss or ignore the information that follows. Give the true facts of history and the individuals that lived that history an opportunity to speak for themselves before you form a final conclusion.

Stunned Amazement

Several weeks into the initial effort of gathering and organizing content for the first edition of this book, the original premise of the

---

[5] Aldous Huxley, *Proper Studies*, (London, Chatto and Windus, 1927), 195.

[6] Ibid, 205.

book was abandoned. A rapidly growing sense of astonishment began to develop as article after article was discovered that exposed an escalating breakdown of the traditional family unit and also a rapid increase in immorality that was taking place in America.

While collating information from dozens of books to construct an outline, an opportune discovery pointed to what might be a partial answer to the question, "What happened?" Was there a driving force that could explain, at least in part, the escalating immorality and violence afflicting America? Yes there was. One book said many Americans no longer believe that we are *one nation under God*. Some do not think about it, some have forgotten it, and some totally reject the notion that America is one nation under God. America is on the verge of abandoning its Christian heritage. Much more information to amplify and support that claim will be offered in later chapters.

One single article containing a lengthy quote attributed to Christopher Columbus put an immediate and final halt to further development of the original premise and outline of the first edition. Numerous *historical revisionists*, and others, claimed, with increasing influence, that America was not and is not a Christian nation and America did not have a Christian founding. The quote attributed to Christopher Columbus completely contradicts the 'revisionists' claims. Here is a small snippet from that quote:

> "It was the Lord who put into my mind (I could feel his hand upon me) the fact that it would be possible to sail from here to the Indies. All who heard of my project rejected it with laughter, ridiculing me. There is no question that the inspiration was from the Holy Spirit, because He comforted me with rays of marvelous inspiration from the Holy Scriptures."[7]

The shocked reaction upon reading those words was, "What?" The entire quote, printed in a little known newspaper, was read two additional times to be certain it had not been misread or

---

[7] Christopher Columbus, Roberto Rusconi translator, *Book of Prophesies*, (Berkeley, California: University of California Press, 1997), 67.

misunderstood. With each reading the reaction was the same -

stunned amazement. Did Columbus really believe that? Did Columbus really say those words? All we had ever been taught in school said Columbus had discovered America *by accident* while trying to sail to the Indies. Why was there no mention of Columbus's faith contained in the history texts? Where did those words come from?

The public school system during the last half of the twentieth century made no mention whatsoever of Columbus's faith, let alone that he believed he had been given that mission by God Himself. Quite the contrary. Many books and articles called him a *mysterious* figure. An official United States Government website called him a *greedy imperialist.* Several biography and history websites said his intent was fame and fortune. A well-known encyclopedia website said he was *deeply flawed.* However, not a single one of those websites listed even one reference to support their assertions.

The citation for Columbus's quote in the newspaper article mentioned above indicated Columbus's quote came from a book written by Columbus himself titled *Book of Prophecies,* which had not been translated into English until sometime after 1971. A lengthy search of available library resources revealed just one copy of the book, published in 1997, existed in the entire United States at the University of California - Berkeley. Much additional information concerning Columbus's words, his faith, and his reason for sailing to the New World appears in a later chapter (see page 108).

Immediately, the first edition's premise switched to one of discovering the Christian founding and heritage of America, the propagation of that heritage, and the continuing attempts to rewrite history and *deceive* the American people into believing America is not and was not founded as a Christian nation.

Let The Truth Speak

In the twenty-first century, Americans are suffering from information and sensory overload. Persuasive advertisers, amazing new products, and innovative ideas clamor for America's attention twenty-fours a day. The world-wide web with its ubiquitous search engines has only intensified the deluge of information. Today's consumer, whether a student searching for reference material for an assignment or report or a consumer searching for products or information, has been conditioned to expect results immediately. A few simple keystrokes can literally put thousands of results at the consumer's fingertips in seconds.

Not all of the available information is reliable. Far from it. A large portion of the information is inaccurate and some is outright false. A significant portion of the articles returned by an internet search contains no citations whatsoever that point to a source of primary information or how the author reached his or her conclusions. That may be acceptable for general information, but it is **NOT** acceptable for '*supposed*' scholarly articles and it is especially **NOT** acceptable for the reporting of history.

To fully understand and evaluate articles and books in the social sciences, natural sciences, and especially history, you *must* be able to differentiate between primary and secondary research. Specifically, the source material that was used to form conclusions or to present 'facts' must be identified. The distinction between primary and secondary research illustrates the degree to which an author is removed from the event or events being described. The difference being whether the author is reporting first hand impressions and experiences or if the author is merely repeating the opinions of others, using material which may be second hand and unverified.

A description of these two information sources follows:

- **Primary Sources**: These are accounts of an event, written by someone who experienced or witnessed the event being reported. They are original documents and are not quotes or material copied from other documents or accounts. These documents include books, diaries, letters, memoirs, journals, speeches, and manuscripts.

- **Secondary Sources**: These are documents that restate information from primary sources. Therefore, they are at least one step removed from the actual events being reported. Secondary sources often interpret, speculate upon, and/or propose differing conclusions regarding the events reported in primary sources. These documents may take the same form as primary sources.

When evaluating primary or secondary sources, to determine the value and *accuracy* of the material being considered, you *must* ask the following essential questions:

- How does the author know the details (persons, places, names, dates, times, etc.)?
- Was the author present at the event?
- Where did the information come from: public record, personal experience, or eyewitness accounts?
- Is the information second-hand; reported or written by others who did not witness the event(s)?
- Are the author's conclusions based on evidence or opinion?

The foregoing explanation of the terms primary and secondary sources was necessary. The stated goal of the research behind this book was to determine the '*true facts*' of history regarding whether America, in fact, does possess a Christian heritage. A second and equally important goal was to examine and then substantiate or refute, if necessary, the claim that several critical events in history coincided with a sudden and rapid increase in America's immorality.

Far from diligently gathering and presenting true and valid information regarding the history of America's founding and its Christian heritage, *historical revisionists* have ignored, dismissed, removed, and/or revised the actual events of history. A large portion of the *revisionist* documents and articles examined for this book could only be *loosely* classified as secondary research in that they contained no citations pointing to *any* source material. A surprising number of the documents and articles that did contain citations to primary sources were not faithful to the original sources. When quoted material is placed inside double quotes, it is expected to be an *exact* quote of the original. The quoted material in those books and articles was checked using the exact book cited, based on author, volume number, publisher, and date.

This book does not use any secondary quotes, except for several quoted conversations reported from television interviews that are no longer available. Using verified material is critically important as any valid history of America's founding must come from the mouths and pens of the people who lived that history. As is stated elsewhere, "The '*true facts*' of history really do matter and the truth that establishes those facts is paramount."

> Nothing is easier than self-deceit. For what each man wishes, that he also believes to be true.
> DEMOSTHENES
> Third Olynthiac, paragraph 19,
> Minor Public Speeches.

The quote above from Demosthenes, a contemporary of Plato and Aristotle, who lived from 384 BC until 322 BC, rings as true today as it did some twenty-three hundred years ago. The things a person wishes (aka their 'cherished beliefs'), they also believe to be true. When an individual believes something to be true without allowing the evidence to speak simply because he or she wishes it to be so, that belief is then, at best, an opinion and, at worst, it is a lie and not a fact.

Writers, historians included, are often guilty of mixing fact and opinion. Some would say it is not always easy to tell whether something is based on facts or whether it is only someone's particular viewpoint or opinion. In view of that, it is important to read with a questioning mind. Just because someone says something is true – it does not

> Everyone is entitled to their own opinion, but not their own facts.
> Daniel Patrick Moynihan

make it true, regardless of how impressive their credentials may be. That is especially true with regard to the subject of history.

No matter how much you may wish to avoid the truth and no matter how much the truth may fly in the face of an opinion or 'cherished beliefs', it is still the truth. Truth absolutely *must* be accepted for what it is.

Former New York Senator Daniel Patrick Moynihan, politician, sociologist, and adviser to U.S. President Richard Nixon, is quoted as saying, "Everyone is entitled to their own opinion, but not their own facts."[8]

Mr. Moynihan's statement certainly seems logical and correct. Why then do those who would revise history, whether it be done deliberately or unconsciously, report erroneous or distorted versions of history? A quote from the American diarist, essayist, and novelist Anais Nin answers that question quite succinctly: "When others asked the truth of me, I was convinced it was not the truth they wanted, but an illusion they could bear to live with."[9]

 The implication behind that quote speaks to the topic of *information avoidance* discussed earlier. Because of ideological biases, also known as 'cherished beliefs', *historical revisionists* minimize or avoid the *true* and *corroborated* facts to produce a version of history that they '*can bear to live with*'; a history that aligns with their worldview and does not challenge their closely held beliefs (aka biases).

The critical task for this book, when reporting history as it relates to America's Christian heritage, is separating the truth of history from assumption and opinion. To accomplish that task, primary sources only were used on the subject of America's founding and heritage in order to allow the eyewitnesses that lived and produced that history to speak for themselves. They were individuals driven by faith, seeking a new land where they could live in freedom. The voices of those brave men and women, many separated from families, that embarked on a hazardous journey fraught with great dangers and many unknowns, must be heard.

---

[8] Timothy J. Penny, *Facts Are Facts,* National Review, September 4, 2003.

[9] Anais Nin, *The Diary of Anais Nin: Vol. 1 (1931-34),* (New York & London: Harcourt, Brace, Jovanovich, 196), 6 .

The truth from *their* mouths *must* be allowed to speak. Any other choice would be to dismiss the toil, struggle, and lives that were sacrificed to plant the seeds of freedom. It is from those sacrifices that America's freedom spread and now exists.

Untruth, falsehood, and lies will not be overcome by mere denunciation. Neither will untruth be overcome by eloquent criticism. Such criticism certainly has its place. However, it must be accompanied by truth. The Scottish philosopher, essayist, and historian Thomas Carlyle said the truth will not be preserved by the act of mangling and slashing asunder the false.[10]

The oft quoted witticism, "Yet it is far better to light the candle than to curse the darkness." first appeared in 1907 in a sermon preached by W. L. Watkinson as recorded in *The Supreme Conquest and other Sermons Preached in America*.[11] Rather than cursing the untruth of revisionist history, this book will light the candle of truth. Now begins an inspiring journey to shine the bright light of truth upon fairy tales, opinions, and deception regarding the Christian founding and heritage of America.

> It takes two
> to speak the truth:
> one to speak and
> another to hear.
>
> Henry David Thoreau
> A Week on the Concord
> and Merrimack Rivers

Before focusing specifically on the threat of *'revisionist history'*, chapters two, three, and four will expose some of the sweeping changes that have led America to the place where it finds itself at the beginning of the twenty-first century, where radical, destructive forces have altered political and societal norms.

The last three chapters of this book will detail the Christian influence behind the discovery of America. Then the Christian intent behind the founding of America and of the great *'experiment'* called the Constitution. Then follows a discussion of the dismantling of Americas Christian heritage due to influences of

---

[10] Thomas Carlyle, *The Works of Thomas Carlyle And Miscellaneous Essays,* Vol. XXVIII, (London: Chapman And Hal, 1899), 166.
[11] W. L. Watkinson, D.D., LL.D., *The Supreme Conquest and other Sermons Preached in America*, (New York & Chicago, Fleming H. Revell Company, 1907), 218.

affluence and a growing modernism. Those final chapters are based on the words of the brave men and women who sacrificed their fortunes and their lives; literally everything they had.

Only through the revealing of the truth of history, shall lies and untruth diminish, grow pale, and fade away.

Will you not join the journey? Will you not let the truth speak?

Chapter Two: Winds of Change

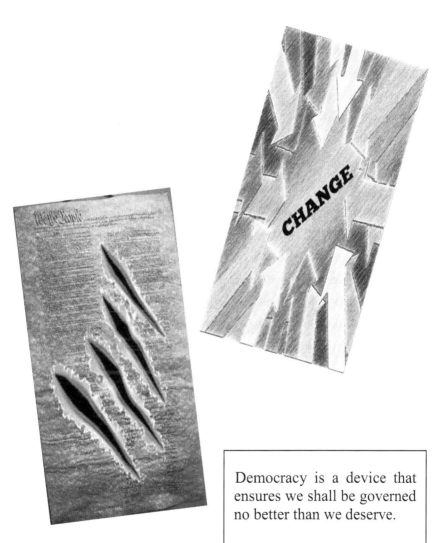

Democracy is a device that ensures we shall be governed no better than we deserve.

George Bernard Shaw

Winds of

> So long as the people do not care to exercise their freedom, those who wish to tyrannize will do so; for tyrants are active and ardent, and will devote themselves in the name of any number of gods, religious and otherwise, to put shackles upon sleeping men.
>
> Voltarine de Cleyre
> Anarchism & American Traditions, 1932, p. 12.

Change

America - Wearing Away

The term *Winds of Change*, used as the title of this chapter, characterizes a tendency or trend; something that disrupts and destroys; destructive forces that have the power to change things. For the narrative that follows, the forces in view are the predominant trends which alter political and societal norms. As was revealed in the previous chapter, the decade of the 1960s experienced the most dramatic moral change in America's history. The 1960s with its affection for drugs, and the distorted reality it produced, had an enormously destructive effect upon society, especially upon its weakest and most naive members.

Beginning in the mid-1960s, hundreds of thousands of teenagers left home chanting their much loved mantra of the day, "turn on, tune in, and drop out". The generation of that decade and those that followed exhibited increased rebellion against authority at all levels. Only intensifying that upheaval, university professors in America championed that new *freedom* and its freethinking philosophy as liberating and beneficial. However, the effects were anything but beneficial. The effects were clearly destructive, contributing to an overall moral decline.

Rather than cite study after study along with their disturbing statistics, the objective here is to identify the force or forces behind the change and then answer the question: where has that dramatic change led America in the twenty-first century?

Consider where America now stands after years of revolt and rebellion. The years of revolt and riots did not result in an immediate transformation. They resulted in a gradual '*wearing away*' of America's moral values.

Mr. Marion Smith, Executive Director of the Victims of Communism Memorial Foundation in Washington, D.C., wrote in May of 2014 that a book which offered purposeful admiration of Karl Marx's book *Das Kapital* was the bestselling nonfiction book in America.[1] The book Mr. Smith was referring to is Thomas

---

[1] Marion Smith, *Thomas Piketty And The Coming Marxist Moment*, https://thefederalist.com/2014/05/29/thomas-piketty-and-the-coming-marxist-moment/ (Accessed 06/21/2018).

Piketty's book, *CAPITAL In The Twenty-First Century*. It is not possible to verify what the book's sales rank was in 2014. However, a check of the book's sales rank on June, 21, 2018, at the nation's largest online book retailer revealed that the book ranked #3, #4, and #5 in three subcategories in the overall category Business & Money.

Mr. Piketty's book was examined to determine if it supported Marxism and its ultimate result Communism. Mr. Piketty, a French economist and economic advisor to several Socialist Party candidates, exhibits an unconditional belief in wealth redistribution. It should then come as no surprise that in his book Mr. Piketty would praise the 'Soviet experiment' for unshackling Capitalism's "chains along with the yoke of accumulated wealth."[2] The book's title is an indisputable admiration of Marx's book of nearly the same title. Piketty believes taxation is not about funding government. Rather, taxation is an instrument for leveling society across economic classes.

During the cold war, just a few short decades ago, it would have seemed unthinkable that such a book would make its way to the top of the nation's bestseller list. The success of Piketty's *CAPITAL* is not a trivial aberration. No, not at all. America is witnessing an exploding enthusiasm for Marxist manifestos like Piketty's *CAPITAL*. In America, it seems there is a troubling and *deliberate* amnesia regarding Communism's history.

Less than a generation ago, just twenty-nine short years, everyone watched as the Berlin wall came crashing down. Everyone thought, or wanted to think, Communism was dead or at least dying. However, the growing appeal of Socialist and Communist propaganda contained in Mr. Piketty's book confirms that Communism is anything but dead. This is especially true among America's younger generations, amply documented elsewhere in this book. To believe Communism is dead and no longer a threat is a seriously dangerous illusion.

So, once again the question is asked, *"What happened in America?"*

---

[2] Thomas Piketty, *CAPITAL In The Twenty-First Century*, Arthur Goldhammer translator, (Cambridge, MA, Belknap Press of Harvard University, 2014), 531.

Mysterious Events

Many hundreds of hours were spent gathering statistical data related to America's decline in morality. The results of the analysis of that data will be discussed in detail in the next chapter. As the raw data was organized, analyzed, and summarized, several gnawing questions began to emerge. Could a source for the *momentum* behind the rapid decline in morality be identified. Where did it originate? Could the decline be tied to a specific time and/or specific events? Could any organization, party, or movement be associated with the decline?

Originally, those nagging questions remained unanswered as they were considered to be beyond the original premise of this book. However, all efforts to overlook and dismiss those questions were unsuccessful because those questions were critically important. Those questions demanded answers. During the search for raw data, an article was discovered that described a U.S. Supreme Court case. The article suggested a potential source, or sources, where answers to those nagging questions could be found. The article also contained several trend charts representing the decline in America's moral attributes presented in a graphic format.

Deeper research and analysis of the source data referenced in the article that was used to create the charts proved fruitless. Many of the tables and charts contained incomplete data, charts that began or ended at different years; or the underlying data had different aggregation levels, missing year(s), different data types, and dissimilar categories, etc. A quest was undertaken to identify, accumulate, and organize verifiable, raw source data to produce accurate charts. The key word here is: *verifiable*. The U.S. Government sources referenced in the article and a number of additional government sources, identified during the gathering of data, were used as sources. The actual 'raw' data that was gathered, including citations, can be found in the Appendix.

The search turned out to be far more complex and time consuming than anticipated. In excess of five hundred hours were expended locating, verifying, gathering, consolidating, and analyzing the raw government statistics from ten separate, official U.S. Government agencies for the six selected 'indicators' of America's declining morality. The six morality 'indicators' to be presented later in this book are listed below:

- Family Stability
- Married vs. Unmarried Households
- Percentage of Births to Unwed Girls
- Sexually Transmitted Disease
- Educational Achievement
- Violent Behavior

Great care was taken to be certain the supporting raw data was complete and present for all years for each one of the six 'indicators', Additionally, all values were required to have the same attributes to allow for accurate aggregation and creation of trend charts. The resulting trend charts will be displayed and explained in the following chapter.

Even after the raw data was gathered and analyzed, there was still a missing element in answering the questions posed earlier in this chapter. The trend charts unquestionably revealed an alarming trend in America's morality, but still the underlying stimulus for the *sudden* increase in decline was missing.

The missing component and inspiration for this chapter arose during the viewing of a video documentary titled "*AGENDA: Grinding America Down*", loaned to me by a friend. Mr. Curtis Bowers, producer and editor of the documentary, made a remarkably compelling statement at the beginning of his introduction. He said, "Since 1960 the whole culture has been transformed."[3] That statement certainly agreed with the trends revealed in the raw data gathered from the U.S. Government agencies. It also agreed with the dramatic changes taking place in the 1960s described earlier.

As the introduction to the documentary continued, Mr. Bowers, and others, made some equally riveting statements. Trevor

---

[3] Curtis Bowers, Producer, *AGENDA: Grinding America Down* DVD, Black Hat Films, 2010.

Louden, a New Zealand author and speaker, said "They [speaking of 'the left'] want change and they will subvert and rob everything good and decent that we believe in. They have a vision for a new society and that must mean the replacement of the old society."[4] If Mr. Louden's statement is true, there are individuals and groups that wanted to accomplish a wholesale change in American society. There is much more going on than just masses of dissatisfied, rebellious youths and liberal college professors. A *wholesale* change of society would require a premeditated and organized effort.

Without a doubt, there will be many who attempt to distort, minimize, or laugh-off the statements in Mr. Bowers's documentary as misleading, silly, dead-horse-beating, and other derogatory comments in an attempt to reduce the impact of the documentary. Mr. Bowers is not a rabid, right-wing fanatic. He is a former Idaho State Representative and winner of 'Best Documentary' at the 2016 Christian Worldview Film Festival. He is also a winner of the 'Jubilee Grand Prize' at the San Antonio Independent Christian Film Festival. Additional information from Mr. Bowers's documentary will be presented later in this chapter.

First, several statements are necessary to define moral decline and morality/immorality. Moral decline (or degeneration) refers to the process of deterioration from a higher to a lower level of morality. The condition of moral decline is seen as preceding or associated with a decline in the quality of life, as well as a decline of the nation as whole. In 1959 British lawyer and jurist Judge Sir Patrick Devlin (1905-1992), in his Maccabaean Lecture, *The Enforcement of Morals*, said "...an established morality is as necessary as good government to the welfare of society. Societies disintegrate from within more frequently than they are broken up by external pressures."[5]

In order for morality to be sustained and for deterioration to be effectively measured, a standard must exist as a point of moral reference. While legal philosophy says immorality is *whatever* a moral person considers immoral, an accurate conclusion must be

---

[4] Bowers, *AGENDA: Grinding America Down*, 2:41.
[5] Sir Patrick Devlin, *The Enforcement of Morals* (Oxford University Press, 1965), 13-14.

based on either a religious foundation or on an established secular ideology. In America, until the middle of the twentieth century, it was widely held that morality was foundationally based upon the Bible. However, as sweeping changes in spiritual demographics occurred, morality, or the lack thereof, became more and more based on the dictates of secularism. The definition of morality from Noah Webster's dictionary of 1828 is:

> The quality of an action which renders it good; the conformity of an act to the divine law, or to the principles of rectitude. This conformity implies that the act must be performed by a free agent, and from a motive of obedience to the divine will. This is the strict theological and scriptural sense of morality. But we often apply the word to actions which accord with justice and human laws, without reference to the motives from which they proceed.

Reread the last sentence of the above definition. The key word in that sentence is *'motives'*. When morality is defined by man's biased perception of what is right or wrong, his motives will most certainly influence his *opinion* of what is or is not acceptable and what 'right conduct' is.

> Conformity to the rules of right conduct.
> Dicionary.com

If man is allowed to define what morality is, you must then answer the following essential questions:

- What individual, or group of individuals, will be allowed to define morality?
- When does the definition change?
- How often will the definition be allowed to change?
- How many definitions will be allowed?

In an opinion piece regarding the definition of morality, national columnist Cal Thomas wrote:

> Ah, but here's the rub. That definition fits a different era. Morality today is personal. It is not a standard to which

one is encouraged to conform for one's own, or society's benefit. Rather, it is about what makes one feel good. By this non-standard, one can easily change one's sense of what is moral as they might a suit of clothes or a pair of shoes and suffer no societal condemnation because that "moral code", such as it is, exists only for the individual.[6]

That speaks directly to and answers the questions posed above:

- Anybody and everybody.
- Whenever they want it to.
- As many times as is convenient.
- As many definitions as there are individuals.

It is truly shocking what beliefs individuals will convince themselves are reasonable, acceptable, and even justifiable. To illustrate just how far some individuals will push the boundaries of reasonableness, here is a statement made by a feminist journalist. The name of the journalist will not be provided due to the disturbing nature of the quote. Here is what she said, "I was always firmly pro-choice until I became pregnant with my own daughter." Later in the same article she said, "I had no doubt that my daughter was human from conception, from Day 1." She continued, "I went through several months of struggling." Then, she said, "I decided I'm going back to being firmly pro-choice."

Here is what she said was her reasoning for the decision to return to being pro-choice: "It's true that the fetus is human and is life from conception, but women will lose too much if we lose the right to control our reproduction." She concludes with a very chilling statement, "Yes; it's killing, but it's a lesser evil."[7]

Killing an unborn child is a lesser evil than what? In her own words she said the fetus inside her was human. Then, by her own definition, it is less evil to engage in sex outside marriage and then

---

[6] Cal Thomas, *Moral relativism one problem politicians will not solve*, Topeka Capital-Journal, April 9, 2016.

[7] Antonia Senior, *Yes, abortion is killing. But it's the lesser evil*, London Times, June 2010, https://www.thetimes.co.uk/article/yes-abortion-is-killing-but-its-the-lesser-evil-f7v2k2ngvf8 (Accessed 08/13/2018).

kill the child that is conceived than it is to act like an adult and bear and love that child. Killing a child all in the name of 'reproductive rights'. Truly hard to believe, but that is where America and the World finds itself in the twenty-first century.

Such is that sad state of morality in America. America is literally awash in conflicting definitions of morality.

Under secular humanism, which includes most forms of secularism, moral values are highly subject to change, because they are based upon the *presumed* superior reasoning of human intellect. Under this system, man is set forth as the supreme lawgiver. Humanism, being basically atheistic, has a materialistic foundation. Hence, it does not have an objective and impartial moral authority. Humanism is totally unable to offer any guarantee of moral stability because it is prone to the whims of moral relativism.

The method secular humanism (aka materialism) uses to assess morality was described by William Provine, a professor from Cornell University:

Modern science directly implies that the world is organized strictly in accordance with mechanistic principles. There are no purposive principles whatsoever in nature. There are no gods and no designing forces that are rationally detectable... Second, modern science directly implies that there are no inherent moral or ethical laws, no absolute guiding principles for human society. Thirdly, human beings are marvelously complex machines. The individual human becomes an ethical person by means of two primary mechanisms: heredity and environmental influences. That is all there is. Fourth, we must conclude that when we die, we die and that is the end of us.[8]

---

[8] Philip Johnson, *Darwin On Trial*, (Illinois: Intervarsity Press, 1993), 126.

Before continuing, it is needful to repeat what Judge Sir Patrick Devlin said in his lecture *"The Enforcement of Morals"* (quoted earlier) about the disintegration of societies. He said societies more frequently disintegrate from within rather than from external forces. It will be vitally important to remember that statement as you read the details regarding the forces operating within America that are contributing to the destruction of America's morality. Remember: it is easier to destroy from within than from without.

As Mr. Curtis Bowers continued the introduction to his documentary, he said the urge to write his story (documentary) began in the summer of 1992. He received a phone call from an older gentleman who was a writer. The writer asked him to attend a meeting for him at the University of California, Berkeley because he could not attend. He said the Communist Party USA had recently split over differences on how to best take America down. Some still wanted to work toward a violent revolution while others wanted to focus their efforts on using public policies to subvert America from the inside. The writer was curious about what they had to say because the whole world was saying Communism was dead. If Communism was dead, why were they meeting and what were they up to?[9]

Mr. Bowers was in graduate school at the time. He said the thought of slipping into a communist meeting undercover sounded intriguing. Expecting to find an auditorium filled with young, long-haired, college radicals, he was stunned to find fifty, sixty, and seventy year olds, professionally dressed, carrying briefcases.[10]

As the weekend meeting unfolded, Mr. Bowers listened intently as the communists outlined their agenda. They explained how they were going to infiltrate the institutions of America. The goals stated during that meeting and additional goals stated in other sources will be mentioned later in this chapter. A full listing of all the communist's goals can be found in the Appendix. A few of the agenda items from the 1992 meeting of the Communist Party USA are listed below:

---

[9] Bowers, *AGENDA: Grinding America Down*, 6:30.
[10] Ibid., 7:20.

- To influence us in the direction they wanted us to go.
- To destroy our families, they wanted to promote cohabitation rather than marriage.
- They wanted to get children into government programs at the earliest age possible.
- They wanted to get behind the feminist movement, because it had been very successful in making women discontent with marriage and motherhood.
- To destroy business, they wanted to get behind the environmental movement because they felt it was the only vehicle capable of creating enough regulation and red tape to discourage business growth.
- To destroy our culture of religion and morality, they said if they could get Americans to accept homosexuality, they thought it would extinguish the traditional moral values Americans held.[11]

Mr. Bowers asked, "Why do the Communists, and the left, want to destroy a free enterprise system that produces more for anyone willing to work than any other system in history? Why is the left still pushing a 'socialist' agenda on America? There are only two possibilities: 1. They are ignorant; or 2. They are evil?"[12]

The Communists most certainly cannot play the *ignorant* card because there is far too much evidence of their often-stated agenda in their books, articles, papers, and speeches. They certainly did not intend to simply waste their time. That leaves only the last possibility Mr. Bowers offered.

So then, what was the objective of the meeting at the University of California – Berkeley in the summer of 1992? Did the Communists really believe they could accomplish the stated goals of that meeting? Yes, they absolutely believed they could accomplish those goals. In fact, it appears they have indeed accomplished many of their stated goals and far earlier than you might suppose. The very *first sentence* in the preface of W. Cleon Skousen's 1958 first edition of *The Naked Communist* says, "One

---

[11] Ibid, 7:45.
[12] Ibid, 3:54.

of the most fantastic phenomenon of modern times has been the unbelievable success of the Communist conspiracy to enslave mankind."[13] Mr. Skousen, a former FBI agent, said the Communist's success was the result of two types of ignorance: 1. Ignorance concerning the constitutional requirements needed to perpetuate freedom, and 2. Ignorance concerning the history, philosophy, and strategy of World Communism.[14] The ignorance noted in point number two above is quite lengthy and beyond the scope of this book. However, the ignorance noted in point number one is exactly in agreement with the premise of this book.

An entire chapter of this book details America's Christian founding and the Christian heritage upon which America was built. Another chapter details the beginnings of the slide toward modernism that not only affected America in general but also began to infect America's churches. Yet another chapter then details the disastrous results of revising history by minimizing, ignoring, and *deliberately* attempting to purge the impact and value of America's Christian heritage. The result described was an ever increasing slide toward immorality.

Were the goals of the Communist Party USA, as stated in Mr. Skousen's book and declared at the meeting at the University of California - Berkeley in 1992, coming to fruition? Even a superficial evaluation of the readily accessible facts would result in a resounding – YES !

As the remainder of this chapter unfolds, a number of the goals of the Communist Party USA will be mentioned as they

relate to specific attributes of the declining morality being discussed. To view all forty-five Communist goals in their entirety, see the complete list in the Appendix.

In a later chapter, irrefutable, statistical facts, obtained from numerous United States Government agencies, will show that many of the Communist Party's goals related to the decline of

---

[13] W. Cleon. Skousen, *The Naked Communist*, (Salt Lake City: Ensign Pub. Co, 1962, 11th ed.), Preface.

[14] Ibid.

morality indeed have been accomplished. It matters little if America's declining morality is a *direct* result of Communist efforts or if the Communists only *assisted* in the decline of morality by taking advantage of and influencing a deteriorating system of moral values. The distressing condition wherein America finds itself at the close of the second decade of the twenty-first century is the same.

Colleges and universities, both public and private, have become the stronghold of the new progressive attitude and its philosophy. Curriculums were revised and new and more freethinking courses became part of the prevailing mind-set, with a resultant disregard of the old core subjects. One state school board went so far as to eliminate completely the requirement for teaching the first one-hundred years of American History. (More detailed information is offered on that catastrophe in a later chapter.) Fewer and fewer teaching positions were offered to conservative or moderate professors.

Those that had 'a vision for a new society', whether they were Socialists or outright Communists, realized they could not win by using a direct attack. Rather, they chose to use the cunning tactics employed in an approach called the *Fabian Strategy*. This strategy was first employed by the Roman military commander and statesman Quintus Fabius Maximus. During the Second Punic War, 218–201 BC, he waged a war of slow attrition, avoiding direct engagement whenever possible. Quintus Fabius Maximus used a cautious delaying tactic of *wearing down* his opponents through a war of attrition, harassing his enemy through skirmishes, trickery, and dishonesty.[15]

Employment of this strategy implies that the side adopting the strategy believes time is on their side. Those that want to fundamentally change America, see the unmistakable discontent, the rebellion against authority, and the erosion of morality. They know that time is on their side. Their strategy is to simply wear America down or in a vein similar to what the documentary mentioned earlier said, they intend to *'grind America down'*.

---

[15] Quintus Fabius Maximus Verrucosus, https://www.britannica.com/biography/Quintus-Fabius-Maximus-Verrucosus (Accessed 09/06/2018).

An Enemy Within

If you were to observe individuals witnessing a discussion regarding Communists working in America, a frequent response would be the big *'eye roll'* and contemptuous expressions of disbelief or denial on their faces. "Preposterous, ridiculous! America would never welcome the Communists!", they would shout. Most believe the very idea of a communist America is the fairytale and make-believe of movies. Do not be fooled. It is not a fairytale nor is it make-believe. Not any longer.

In America today, the philosophy of Socialism is no longer soundly rejected by most Americans. Surprisingly, a significant percentage of America's youth would rather live under Socialism (see chapter Four, page 89). Even Communism, with its undeniable history of brutality, gulags, oppression, and re-education camps, is no longer feared like it once was. How did America reach such a state? By subscribing to the attitude described in the paragraph above. The motives of Socialism, and its ultimate conclusion - Communism, do not change simply because people are ignorant of them and choose to scoff at those who see the dangers.

Slightly over two thousand years ago, seventy years before the birth of Christ, a young law student suffered great disillusionment over the eroding government of his day. Rome, by force of arms, cunning, and deceit, dominated the then-known world. The citizens of Rome, especially its leaders, had grown lazy and fat. The Romans had also grown careless regarding their rights and duties as citizens, falling victim to ruthless, lying politicians who craved ever increasing power and riches.

On numerous occasions the young law student argued before the Roman Senate against confiscatory taxation, integrity and fair dealing, and the curtailing of the rights of those who disagreed with them. Despite his valiant efforts, Rome continued to decay. The ambitious and powerful grew fatter and fatter upon the backs of its citizens. The civil liberties of the people were pilfered one by one in the name of this or that emergency.

Keith Hoar

That young law student was Marcus Tullius Cicero. Many sources, scholarly books included, assert that during Cicero's Second Oration Against Catiline, given before the Roman Senate, he said, "*A nation can survive its fools and even the ambitious. But it cannot survive treason from within. An enemy at the gates is less formidable, for he is known and he carries his banners openly against the city. But the traitor moves among those within the gates freely, his sly whispers rustling through all alleys, heard in the very halls of government itself. For the traitor appears no traitor; he speaks in the accents familiar to his victim, and he wears their face and their garments and* he appeals to the baseness that lies deep in the hearts of all men.

He rots the soul of a nation; he works secretly and unknown in the night to undermine the pillars of a city; he infects the body politic so that it can no longer resist. A murderer is less to be feared. The traitor is the plague." [16]

Treason is a strong word. Are there individuals operating within the United States that could be accused of treason? Yes, more than you might think. There are individuals, some well hidden and some not so much, that are waging war against the ideals and values that established and built America. As stated earlier, those individuals wish to undermine

> **Treason**
>
> The betrayal of one's own country by waging war against it or by consciously or purposely acting to aid its enemies.

---

[16] Marcus Tullius Cicero, *Orations of Marcus Tullius Cicero*, Charles Duke Yonge A.B. Translator, (New York, Colonial Press), Revised Edition, 1900, 21-31. Note: Cicero's Second Oration was said to be recorded in approximately 42 B.C. by Sallust, aka Gaius Sallustius Crispus. Twelve sources, dated 1922 or earlier, were searched and the words in the above quote do not appear anywhere in any of them. In fact, it is impossible to match any of the words to a specific section. However, the basic concept of the quote seems to come from several different sections of the oration. It may be a bit of a stretch but the quote does 'mostly' seem to convey Cicero's intended thought.

America's culture. They have a vision for a new society and wish to '*completely transform*' America.

As the definition of treason indicates, it occurs when an individual consciously aids an enemy of his or her country. Communism *is* an evil force and has always been and will always be an enemy of the United States. The ultimate, stated goal of Communism is a *New World Order*; a dreamed of utopia. Hence, a whole new society. That evil force is active and it is operating in America.

The Communist Party USA (CPUSA), inspired by Russia's October Revolution of 1917, was formed in Chicago in 1919 after a split with the Left Wing section of the Socialist Party of America.[17] John Bachtell, the national chair of the Communist Party USA, said he wholeheartedly agreed that America needs a radical, third party. Mr. Bachtell wrote the following in an article, titled "*A radical third party? I agree!*" posted on a Communist Party propaganda website:

> Second, our objective is *not* to build the Democratic Party. At this stage we *are* about building the broad people's movement led by labor that utilizes the vehicle of the Democratic Party to advance its agenda. We are about building the movements around the issues roiling wide sections of people that can help shape election contours and debates.[18]

The word 'roiling' in the last sentence in the quote above means: in a state of agitation or disorder, disturbed or irritated. The Communist Party openly states they intend to use individuals or groups that are angry and agitated to advance their agenda.

Bearing in mind the candid statements from communist founders and leaders regarding their goals, affirmed in their speeches, and written in their books, you might be tempted to ask, "*How could men and women, raised in a free and open society,*

---

[17] The Communist Party of America - *Party History*, https://www.marxists. org/history/usa/eam/cpa/communistparty.html (Accessed 06/28/2018).

[18] John Bachtell, *A radical third party? I agree!*, http://www.peoplesworld. org/article/a-radical-third-party-i-agree/ (Accessed 06/25/2018).

especially scientists, politicians, and leaders, be converted by communist ideology to believe that by espousing and actively pursuing stated communist goals they would actually be helping humanity?" No doubt you would answer that it is simply not possible they could not be so easily duped.

You might also be tempted to say, *"That may be true but the communist activists and sympathizers cannot rise to levels of power high enough to instigate real change."* About both questions, you would be wrong. Very, very wrong!

There is an extremely enlightening narrative from the near past recorded in the Canadian *'Report of the Royal Commission'* that describes the case of Igor Sergeievitch Gouzenko, military attaché of the Soviet Embassy to Canada. Mister Gouzenko observed that even during a time of war, the Canadian people enjoyed freedom, they were a happy people, and the government served the people rather than vice versa. Most of all he was quite impressed by the way democracy worked. Over a period of two years, Gouzenko discovered that top Canadian scientists and high-ranking officials were cooperating with Communist agents and were providing them with highly secret government data.

Gouzenko was puzzled because he was certain those scientists and officials were aware that the ultimate aim of the Communists was world-wide revolution. Having made up his mind he would never go back to Russia, Mister Gouzenko smuggled out a large number of documents that would expose the espionage. He went to the Canadian officials, confident they would welcome the information. Gouzenko was horrified and genuinely frightened when he realized they did not believe him. He was deeply concerned he had put himself in grave danger. Just moments before being apprehended by Russian agents, some of the Canadian officials had finally admitted Gouzenko's story might be true. Gouzenko was taken into protective custody and a formal investigation was launched.[19]

Here is a portion of what Mr. Gouzenko testified to under oath regarding the depth of the Soviet Government's spying:

---

[19] Honorable Robert Taschereau, Honorable R. L. Kellock, et.al., *The Report of the Royal Commission* Appointed Under in Council P.C. 411, (Ottawa: Edmond Cloutier), June 27, 1946, 7-14.

They (the Soviet Government) were trying to establish a Fifth Column in Canada. What transpired is only a modest or small part of all that is really here. You may have discovered fifteen men but it still leaves in Canada this dangerous situation because there are other societies and other people working under every Embassy, under every Consul in each place where there is a Consulate. It is just like a number of small circles. There are parallel systems of spies or potential agents.[20]

The Canadian government's investigation revealed an unbelievable trail of treason at the highest levels of government. The list of high-level positions held by the fifteen sympathizers (aka traitors) that were identified during the investigation was startling to say the least! Here are a few of the positions held by those Soviet collaborators: a senior supervisor on the National Research Council, a graduate of McGill and Harvard serving in a top position of the Industrial Development Bank, a professor doing research for the Directorate of the Artillery, a scientist doing research on advanced radar, an officer in the Directorate of Intelligence of the Royal Canadian Air Force, an Executive Secretary of the Interdepartmental Committee on Psychological Warfare, and a Squadron Leader in the Royal Canadian Air Force.[21] This list is not just filler. It is included to demonstrate just how alluring the insidious and devious enticements of Communism can be and how even the most educated and most trusted individuals can fall victim to Communism's subtle offer of a *New World Order*.

The most startling, single aspect that can be gleaned from the account of Igor Gouzenko detailed above is the incredible success with which the Soviet agents were able to find Canadians who were willing to betray their country. The traitors, for that is *exactly* what they were, supplied secret information to which they had access in the course of their work to agents of a foreign

---

[20] Ibid., p 18.
[21] Ibid., p 58.

government, despite the oaths of allegiance and secrecy to which they had sworn.

Mr. Gouzenko further testified:

> Then according to conversations between Sokolov and Zabotin, I think they suspected that there existed a parallel military intelligence system, parallel to Zabotin's. *The same thing was true in the United States,* [emphasis added] according to a telegram I saw. The chief of the Technical Bureau is head of one parallel system; military intelligence has another system.[22]

There is no reason to believe Americans in similar positions were not wooed by Soviet agents into betraying their country. Long before the story narrated above, the Communist Party USA began in Chicago in 1919, (see pg. 33). Without a doubt the Communists charmed many individuals and infiltrated many organizations using the same tactics employed in Canada in the 1940s.

First, several statements from the *Report of the Royal Commission* regarding the methods the Communist Party used in Canada to recruit what they called 'adherents'. Mr. Gouzenko, in a statement which he wrote on October 10, 1945, summarized what he had said to Canadian police officials on September 7th:

> To many Soviet people abroad it is clear that the Communist Party in democratic countries has changed long ago from a political party into an agency net of the Soviet Government, into a fifth column in these countries to meet a war, into an instrument in the hands of the Soviet Government for creating unrest, provocations, etc., etc. . . .[23]

---

[22] Ibid., p 20.
[23] Ibid., p 29.

According to the report, a basic technique of the Communist

Fifth Column
A clandestine group or faction of subversive agents who attempt to undermine a nation's solidarity by any means at their disposal.

Party was to organize and encourage membership in *secret* cells, and study-groups. The objective was to gradually accustom the young adherents to an atmosphere and an ethic of conspiracy. The general effect on the young men and women over a period of time of *secret* meetings, *secret* acquaintances, *secret* code names, and *secret* objectives, could easily be imagined. Those techniques were designed to develop the psychology of a double life and double standards.[24]

Regarding the scheme of secrecy, the report said: "An inevitable result of this emphasis on a conspiratorial atmosphere and behavior even in political discussions, correspondence, and meetings which are in themselves perfectly legal and indeed are the cherished right of everyone in a democratic society, would seem to be the gradual disintegration of normal moral principles such as frankness, honesty, integrity, and a respect for the sanctity of oaths."[25]

The investigation found it quite significant that not a single one of the individuals who were approached by members of the Communist Party to engage in espionage reported it to any agency or department in which they were employed.

Not even one of those individuals, from evidence in sworn testimony, described any hesitation or struggle with their conscience before they agreed to act as spies against Canada. This serves as a striking exhibition of the effectiveness of the Communist's study-groups in inducing individuals to participate in clearly illegal activities directed against their country.[26]

The communist agents used carefully selected political and philosophic words and works to develop in their adherents a critical attitude and dislike towards Western democratic society. The adherents were persuaded to engage in illegal activities by

---

[24] Ibid., p 71.
[25] Ibid., p 72.
[26] Ibid., p 77.

speaking to their desire to advance causes which they considered worthy. For example, a highly respected scientist with an international reputation and member of the National Research Council stated, under oath, that he gave secret information to a known, code-named Soviet agent despite the oath of secrecy which he had taken, believing that his action would further 'international scientific collaboration'.[27] Regardless of any *assumed* goal or the *sincerity* of his motives, his actions constituted a direct breach of his oath and amounted to treason against his own country.

The rather lengthy narration of Mr. Igor Gouzenko's story and portions of the outcome of the subsequent investigation that resulted, was necessary to demonstrate how mesmerizing and powerful the rhetoric of socialist and/or communist agents is when targeted at individuals who are angry, despondent, or disillusioned. However, as the testimony above confirms, it is not just individuals who are angry, despondent, or disillusioned that can be swayed. It can and does influence highly educated individuals. The carefully targeted propaganda, albeit subtle, can even manipulate individuals in high-level, sensitive government positions, those with access to top secret material. No one is immune.

Mr. Gouzenko's testimony revealed, based on a telegram he viewed, that the same situation as happened in Canada, was occurring in America (see page 36). That requires an answer to the question, "Are there Communists operating in America?" Yes, absolutely, there are Communists operating in America! As stated earlier, the Communist Party USA was formed in 1919 in Chicago. Their own statements admit they intended to use the Democratic Party to advance their agenda (see page 33).

To the unbelievers and naysayers: Communism is not nor was it ever dead! It is alive and breathing and working diligently to destroy capitalism in America. Everyone must bear in mind the words of those that suffered at the hands of Communism. The Victims of Communism Memorial Foundation website states, "Communism isn't back: It never left. We simply forgot about it. And as it rears its ugly head once more, openly and shamelessly,

[27] Ibid., p 74.

we seem far less prepared to meet the challenge in this century as we did in the last."[28]

America certainly appears to be totally unprepared to stand up to the threat that Communism presents. The younger generations know virtually nothing of the old, hard-line Communism of the cold-war era. No other conclusion can be drawn when the results of a recent survey confirm that slightly over half of millennials would prefer to live in a socialist or communist country than a capitalist democracy like America (see page 89).

While there may be some individuals who are willing to acknowledge Communism is a threat, they are reluctant to concede it has had a significant impact on America's morals. That is *exactly* what the Communists want Americans to think. Knowing they could never win an outright conflict, they chose rather to infiltrate America's institutions and work from the inside. Listed below are a few excerpts of the Communist goals officially affirmed during a 1992 meeting of the Communist Party USA.

- Capture one or both of the political parties in the United States.
- Get control of the schools. Use them for Socialism and current Communist propaganda.
- Get control of teachers associations. Put the party line in textbooks.
- Use student riots to foment public protests.
- Infiltrate the press.
- Gain control of key positions in radio, TV, and movies.
- Continue discrediting American culture.
- Eliminate all laws governing obscenity by calling them "censorship".
- Break down cultural standards of morality by promoting pornography and obscenity.
- Infiltrate the churches and replace revealed religion with "social" religion.
- Eliminate prayer or any phase of religious expression in the schools.

---

[28] All contact names at https://www.victimsofcommunism.org/, their official website, were contacted for a source for the quote. No response.

- Discredit the American Constitution by calling it inadequate and old fashioned.
- Belittle all forms of American culture and discourage the teaching of American history.
- Dominate the psychiatric profession.
- Discredit the family as an institution. Encourage promiscuity and easy divorce.
- Create the impression that violence and insurrection are legitimate aspects of the American tradition.

Even though these and other goals were openly stated in January 1961 (officially read into the Congressional Record), they have been in play in different forms much earlier than that. The Chairman of the Communist Party USA from 1945 to 1957 and militant union organizer, William Z. Foster, in his book, titled *Toward Soviet America*, (full citation elsewhere, see page 58) wrote this in regard to furthering the cultural revolution:

> "...schools, colleges and universities will be coordinated and grouped under the National Department of Education and its state and local branches. The studies will be revolutionized, being cleansed of religious, patriotic and other features of the bourgeois ideology..."

Mr. Foster, also a member of the Socialist Party of America and the Industrial Workers of the World, published his book in 1932. Therefore, at least as early as 1932, Communists were at work, pushing to revolutionize public education by cleansing it of all things religious and patriotic.

Can those that question whether Communism has had any *real* influence on American morality continue to hold that position after considering Mr. Foster's statement and the excerpts of the stated Communist goals listed above? For a complete listing of the forty-five Communist goals as read before Congress, see the Appendix, page 209.

Do not forget what happened in Canada in the 1940s. Mr. Gouzenko testified it was also happening in America. The Communist Party USA was organized and started operating in

1919. Over the years, Communists adherents and sympathizers have risen to high-level positions in education, unions, government, and business organizations. The Communists have used turmoil, riots, unrest, anger, and disillusionment to influence entire generations toward acceptance of Socialism and Communism.

A few brief descriptions of some of the accomplishments of the Socialist Party USA and the Communist Party USA are necessary to confirm the successes they have had in spreading their agendas.

First, and most revealing, is a news conference that occurred in May 2015, outside the U.S. Capitol with labor leaders, Democratic lawmakers, and liberal activists. The far-left, progressive mayor of New York City was there to unveil his thirteen-point 'Progressive Agenda to Combat Income Inequality'.[29] Mr. Will Bredderman of *The Observer* reported the mayor as saying, "I can't think of anything more important." and that as mayor he feels it "…is important and appropriate to his duties as mayor, despite complaints that he is neglecting the bread-and-butter issues of every day New Yorkers"[30] Mike Lux of the *Huffington Post*, referring to this same news conference said, "…there is something exciting going on, a political and policy movement bubbling up that historians may well someday look back on and call the most important development of 2015"[31] The forgoing reports describing the news conference very clearly show how important this meeting was to the progressive movement.

The revealing aspect of the progressive, thirteen-point agenda is how eerily similar it is to the agendas of the Socialist Party USA (SPUSA) and the Communist Party USA (CPUSA). A complete

---

[29] City of New York, Transcript: *Mayor de Blasio and National Progressive Leaders Unveil the Progressive Agenda*, https://www1.nyc.gov/office-of-the-mayor/news/307-15/transcript-mayor-de-blasio-national-progressive-leaders-the-progressive-agenda-to#/0 (Accessed 07/06/2018).

[30] Will Bredderman, *De Blasio 'Can't Think of Anything More Important' Than Going to D.C.*, http://observer.com/2015/05/de-blasio-cant-think-of-anything-more-important-than-going-to-d-c/, (Accessed 07/06/2018).

[31] Mike Lux, *A Bold New Agenda Bubbling Up From the Grassroots*, (https://www.huffingtonpost.com/mike-lux/a-bold-new-agenda-bubblin_b_8205232.html (Accessed 07/06/2018))

comparison can be found in the Appendix (see page 220). During the news conference the mayor encouraged everyday people to go to their website and sign up. An attempt to access the Progressive Agenda website to verify the list of original signers revealed that the website has either been taken down or abandoned. Attempts to find a website with a similar name were also unsuccessful. Remember, the mayor said he could not think of *anything more important* and others described it as *the most important development of 2015.* If that is true, does it not seem quite odd that only three years later the website no longer exists.

The complete list of original signers of the progressive agenda, duplicated on a different website, listed the source as http://progressiveagenda.us/signers. Since the source website no longer exists, the names of the signers will not be revealed. Only the stated positions of the signers will be listed. Here is a sampling from the eighty-four original signers of the progressive agenda:

- Mayor of Newark, New Jersey
- U.S. Representatives from New York & Connecticut
- Governor of Minnesota
- U.S. Representatives from Minnesota & Pennsylvania
- President, National Education Association
- President, United Steelworkers
- President, Service Employees International Union
- President, American Federation of State, County and Municipal Employees
- U.S. Representatives from Texas & Arizona
- U.S. Senators from Iowa & Oregon
- President, Young Democrats of America
- President, American Federation of Teachers
- President, AFL-CIO

Many mayors, U.S. representatives, congressmen, educators, and others were included in the list of signers. The positions listed above clearly demonstrate that a progressive, socialistic, and often communistic attitude has permeated top levels of the education, government, and labor (union) sectors. Those occupying the positions listed above wield great power and influence over their memberships.

The question posed earlier is repeated, *"Can those that question whether Communism has had any real influence on American morality continue to hold that position after considering the deep penetration the progressive, socialist, communist agenda has had in the organizations listed above?"* The Socialists and Communists have been hard at work deep within American organizations and communities since the early twentieth century. They have had *far* greater success than many are willing to admit and they have poisoned multiple generations of American youth.

On October 13, 1960, before the UN General Assembly of the United Nations, Russian Premier Nikita Khrushchev banged his shoe on the podium. America, fearing an invasion from Russia, built the most powerful military machine in history. However, while building that military machine, America forgot to guard its educational and political home front from being taken over by socialistic, liberal activists.

Sadly, too many Americans naively still believe that Communism is dead because the Berlin Wall came down and the Iron Curtain has supposedly been removed. The actual truth is that Communism is not dead. Far from it! It has just switched names and gone underground. The face Communism now presents to an uninformed public is one of 'political correctness' and 'defense of the oppressed worker'!

A confirmation that Socialism/Communism continues to grow within the Democratic Party, was the stunning primary election defeat on June 26, 2018, of a ten-term incumbent, once seen as a likely replacement for House Minority Leader, by a self-described and incredibly inexperienced socialist. In the spring of 2017, before she ended the twenty-year congressional career of her opponent, she was working behind a bar and taking brunch orders.[32]

[32] David Weigel, *Alexandria Ocasio-Cortez: The Democrat who challenged her party's establishment — and won*, https://www.washingtonpost.com/news/powerpost/wp/2018/06/27/alexandria-ocasio-cortez-the-democrat-who-challenged-her-partys-establishment-and-won/?noredirect=on&utm_term=.2a610513f0a1 (Accessed 08/02/2018)

One must ask, "Does tending bar and taking bunch orders qualify her for a position in Congress?" Her victory does not speak to her qualifications, Rather, it speaks to her support for liberal social programs. Her politics are substantially to the left of most of the Democratic Party, and even to the left of its previously most popular Socialist. In her campaign videos and posters, she came out for universal Medicare, a federal jobs guarantee, free college tuition, forgiveness of all student loan debt, and other issues. She said the posters used for her campaign were designed to look 'revolutionary'. In an interview she also said, "We are fighting for an unapologetic movement for economic, social, and racial justice in the United States,"[33]

Albeit the congressional district in which she won gave seventy-eight percent of the vote to the democratic candidate for president in the 2016 election, her victory was significant in that she defeated a candidate who had never even come close to losing in New York's 14th Congressional District. Remember, she is inexperienced and cannot explain how her definition of 'Democratic Socialism' differs from the murderous socialist regimes in Cuba, Nicaragua, Venezuela, and others.[34] What propelled her to victory is the promise of 'free stuff' and speaking to the anger and discontent of the social and racial justice movements.

The website of the Democratic Socialists of America in defining what socialism means says both the economy and society should, "meet public needs, not to make profits for a few. To achieve a more just society, many structures of our government and economy must be radically transformed". On the same webpage they claim, "Democracy and socialism go hand in hand. All over the world, wherever the idea of democracy has taken root, the vision of socialism has taken root as well—everywhere but in the United States."[35]

---

[33] Ibid.

[34] Jorge Bonilla, Alexandra Ocasio-Cortez Struggles to define 'Democratic Socialism', https://www.newsbusters.org/blogs/latino/jorge-bonilla/2018/07/18/alexandria-ocasio-cortez-struggles-define-democratic-socialism (Accessed 07/25/2018)

[35] Democratic Socialists of America, *What is Democratic Socialism?* https://www.dsausa.org/what_is_democratic_socialism. (Accessed 07/25/2018)

On August 1, 2018, Megan Day in the article titled, *Democratic socialism, explained by a democratic socialist,* wrote that the Democratic Socialists of America (DSA) is the country's largest socialist group and its membership has exploded from 6,000 in the summer 2016 to more than 45,000 today.[36] Later in that article she made this extremely revealing statement:

> I'm a staff writer at the socialist magazine Jacobin and a member of DSA, and here's the truth: In the long run, democratic socialists want to end capitalism. And we want to do that by pursuing a reform agenda today in an effort to revive a politics focused on class hierarchy and inequality in the United States. The eventual goal is to transform the world...[37]

Later Ms. Day states that even Medicare-for-all would not be enough as that would only nationalize insurance and not the whole health care system because they want to own the health care providers and hospitals as well. Two paragraphs later she says:

> Of course, even socializing a whole industry like medicine wouldn't automatically lead to the socializing of others. But through the process of the campaign, democratic socialists want to build into the popular consciousness an awareness that the market is not capable of meeting society's needs. This sets us up for other fights, whether something defensive such as *stopping school privatization* [emphasis added] or something proactive such as *nationalizing energy companies* [emphasis added].[38]

---

[36] Megan Day, *Democratic socialism, explained by a democratic socialist,* August 1, 2018, https://www.vox.com/first-person/2018/8/1/17637028/bernie-sanders-alexandria-ocasio-cortez-cynthia-nixon-democratic-socialism-jacobin-dsa (Accessed 08/23/2018).

[37] Ibid.

[38] Ibid.

The article uses inciteful phrases such as: 'corporate power', 'wage slavery', and 'capitalist Goliaths'. Those rallying phrases go along with their desire to use class warfare. She says, "To marshal the kinds of forces that can achieve such policy victories, we need to get working Americans comfortable thinking about class in a broader sense." and "Fighting for Medicare-for-all can teach Americans the value of uniting over the working-class majority's interests."[39]

That philosophy is a typical ploy direct from the Communist play book; little steps as they condition their followers to their full goal of complete and total Socialism, see Communist goals 19, 32, and 42 in the Appendix.

The 'About' page on the Jacobin Magazine website for which Ms. Day writes says, "Jacobin is a leading voice of the American left, offering socialist perspectives on politics, economics, and culture"[40] The name 'Jacobin' chosen for their magazine name is quite informative. The Jacobins were the most violent and radical political group of the French Revolution. The Encyclopedia Britannica says this about the Jacobins, "Jacobins were the most famous political group of the French Revolution, which became identified with extreme egalitarianism and violence and which led the Revolutionary government from mid-1793 to mid-1794."[41] The Jacobin Magazine website says this in an article on their website, "Above all else, the Jacobins were intensely concerned with translating the revolutionary fervor of 1789 into a durable and sustainable revolutionary society."[42]

An organization that would choose to name their magazine after such a violent group indicates that, like socialist movements of the past, they likely agree with the traditional method for socialist revolution – oppression, bloodshed, and violence.

The question that **MUST** be answered is:

---

[39] Ibid.

[40] Jacobin Magazine, https://www.jacobinmag.com/about (Accessed 08/18/2018).

[41] Encyclopedia Britannica, *Jacobin Club*, https://www.britannica.com/topic/Jacobin-Club (Accessed 08/21/2018).

[42] Jonah Walters, *A Guide to the French Revolution*, https://www.jacobinmag.com/2015/07/french-revolution-bastille-day-guide-jacobins-terror-bonaparte/ (Accessed 08/21/2018).

When Democratic Socialists have destroyed capitalism and the profits are gone and the companies have either failed or fled the country and they run out of other people's money, what source of revenue will Socialism feed off of then?

Perhaps America will turn to the bread lines and empty shelves like the old USSR. Or perhaps America will become like socialistic Venezuela where the people eat rats or break into zoos to eat the animals because the market shelves are empty?[43]

The reason that Socialism has not taken root in America, at least as yet, is because Democratic Socialism conflicts with the U.S. Constitution. However, as liberal, activist judges continue to chip away at the Constitution and render decisions based upon what they '*want*' the Constitution to mean rather than what it actually says, the Constitution will become nothing more than another dry, dusty document to be ignored. Will the grand 'experiment' born in the minds of the *Framers* ultimately fade away? Will the United States become another Third World country? Only time will tell.

A Failed Experiment?

As the end of the second decade of the twenty-first century approaches, is America poised to become a 'failed experiment'?

As Benjamin Franklin left Independence Hall on the final day of deliberation at the Constitutional Convention of 1787, Mrs. Powell of Philadelphia asked Dr. Franklin, "Well Doctor, what have we got a republic or a monarchy?" Dr. Franklin replied, "A republic if you can keep it."[44]

Dr. Franklin understood quite well that it would require great diligence and effort to maintain the 'experiment' that had just

---

[43] John Kass, *Eating the zoo creatures in Venezuela*, http://www.chicagotribune.com/news/columnists/kass/ct-venezuela-zoo-animals-kass-0818-20170817-column.html (Accessed 08/23/2018).

[44] Max Farrand, Editor, *The Records of the Federal Convention of 1787* Vol. III, (New Haven: Yale University Press, 1911), 85.

begun in America. Because so few Americans, especially the younger generations, know anything about true history and correctly understand its lessons, an explanation of the question that opens this section is warranted. The *Founders* considered the United States an experiment in self-government. Never before anywhere had such a form of government been attempted. It truly was an 'experiment' to see if a group of people could form and *maintain* a government 'of the people, by the people, and for the people'.

Mr. James Parton in his book, *The life of Thomas Jefferson*, described a hostile debate in the House regarding centralism versus the rights and dignity of the State governments, "But why so much ill-humor? Because Hamilton and his friends, the men who were conducting the *experiment of Federal government* [emphasis added] by the people, had no faith in the principle. It was not in their blood to submit at once, without a word, to the decision of a majority."[45]

Later in the same book, Mr. Parton writes, "Again, in his second inaugural, he spoke of the importance to mankind of this *experiment* [emphasis added] to ascertain whether a government that did no act which it would be unwilling the whole world should witness could be written down. 'The *experiment* [emphasis added] has been tried,' said he."[46]

Mr. Jared Sparks in his book, *The Life of George Washington*, wrote regarding Washington's exasperation after learning of a plan to make him king:

We have seen with what a stern rebuke the proposal to be a king was met by him, even when he literally had the power of the nation in his hands. From the beginning of the revolution to the end of his life, he was an uncompromising advocate for a republican system. In the abstract he regarded it as the best; and he had faith enough in the virtue of the people, and in the efficacy of their former habits, to convince him that it might be

---

[45] James Parton, *The life of Thomas Jefferson*, (Boston: James R. Osgood and Company, 1874), 391.
[46] Ibid., 634-635.

successfully established. At all events he was for having the *experiment* [emphasis added] thoroughly tried; and his whole conduct proves, that, in regard to himself, he was ready to risk his reputation, his property, and his life, if necessary, in a cause so momentous to the welfare of his country and to the social progress of mankind.[47]

The word 'virtue' as used by George Washington in the quote above means: good value or high merit. Mr. Washington believed the virtue of American citizens would successfully establish the 'experiment' called the United States. Not only would it be required to establish it, it would also require virtue and high merit for the experiment to flourish and continue.

More quotes could be presented to show that the *Founders* considered the founding of the United States of America to be a grand experiment in self-government. However, the foregoing quotes from two of the leading *Founding Fathers* should be sufficient.

The principle underlying the answer Dr. Franklin gave to Mrs. Powell, as quoted above, meant that it would be up to America's citizens to:

- Learn what the United States stands for.
- Come to understand its philosophy and governing systems.
- Then, vote accordingly.

America has now come to a time when only a handful of its citizens have a genuine understanding of its history and a high percentage of those that do vote are uninformed. But worse than that; many are not just uninformed, they are uninterested in the true facts of history.

Considering the information on the foregoing pages, it seems incredibly difficult to refute the belief that modern society is in sharp decline. Among the ills that demonstrate that belief are: skyrocketing rates of crime, divorce, teenage sex, teenage births,

---

[47] Jared Sparks, *The Life of George Washington*, (Boston: Ferdinand Andrews, 1839), 401

drug abuse, and a general decline in personal morality and religiosity.

Using irrefutable government statistics, the next chapter will present a sad and disheartening picture of America's morality at the end of the twentieth century and into the beginning of the twenty-first century.

Numerous trend charts, discussions, and supporting statistics in the following chapter will present clear and irrefutable evidence that a startling increase in the rate of America's moral descent can be traced to a specific point in time and, thereby, several noteworthy events in history.

Chapter Three: Morality - Decades of Decline

Men do not differ much about what things they will call evils; they differ enormously about what evils they will call excusable.

G. K. Chesterton
The Illustrated London
News, 10/23/1909

Decades

A system of morality which is based on relative emotional values is a mere illusion, a thoroughly vulgar conception which has nothing sound in it and nothing true.

Socrates
Quoted in Plato's - Phaedo Sec. 68c-69d

Of Decline

Departure From Principle

The trend charts and related discussions that follow will present a shocking and frightening trend in morality that began after the United States Supreme Court made a number of extremely damaging decisions disallowing God and the Bible to be used or mentioned in our public school system and eventually nearly all facets of public life. The charts below, built upon raw government statistical data, are the eye-opening results of locating, gathering, consolidating, and analyzing government statistics. Those statistics were gathered from the following ten official government sources:

- Numerous annual issues of "The Statistical Abstract of the United States"
- U. S. Census Bureau
- FBI Crime Statistics Database
- U. S. Department of Health, Education, & Welfare
- U. S. Department of Health and Human Services
- U.S. Department of Commerce
- U.S. Department of Justice
- National Center for Health Statistics
- National Center for Education Statistics
- National Centers for Disease Control

It is no mere coincidence that the underlying moral values that lie beneath the statistical trends, exposed by the following charts, all seemingly went '*haywire*' at the same time. It is an undeniable fact that if you remove God from public life, its moral foundation will crumble.

There are three landmark cases that went before the U.S. Supreme Court that changed the meaning of the First Amendment as it was previously understood and practiced in America. In those three cases, one parent of a child petitioned the courts to stop the school from exposing their child to prayer in school. ACLU lawyers, as they had many times in the past, misused a letter from Thomas Jefferson in the argument for the plaintiffs. As so many other have, they used the erroneous claim that the founding fathers wanted a '*wall of separation between church and State*'. That was *never* the case as explained in detail in Chapter Five, see page 121 and following.

The three pivotal U.S. Supreme Court cases that began the removal of God from public life and its resultant deterioration of America's moral fabric are listed below:

- *Engel vs. Vitale* "The Regents School Prayer" - 1962
- *Murray vs. Curlett* "School Prayer" - 1963
- *Abington Township School District vs. Schempp* "Bible reading in school" - 1963

The first of the cases listed above, *Engel ET AL. vs. Vitale ET AL.* "The Regents School Prayer", argued April 3, 1962, decided June 25, 1962, began the elimination of prayer in public schools. Supreme Court Justice Black delivered the majority opinion of the Court in this case. In the majority opinion, regarding the *purposes underlying* the Constitution's Establishment Clause, Justice Black wrote, "Its first and most immediate purpose rested on the belief that a union of government and religion tends to destroy government and to degrade religion."[1] That statement is emphatically untrue. There are many statements, some quoted later in the this chapter, that fly in the face of the statement written by Justice Black. I repeat the question Mr. David Barton asked in his book *Original Intent*, (for citation see page 125) "Why doesn't the current Supreme Court quote the early Court Justices such as Justice John Jay?" It is perhaps that the writings and rulings of those early justices who understood constitutional *intent* would challenge the twentieth and twenty-first century Court efforts to *make* law rather than interpret law?

A few sentences later in the majority opinion, Justice Black continued, "It has been argued that to apply the Constitution in such a way as to prohibit state laws respecting an establishment of religious services in public schools is to indicate a hostility toward religion or toward prayer. Nothing, of course, could be more

---

[1] *Engle v. Vitale*, 370 U.S. 421 (1962), 370, Supreme Court of the United States, https://supreme.justia.com/cases/federal/us/370/421/case.html, (accessed 8/16/2017).

wrong. The history of man is inseparable from the history of religion."[2] First, a simple prayer to and acknowledging God is not a religious service. Second, prohibiting prayer absolutely does demonstrate a hostility toward religion. Third, it is quite informative to note that Justice Black says, "...man is inseparable from the history of religion." It certainly seems that Justice Black said we can consider the *history* of religion but we should not *practice* religion. At least not in school where the next generation of leaders is being trained and equipped for the future.

The *Abington Township School District vs. Schempp* ruling involved two cases: its namesake and *Murray vs. Curlett*, 228 Md. 239, 179 A. 2d 698 (Md. 1962). The U.S. Supreme Court agreed to hear *Abington Township School District vs. Schempp* along with *Murray vs. Curlett* as a consolidated case. Madalyn Murray O'Hair and her fourteen-year-old son, William Murray, were atheists. They challenged a 1905 Baltimore school board rule requiring each school day to start with Bible reading or prayer. An attorney herself, Murray brought the suit after protesting to officials, stirring up media attention, and encouraging her son to protest in a controversial strike. The Murray suit, as others, claimed the school's action transgressed the Establishment Clause by requiring compulsory religious education.

Supreme Court Justice Thomas Clark delivered the majority opinion of the Court for the combined cases. The full text of the document of the cases contains many pages of "snippets" from other Supreme Court and State Court cases. Buried within all those "snippets", supporting the majority opinion, is a quoted section from the U.S. Supreme Court case *"Everson v. Board of Education*, 330 U.S. 1 (1947)":

The Amendment's purpose was not to strike merely at the official establishment of a single sect, creed or religion, outlawing only a formal relation such as had prevailed in England and some of the colonies. Necessarily, it was to uproot all such relationships. But the object was broader than separating church and state in this narrow sense. It was to create a complete and permanent separation of the

---

[2] Ibid, *Engle v. Vitale*, 370 U.S. 421 (1962), 370

spheres of religious activity and civil authority by comprehensively forbidding every form of public aid or support for religion.[3]

The quoted section in the *Abington Township School District vs. Schempp* ruling, shown above, once again singled out the Establishment Clause of the First Amendment.[4] Based on the *Everson v. Board of Education* quote, and earlier cited quotes from the *Engel vs. Vitale* case, it seems extremely difficult, if not impossible, to take any other position than the Supreme Court has become openly hostile to religion, except, perhaps, to the religion of humanism.

The trend charts that follow will provide more than ample proof that America's morality has taken a drastic turn for the worse. A vertical reference line has been added to all charts, where applicable. The reference line aligns with the years 1962 and 1963, the years when the damaging U.S. Supreme Court cases were decided. It is *instantly* obvious that the rate of decline in morality for all six "indicators" exhibits a sudden and dramatic change at the exact time of those damaging decisions. To eliminate any potential argument that the Unites States population increase impacted the rate of change, a population trend line for total US population was added for comparison to those charts, where appropriate.

Discerning The Times

The seed for the rapid upsurge in the rate of America's moral decline existed in the hearts of the American people long before the damaging U.S. Supreme Court decisions, described in the

---

[3] *Everson v. Board of Education*, 330 U.S. 1 (1947), Supreme Court of the United States, https://supreme.justia.com/cases/federal/us/330/1/case.html#3, (accessed 8/16/2017).

[4] *School Dist. of Abington Tp. v. Schempp*, 374 U.S. 203 (1963), Supreme Court of the United States, https://supreme.justia.com/cases/federal/ us/374 /203/case.html, (accessed 8/18/2017).

previous section, were handed down. To the surprise of many, the Communist Party had been operating in the United States long before that time. Harold Lasswell and Dorothy Blumenstock confirm that fact in their book, *World Revolutionary Propaganda: A Chicago Study*. They stated the American Communist Party began in Chicago in 1919:

> FROM the birth of the American Communist Party in Chicago in 1919 Chicago has been one of the chief radiating centers for Communist propaganda in the United States. Although the political capital of the party was removed to New York about 1924, and the Midwest center declined in national importance, it has always remained a stronghold of the party. During the period with which we are concerned, Chicago continued to be an active relay center for propaganda directed from Moscow, and an important congregating center for party specialists.[5]

Earlier in their book, they wrote, "Before the splits of 1919 began, [referring to the Industrial Workers of the World and the Socialist Party] there were 28 radical magazines and newspapers published in Chicago."[6]

Even before the birth of the American Communist Party, the communists were hard at work spreading their propaganda.

To understand how the U.S. Supreme Court decisions stirred the underlying propensity toward immorality and precipitated a rapid increase in the rate of moral decline, you must first understand the mission of Communism. Most adherents of Communism and/or Socialism greatly misunderstand the mission of Karl Marx, considered to be the father of Communism, and other atheistic writers. Those adherents mistakenly believe the mission of Marx and his followers to be economic in nature and for the good of the people. However, their real mission, like all

---

[5] Harold D. Lasswell and Dorothy Blumenstock, *World Revolutionary Propaganda: A Chicago Study,* (New York, New York: Alfred A. Knopf, 1939), 271.

[6] Ibid, 61.

materialists, is not economic but rather their mission is to gain power through ideological warfare. The idealistic expression of Marxism and Marxism-Leninism is *dialectical materialism*. Dialectical materialism holds that the world, including human beings, is 'matter in motion' and that progress occurs through struggle.[7] Dialectical simply means the process of change through the conflict of opposing forces.

Vladimir Ilyich Ulyanov, also known by the alias Lenin, was a Russian, communist revolutionary, politician, and political theorist. Writing in regard to Marxism and the conflict needed between opposing forces he said, "We must combat religion – that is the ABC of all materialism, and consequently of Marxism. But Marxism is not a materialism which has stopped at the ABC. Marxism goes further. It says: We must know how to combat religion, and in order to do so we must explain the source of faith and religion among the masses in a materialist way."[8]

William Z. Foster (1881-1961) was a militant union organizer and Marxist politician, whose career included serving as Chairman of the Communist Party USA from 1945 to 1957.[9] As chairman of the Communist Party USA, Mr. Foster's words can be taken as accurate when describing the communist policies for altering America. In the preface to his book, *Towards Soviet America*, Mr. Foster wrote, "It outlines simply the program, strength, strategy and perspectives [Communist policy] of the Communist party of the United States. It undertakes to point out what is the matter with capitalism and what must be done about it."[10] In the fifth and final section of his book, THE UNITED SOVIET STATES OF AMERICA, Mr. Foster, describing the measures his desired 'American Soviet government' would use:

[7] New World Encyclopedia, *Dialectical Materialism*, http://www.newworldencyclopedia.org/entry/Dialectical_materialism, (accessed 8/21/2017).

[8] V. I. Lenin, *Religion*, (New York, New York, International Publishers, 1933), 21.

[9] Encyclopedia Britannica, William Z. Foster, https://www.britannica.com/biography/William-Z-Foster, (accessed 8/21/2017).

[10] William Z. Foster, *Toward Soviet America*, (Coward – McCann, Inc., 1932), vi.

...to further the cultural revolution are the following; the schools, colleges and universities will be coordinated and grouped under the National Department of Education and its state and local branches. The studies will be revolutionized, being cleansed of religious, patriotic and other features of the bourgeois ideology. The students will be taught on the basis of Marxian dialectical materialism, internationalism and the general ethics of the new Socialist society.[11]

On the next page, Mr. Foster said, "The whole basis and organization of capitalist science will be revolutionized. Science will become materialistic, hence truly scientific; God will be banished from the laboratories as well as from the schools."[12]

The measures Mr. Foster advocates, as do all of the 'true' believers of Communism, are based on power. Elsewhere in his book, Mr. Foster wrote, "The relations between them [the poor, the workers, the exploited, etc.] depend upon the question of power. The workers can get from the employers only what they have the power to take."[13] Mr. Foster knew the American worker would not readily accept the revolutionary struggle he advocated. He stated, "The application of the 'Class Against Class' policy requires the making of united front movements with workers who, while not prepared to accept the whole revolutionary program of the Communist party, nevertheless are willing to struggle for immediate, partial demands."[14] The leaders of Communism carefully and subtly pushed and goaded the lower classes further and further toward their goal of taking over America from within.

One more statement from Mr. Foster will establish his, and those he learned from, desire to revolutionize and overthrow the American culture: "Superstition, and ignorance will vanish in a realm of science; Culture will become the acquirement of all and

---

[11] Ibid, 316.
[12] Ibid, 317.
[13] Ibid, 252.
[14] Ibid, 253.

the class ideologies of the past will give place to scientific materialist philosophy."[15]

One more quote from the founders of Communism is necessary to firmly establish their ungodly aims: "There are, besides, eternal truths, such as Freedom, Justice, etc., that are common to all states of society. But Communism abolishes eternal truths, it abolishes all religion and all morality, instead of constituting them on a new basis; it therefore acts in contradiction to all past historical experience."[16]

Remember William Foster's statement that the classes they targeted would not accept Communism's 'whole revolutionary plan' but they would accept their 'immediate, partial demands'. Do not forget that Marx and Engels said they intended to abolish eternal truths, religion, and morality by acting in contradiction to all past historical experience.

The statements, concepts, goals, and teachings the Communists illustrated so far in this chapter are critically important as the discussion now turns to U.S. Government statistics that confirms an identifiable, and sudden increase in the rate of America's moral decline.

A statement was made earlier in this chapter that the seed for the rapid upsurge in the rate of America's moral decline existed in the hearts of the American people long before the damaging U.S. Supreme Court decisions described earlier. Clear evidence was given proving the Communist Party was at work long before those Court decisions. Not long after the Court decision of 1962, 63, the 'hippy movement' with its violent protests and *question everything'* attitude was in full swing. In April of 1966, *Time Magazine's* cover asked the question, "Is God Dead?"

There were certainly a number of negative forces already at work, ripping away at America's moral fabric. Then the U.S. Supreme Court removed God from public school and, in essence, said God and religion do not belong in public life. The court said to America's parents and children, *"Morality is not based on God's Law but, rather, it is based on how human intellect defines it."* The

---

[15] Ibid, 316.
[16] Karl Marx and Friedrich Engels, Samuel Moore translator, *Manifesto of the Communist Party*, (Moscow, USSR: Progress Publishers, 1971), 58.

statistical evidence that follows certainly seems to indicate that those Court decisions acted as a 'release of the flood gates'. The following charts and discussions will confirm that America's moral values began a precipitous decline precisely at the time of those Supreme Court decisions.

Desertion From Family Stability

The first attribute indicating America's decline in morality that will be examined is "Family Stability", where children are present. A lengthy search of the internet netted next to nothing with regard to a *formal* definition of family stability. Many websites, including non-profit organizations and governmental agencies, pointed out the great need for family stability and indicated they had programs to encourage it, but nowhere did they define exactly what that desired stability entailed. Definitions from the few that did define family stability are listed below:

- The consistency of family activities and routines.
- The regularity of daily family events and activities.
- Regularity of family activities that occur on a daily basis, within the home, and those that are more social in nature and occur outside of the home.
- The consistency in which routines and activities occur in a family.[17]

While it can certainly be said that regular family events and activities, of the proper kind, can add to and enhance family stability, that is not even close to a proper definition of family stability. Research shows that children born to cohabiting, unmarried parents face an elevated risk of family instability relative to children born to married parents because cohabitation is

---

[17] One definition was from a college honors thesis, one was from a major university, while the rest were from commercial websites touting their family stability programs listed for sale.

less stable than marriage, even when children are present.[18] This same study states in the "Executive Summary", "...marriage seems to be associated with more family stability for children across much of the globe, whereas cohabitation is typically associated with more instability." Therefore, for the trend chart below labeled Family Stability, family stability will be defined as a traditional, two parent household, consisting of a mother and a father.

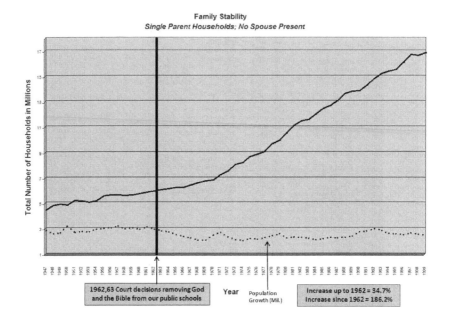

Figure 1 - Family Stability

On the chart above, a vertical line has been added to represent the point-in-time when the U.S. Supreme Court decisions were handed down. The chart above plots two values: 1.) The number of single parent households, and 2.) U.S. population growth. The population growth values were added to show that the increasing number of single parent households was not simply due to increasing population. The text block at the lower right corner of

---

[18] Laurie DeRose, Mark Lyons-Amos, W. Bradford Wilcox, Gloria Huarcaya, *THE COHABITATION-GO-ROUND: COHABITATION AND FAMILY INSTABILITY ACROSS THE GLOBE*, (New York, New York, Social Trends Institute, 2017), 7.

the chart lists the percentage of increase from 1947, the starting year of available data, up to 1962 and from 1962 to 1999, the ending year of available data. For anyone interested, the raw data, including citation of sources, for all trend charts can be found in the appendix at the end of the book.

It would seem the communists, directly or indirectly, have been quite successful in realizing one of their stated goals, namely to "Discredit the family as an institution. Encourage promiscuity and easy divorce.", goal number 40 in the list that was officially read into the United States Congressional Record in 1963 (see the complete list of Communist goals in the appendix).

Dissolution of Marriage

The next attribute indicating America's decline in morality that will be examined is the overall category of "Married vs. Unmarried Households". Strong family unity is not only part of America's religious strength it is also part of America's national strength. Family unity is despised by the materialism of Communism. Marx and Engels wrote in their *Manifesto of the Communist Party* that they stood for "the abolition of the family"[19].

Cohabitation is an increasingly common circumstance for the bearing and rearing of children, especially in America. Table 4.2 "Married vs. Unmarried Households", shown below, provides irrefutable evidence of that fact. A recent 2017 study also finds that family instability is higher in countries where more children are born to single mothers and cohabiting couples.[20] The authors of the study confirm that the data they gathered shows that "growth in cohabitation predicts growth in family instability"[21]. They also confirmed, unsurprisingly, that children born to single mothers have the least stable family lives [22]

---

[19] Marx and Engels, *Manifesto of the Communist Party*, 55, 71.
[20] Laurie DeRose, et. al., *THE COHABITATION-GO-ROUND: COHABITATION AND FAMILY INSTABILITY ACROSS THE GLOBE*, Executive Summary.
[21] Ibid, 20.
[22] Ibid.

Keith Hoar

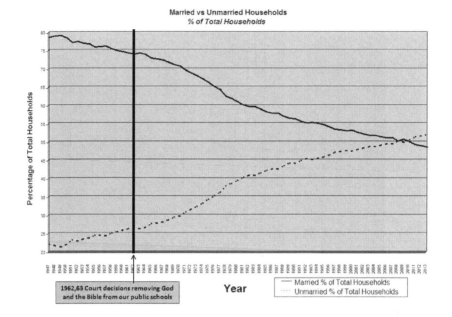

Figure 2 - Married vs. Unmarried Households

A vertical line has been added to represent the point-in-time when the U.S. Supreme Court decisions were handed down. The chart above plots two values: 1.) The percentage of married households, and 2.) The percentage of unmarried households. From 1947 to 1963 the percentage of unmarried households increased by 4.3%, representing an increase of 0.25% per year. From 1962 to 2013 the percentage of unmarried households increased by 25.6%, representing an increase of .50% per year. Three disconcerting observations arise from the above chart. 1. The rate of increase in unmarried households has doubled. 2. The number of unmarried households now exceeds the number of married households. 3. The perceived value of marriage is decreasing in America.

Considering the findings of the *COHABITATION-GO-ROUND* study, cited earlier, that confirmed growth in cohabitation (unmarried households) predicts growth in family instability. Once again, the data shows the communists, directly or indirectly, have been successful in realizing their stated goal of discrediting the family as an institution.

Demise of Traditional Values

The next attribute indicating America's decline in morality to be examined is the category of "Percentage of Births to UnWed Girls". Frank Newport in a Gallup article, referencing a May 2015 Gallup Values and Beliefs Survey, reveals a significant shift to the left in what Americans find morally acceptable. The article says, "Americans are becoming more liberal on social issues, as evidenced not only by the uptick in the percentage describing themselves as socially liberal, but also by their increasing willingness to say that a number of previously frowned-upon behaviors are morally acceptable."[23] The survey reports the *shocking* reality that only 29% of those surveyed responded that sex between an unmarried man and woman is morally wrong and only 20% responded that divorce is morally wrong! The survey indicates the percentage of respondents that say they believe having a baby outside of marriage is morally acceptable has increased an *astonishing* 16% in just fourteen years (2001-2015).

In a related Gallup article, Jeffery Jones, describing the same 2015 Gallup survey, shows that for the first time in Gallup records Americans who consider themselves generally liberal on social issues equal those who identify as social conservatives. In a chart comparing liberal vs. conservative identification for the years 1999-2015, for the year 2015 those that identify as Very Liberal/Liberal equals 31% and those that identify as Very Conservative/Conservative also equals 31%.[24]

---

[23] Frank Newport, *Americans Continue to Shift Left on Key Moral Issues*, (Gallup, 2015), http://www.gallup.com/poll/183413/americans-continue-shift-left-key-moral-issues.aspx, (accessed 8/24/2017).

[24] Jeffery Jones, *On Social Ideology, the Left Catches Up to the Right*, (Gallup: 2015), http://www.gallup.com/poll/183386/social-ideology-left-catches-right.aspx?utm_source=Politics&utm_medium=newsfeed&utm_campaign=tiles, (accessed 8/24/2017).

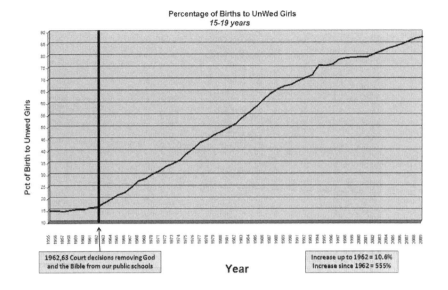

Percentage of Births to UnWed Girls
15-19 years

1962,63 Court decisions removing God and the Bible from our public schools

Year

Increase up to 1962 = 10.6%
Increase since 1962 = 555%

Figure 3 - Percentage of Births to UnWed Girls

As in previous charts, a vertical line has been added to represent the point-in-time when the U.S. Supreme Court decisions were handed down. From 1955 to 1963, the percentage of births to unwed girls increased from 14.2% to 17.4%, representing an increase of 0.36% per year. From 1963 to 2009, the percentage of births to unwed girls increased from 17.4% to 87.2%, representing an increase of 1.49% per year. The "per year" increase since 1963 represents a *staggering* fourfold increase!

Some portion of this rapid increase can likely be attributed to decreasing family stability. However, the majority of the increase is more likely due to an increasing acceptance of promiscuity in American society. An article in the *Los Angeles Times*, citing data from the Centers for Disease Control and Prevention, confirmed that the United States has the highest teen pregnancy rate in the entire industrialized world. The article also mentioned a controversy that resulted from the federal government's refusal to allow emergency contraceptive pills to be sold over-the-counter to girls age sixteen and younger.[25] The fact that a controversy could

---

[25] Shari Roan, *U.S. teen pregnancy rate remains highest in developed world*, Los Angeles Times, January 19, 2012, http://articles.latimes.com/2012/jan/19/news/la-heb-teen-pregnancy-20120119, (accessed 8/24/2017).

develop because the government will not allow *over-the-counter* sales of a pill to terminate teen pregnancies to "children" fifteen and younger certainly speaks to a decreasing morality in America.

Once again, the data in this chart shows the Communists, directly or indirectly, have been successful in realizing not only their stated goal of discrediting the family as an institution but also their goal of presenting promiscuity as "normal, natural, and healthy", see Communist goal #'s 40 and 26 in the appendix).

Dividend of Immoral Behavior

The next attribute indicating America's decline in morality that will be examined is labeled as the broad category "Morality". This broad category is composed of only cases of Gonorrhea. Other types of sexually transmitted diseases exhibit similar statistics. The chart below reveals an *absolutely shocking* increase in sexually transmitted disease.

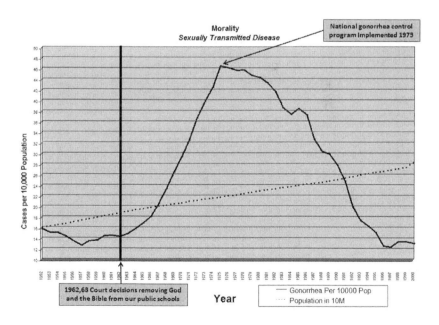

Figure 4 - Morality - Sexually Transmitted Disease

As in previous charts, a vertical line has been added to represent the point-in-time when the U.S. Supreme Court decisions were handed down. The chart above plots two values: 1.) Gonorrhea Cases per 10,000 population, and 2.) U.S. Population in 10M. The total Unites States population indicate a steady growth rate while the number of STD cases (specifically gonorrhea) exhibits a dramatic increase at the exact time of the Supreme Court decisions. The increase in the number of cases was increasing rapidly until 1975 when the National Gonorrhea Control Program was implemented. The government control program required twenty years to reduce the number of cases to the level of 1963.

After seemingly being under control, the incidence of sexually transmitted diseases is sadly once again on the rise. On November 17, 2015, in a NBC news report, the CDC's Dr. Gail Bolan said, "This is the first time since 2006 that all three of our notifiable [sp] sexually transmitted diseases have increased," Doctor Bolan went on to say in that report, "Some of the increases are quite alarming."[26] The report said, "Most of the increases have been seen in young adults, who get infected soon after they first begin having sex. The CDC estimates that half of the 20 million new sexually transmitted infections that occur every year are among people aged 15–24."[27]

The evidence presented in the chart above provides glaring proof that decades of increasing acceptance of immorality amongst American society has produced, and is producing, a serious negative consequence. The statement from a CDC official in the NBC News story paints a grim picture of the state of morals amongst America's most vulnerable youth – those, ages 15-24. An ever increasing advance toward liberal acceptance of immoral behavior and a court system that is telling our children God and Bible-based morality have no place in America's public education

---

[26] NBC News, Maggie Fox, *CDC Sees 'Alarming' Increase in Sexually Transmitted Diseases, https://www.nbcnews.com/health/sexual-health/cdc-sees-alarming-increase-sexually-transmitted-diseases-n465071* (Accessed 08/08/2018).
[27] Ibid.

system is having just the effect the communists laid out as their goal in the early part of the twentieth century.

Decline in Educational Achievement

The next attribute indicative of America's decline in morality that will be examined is the category 'Educational Achievement'. In May of 1994, Donald E. Simanek, Retired Professor of Physics, Lock Haven University of Pennsylvania, delivered a paper titled, *'Over the years we learn a thing or two!'* to the Indiana University (of PA) Physics Alliance meeting. The paper was also delivered two months earlier at the American Association of Physics Teachers (AAPT) regional meeting at Princeton University. In that presentation, Mr. Simanek said, "When I began teaching college physics nearly 30 years ago, we could count on perhaps 5 to 10 percent of the students in freshman physics being well-prepared, bright, intellectually curious, and hard working—capable of earning an honest A grade."[28]

Thirty years later he said, "Now, in the school where I teach, it's not uncommon to have a class in which there's **not one** student meeting this **outmoded** criterion for an A or B student. One is faced with an entire class of the caliber of those we used to 'write off' and ignore [emphasis added]." At the end of his paper, Mr. Simanek said his paper files were bulging with clippings and photocopies of articles from the 1970s when many observers were sounding the alarm about the impending problems in education. At the end of the paper, he lists citations to thirteen articles, dated from 1970 to 1990, describing the looming disaster.[29]

The following year, Mr. Simanek authored part 2 of the paper described above because he had conversations with college faculty, admissions directors, and administrators regarding the declining

---

[28] Donald E. Simanek, *The Decline of Education 1*, Lock Haven University, 1, https://www.lhup.edu/~dsimanek/decline1.htm (accessed 8/25/2017).
[29] Ibid, 17.

quality of students attending colleges.[30] He confirmed a distressing fact regarding college admissions, "Administrators have privately admitted to me that admissions standards have dropped to the point where 'any warm body' can get in. They say this is necessary to maintain enrollments and avoid catastrophic 'downsizing',..."[31]

As the paper continues, Mr. Simanek lists many complaints from college faculty regarding how poorly prepared entering freshmen were, the failure of high schools, and how he personally feels schools must be purged of the scourge of sports to reverse the decline in academic achievement. No doubt high schools poorly preparing students and the dominating influence of sports contributes to declining educational achievement. However, the real culprit is deeper than that. Students have become *aggressively* indifferent to honest learning. They believe they can learn without any effort on their part.[32]

Mr. Simanek said students actually came to him with the following requests and complaints:

- Will you grade it right/wrong, or just 'attempted'?
- You can't expect us to do homework problems, because we are working.
- I can't understand the textbook unless you go over it.
- We ought to get partial credit if we write down the correct equation.
- I understand the material, but I can't do the problems or answer the questions.[33]

In the twentieth and twenty-first centuries, education has become a *right* rather than a privilege. For some unknown reason students feel they *deserve* to receive good grades even though they refuse to put in the effort required to actually earn them.

---

[30] Donald E. Simanek, *The Decline of Education 2*, Lock Haven University, 1, https://www.lhup.edu/~dsimanek/decline2.htm (accessed 8/25/2017).
[31] Ibid.
[32] Ibid.
[33] Donald E. Simanek, *The Decline of Education 2, 4.*

Much more could be quoted related to the declining educational achievement and the methods offered to correct it and reverse the decline. The real purpose here is to simply reveal that there is an alarming decline in educational achievement. The chart below uses SAT scores as an indicator of declining educational achievement. The SAT test is a standardized test that colleges use to evaluate applicants. It is used by nearly every college in America for evaluating a student's college preparedness. It is designed to measure a student's ability to understand and process elements in three subjects: reading, writing, and math, hence, his or her educational achievement.

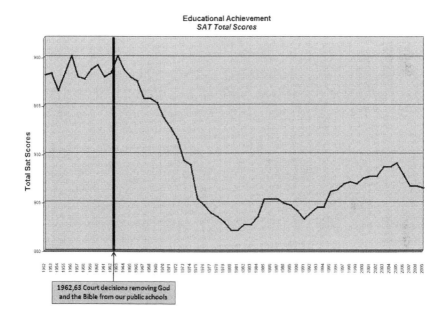

Figure 5 - Educational Achievement

As in previous charts, a vertical line has been added to represent the point-in-time when the U.S. Supreme Court decisions were handed down. The chart above plots a single value, SAT Total Scores. From 1952 to 1963, the average SAT Total Scores actually increased slightly (from 970 to 980). From 1963 to 1981 the SAT Total Scores showed a significant decline. Then from 1981 to 2006 there was some modest improvement in SAT Total

Scores. However, in 2006 it appears SAT Total Scores appear to again be declining.

The educational crisis is continuing well beyond the end of the data represented in the chart above. David Dorsey, a senior education policy fellow, in an article titled, '*A Crisis in Student Achievement*', wrote "Only 31 percent of students who took the ACT are considered college-ready in English, reading, math, and science."[34]

Once again it would seem the communists have been successful, directly or indirectly, in weakening and/or destroying America's educational system. Specifically, consider goal #17, where they say they want to get control of the schools to use as transmission belts for Socialist and Communist propaganda. Or goal #32, where they say they support any socialist movement to give centralized control over any part of the culture - education, etc. Or goal #31. Where they want to belittle all forms of American culture and discourage the teaching of American history. There are a number of other goals that, if successful, eat away at America's culture and foundation. The result is students that are aggressively hostile to authority, teachers, law enforcement, parents, and others. With such a hostile attitude, learning becomes nearly impossible. The decline of SAT Total Scores as shown in the chart above testifies to that fact.

The situation in colleges and universities has gotten far worse than what Mr. Simanek complained about in his two papers described above. Recent polls indicate that most Americans no longer believe acquiring a higher education is worth the time or money it requires. Possessing a college degree once provided the graduate with the opportunity to get a well-paying job. However, modern employers are no longer impressed. The job market is filled with college graduates who are simply not qualified for higher paying positions. Believing that people with college degrees are smarter than people who have not graduated from college is no longer a safe assumption.

Studies show that college and university services are less geared for student needs than for the needs of administrators and

---

[34] David Dorsey, *A Crisis in Student Achievement*, Topeka Capital-Journal, Jan. 19, 2017.

professors. Far too many college courses reflect the interests of the people who teach them rather than the needs of the students who take them. Many courses are designed, not for the teaching of useful and demanding subjects, but to draw students or to promote a liberal agenda.

It would seem that everyone mostly understands that except for those who are running the colleges and those that are paying the bill. If provosts or academic administrators were asked to grade themselves on how well they are preparing students for success in the workforce, they would likely give themselves an A. In fact, they did. Scott Jaschik reported in a 2014 survey of chief academic officers performed by Inside Higher Ed that an astounding ninety-six percent responded that they were doing a good job.[35]

Somewhere there is a rather large disconnect. A Gallup study performed on behalf of the Lumina Foundation, measured how business leaders and the American public viewed the state and value of higher education. The survey revealed that just fourteen percent of Americans and only eleven percent of business leaders strongly agreed that graduates had the necessary skills and competencies to succeed in the workplace.[36]

One report describing some of the ridiculous courses also included the cost per year to attend the school. The cost to attend for one year at many of the schools was in excess of $65,000 per year. That equates to a staggering cost to obtain a four-year education at some of those schools in excess of $260,000. So, in some cases, students, or their parents, are spending in excess of one quarter of a million dollars for an education that eighty-nine percent of business leaders believe does not provide them with the required competencies to succeed in the workplace.

Throughout their entire school years, American school children are told that to succeed in life, they **must** go to college. They are driven to work hard to get there. Some parents decimate

[35] Scott Jaschik, *Pressure on the Provosts*, http://www.insidehighered.com/news/survey/pressure-provosts-2014-survey-chief-academic-officers (Accessed 08/09/2018).
[36] Gallup Inc., *What America Needs To Know About Higher Education Redesign*, https://www.gallup.com/services/176759/america-needs-know-higher-education-redesign.aspx (Accessed 08/09/2018).

their savings accounts and some parents or students sign up for enormous loans to pay for that education. But, are the students *really* learning anything and is it *really* worth it? Maybe or maybe not!

Richard Arum and Josipa Roksa in their book, *Academically Adrift: Limited Learning on College Campuses*, reported on a study that assessed the gain in reasoning and writing skills of more than 2,300 undergraduates at the end of their sophomore year. Here is what they said:

> Another way to assess the magnitude of learning during the first two years in college is to estimate how many students experience gains that fall below the level of statistical significance, or in other words are statistically not above zero. With a large sample of more than 2,300 students, we observe no statistically significant gains in critical thinking, complex reasoning, and writing skills for at least 45 percent of the students in our study.[37]

In a footnote to the statement above, the authors discuss paired-sample, other estimation strategies, and confidence intervals that would demonstrate even higher rates of 47 percent or 53 percent. In regard to questions of reliability, they say any errors would likely pertain to the other half of the distribution as well.[38]

Another disturbing fact is that a substantial portion of the high cost of college education will likely fall on the shoulders of taxpayers. According to the non-profit organization Student Loan Report, as of March 2018, there were 16.9 percent (7.6 million) federal student loan borrowers who were either in default or were in excess of ninety days delinquent. They reported a staggering total student load debt of 1.52 Trillion dollars! The total amount of student loans in default is then approximately 175 Billion dollars.[39] This troubling situation cannot be understated. Student load debt is

---

[37] Richard Arum and Josipa Roksa, *Academically Adrift: Limited Learning on College Campuses,* (Chicago and London: University of Chicago Press, 2011), 36.
[38] Ibid., 219.
[39] Student Loan Report, *Student Loan Debt Statistics 2018*, https://studentloans.net/student-loan-debt-statistics/ (Accessed 08/10/2018).

the second leading form of debt in the United States, second only to mortgage debt. Most of those loans in default, the majority with some form of Federal guarantee, will never be paid and taxpayers will be left to bear the cost.

Nationwide, colleges and universities have become far less interested in preparing students for careers and are more concerned with offering classes steeped in identity politics and liberalism. A thirty-three page report published by Young America's Foundation, titled '*Comedy & Tragedy: College Course Descriptions and What They Tell Us About Higher Education Today*' contains a lengthy list of college courses that defy belief. The report stated:

> It's no secret that America's colleges and universities have operated as bastions of radical liberal thought and activism for at least the last half century. Despite increased public pressure for intellectual balance, however, higher education is only devolving further into ideological monopoly. No longer are our nation's professors teaching students material that is simply biased, they're also teaching students material that is nonsense, and increasingly beneath the dignity of the degrees they're working to earn.[40]

The final twenty-eight pages of the report presents a lengthy list of radical courses and their course descriptions exactly as they were listed on each school's website. A few of those courses are:

- Interrogating Gender: Centuries of Dramatic Cross-Dressing
- God, Sex, Chocolate: Desire and the Spiritual Path
- Tattoos, Piercing, and Body Adornment
- Queer Musicology
- The Sociology of Miley Cyrus
- Queering the Bible

---

[40] Young America Foundation, *Comedy & Tragedy: College Course Descriptions and What They Tell Us About Higher Education Today*, 1.

- Rednecks, Queers, and Country Music:
- The Unbearable Whiteness of Barbie

The courses listed above are just a few of the ridiculous and nonsensical courses exposed in the full study. Fifty of those courses and the schools that offer them are listed in the appendix in this book. To view the complete list of courses with full course descriptions, use the webpage address from the citation in the bibliography to download a copy of the study described above. Note: In the course description provided for each course, the full study includes a webpage address for the entry in each school's online course catalog.

The threat of far-left, radical course material and its influence is not just confined to college campuses. Education and administration majors are educated at colleges and universities where the ideology is overwhelmingly far-left.

Mitchell Langbert, associate professor of business management at Brooklyn College, authored an article titled, *Homogeneous: The Political Affiliations of Elite Liberal Arts College Faculty*. In that article Mr. Langbert details the results of his survey of 8,688 tenured professors from fifty-one of the top sixty-six ranked liberal arts colleges in the U.S. News 2017 report. He reports the ratio of democratic/liberal professors to republican/conservative professors across twenty-four academic departments. The survey results show a great disparity as you move from the STEM subjects, such as Engineering, Chemistry, Economics, Mathematics, and Physics, toward the social sciences and humanities. The STEM subjects show a D:R ratio that ranges from 1.6:1 to 6.2:1. The results are markedly lopsided when you reach the four humanities, English, Religion, Anthropology, and Communications. They show a D:R ratio that ranges from 48.3:1 to 108:0.[41] While it is not unexpected that the ratio of democratic to republican professors at liberal arts colleges would highly favor

---

[41] Mitchell Langbert, *Homogeneous: The Political Affiliations of Elite Liberal Arts College Faculty*, National Association of Scholars, https://www.nas.org/articles/homogenous_political_affiliations_of_elite_liberal (Accessed 09/04/2018)

a democratic political philosophy, the D:R ratio at other colleges is likely very similar.

Many of those graduates then assume teaching or administrative positions in public middle and high schools and they bring their liberal philosophy with them. Nowhere is that more clearly demonstrated than by the sessions and workshops offered at the 2017 Annual Convention of The National Council of Teachers of English. Listed below are a few of those sessions and workshops (snippets of the descriptions are in italics):

- D.01 - FEATURED SESSION: Queering English Studies: Navigating Politics, Policies, and Practices in ELA, Learning Spaces: "...*pursuing research agendas that move English studies from "preservation to transformation."...*"
- B.50 - Who Are We as Activist Allies? Storying Our Work as Social Justice Educators: "...*impact social justice education. Presenters will weave stories of being and becoming activist allies...*"
- C.35 - Teaching Compassion by Advocating for Peace and Social Justice through Children's Literature: "...*use social justice literature to change the world... explore selections of social justice children's literature and ways to integrate them into the curriculum...*"
- A.40 - Why Are All the Trans Youth So "Normal"?: Intersectionality and Absence in Current Trans Fiction for Youth: "...*current lack of engagement with racial and class difference...*"
- E.46 - Using LGBTQ Texts in Middle School to Cultivate Passion, Rigor, and Inclusion: "...*explore teaching LGBTQ texts in the middle school...* "
- J.38 - Creating Agents of Change: Navigating through and Responding to LGBTQ Literary Texts: "...*gain insight into preparing their students to be agents of change.*"[42]

---

[42] The National Council of Teachers of English, 2017 National Convention Agenda, https://ncte2017.zerista.com (Accessed 09/01/2018).

The first paragraph of the NCTE vision says:

NCTE and its members *will apply the power of language and literacy to actively pursue justice and equity* [emphasis added] for all students and the educators who serve them. As the nation's oldest organization of pre-K through graduate school literacy educators, NCTE has a rich history of deriving expertise and advocacy from its members' professional research, practice, and knowledge. Today, we must more precisely align this expertise *to advance access, power, agency, affiliation, and impact for all learners* [emphasis added].

The session and workshop descriptions are littered with the familiar phrases of the far-left: pursuing agendas, transformation, impact social justice, racial and class difference, sociopolitical consciousness, and others. However, what is glaringly missing is any mention of actually teaching English and language skills. The socialist-leaning educator's agenda is all about transformation and change. Is it any wonder that academic quality continues its downward slide toward failure?

Deluge of Violence

The final attribute indicating America's decline in morality that will be examined is the category 'Violent Behavior'. A search of the internet using the search parameter "increasing violence" returns hundreds of thousands of results. Most of the resulting articles that were viewed referred to gun violence and many others to violence in schools or at the workplace. Rather than cite numerous articles on violence and what the author thinks is the cause, it is more relevant to point out a deeper underlying cause. Mr. Skousen, in his book, *The Naked Communist*, did an excellent job of distilling the beliefs of dialectical materialism, the heart and soul of Communism, down to four major premises. They are the excuse which gives validation to the revolutionary violence and amoral conduct of Communism. Acceptance of the ideology behind those premises persuades some intellectuals and wealthy individuals to believe Communism is the great hope of the modern world. Understanding the forces at work behind the scene is critical when evaluating the sudden increase in the decline of America's moral values. Those four major premises Mr. Skousen listed are:

1. Everything in existence came about as a result of ceaseless motion among the forces of nature.
2. Human beings are only graduate beasts.
3. There is no such thing as innate right or wrong.
4. That all religion must be overthrown because it inhibits the spirit of world revolution.[43]

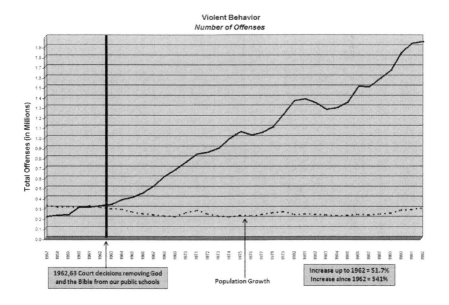

Figure 6 - Violent Behavior

As you can see in the chart above, the percentage increase in the number of violent offenses has increased dramatically since 1963. From 1957 to 1963 the percentage increase in number of violent offenses was 51.7% while from 1963 to 1992 the percentage increase was 541%, representing a *startling* tenfold

---

[43] W. Cleon Skousen, *The Naked Communist*, 354-356

increase. Hate and the violence it provokes are major tenets of the Communist agenda. V. I. Lenin, in his book, *"Left-Wing" Communism: an Infantile Disorder"*, writing in regard to the hate towards class politicians and the bourgeoisie said, " This hatred of the representative of oppressed and exploited masses is, indeed, 'the beginning of all wisdom'; it is the basis of every Socialist and Communist movement and of its success."[44] Two of the stated Communist goals in Mr. Skousen's book speak specifically to the hate Lenin wrote of. Goal #19 says, "Use student riots to foment public protests against programs or organizations." Goal #42 says, "Create the impression that violence and insurrection are legitimate aspects of the American tradition." (See the appendix for a complete list.) Couple those two goals with other goals that say, "eliminate all laws governing obscenity", "break down cultural standards of morality", and "infiltrate the churches and replace revealed religion with 'social' religion". When cultural standards and morality are destroyed, society disintegrated from within. Is it any wonder that violence has increased significantly in America?

Decided Fate

If you understand the objectives behind the four major premises of the Communist Party listed earlier, you will come to understand how supposed, *well-meaning* individuals have become involved in pushing forward the Communist agenda. Those individuals were converted to Communist *objectives* because they accepted seemingly superficial Communist *slogans*. Over time they began to think exactly the way the Communists wanted them to think.

America's public school system is teaching the '*Theory of Evolution*' as a fact. By teaching evolution as fact and the **ONLY** possible explanation for man's existence, public schools have now taught multiple generations of children that man is just a 'graduate beast', satisfying premise numbers one and two. The phrase '*graduate beast*' simply means: to develop by degrees; to change

---

[44] Lenin, *Left-Wing" Communism: an Infantile Disorder*, (Detroit, Michigan: The Marxian Education Society, 1921), 78.

gradually. This aligns with the *evolutionists'* theory that everything you see around you simply evolved over billions and billions of years through accidental, undirected, random processes. Man certainly becomes a beast if you believe, even at his best, man is no better or worse than an animal. Then through sex education, public schools have instructed children how to live immorally, and using 'values clarification' and 'situational ethics' they have taught children how to rid themselves of any guilt feelings, satisfying premise number three.

The catastrophe that is looming in American culture is that America's citizens are losing, or have lost, their grasp of the difference between the freedom produced by America's Christian heritage and the slavery produced by materialism and atheism. America is rapidly approaching the tipping-point where no amount of effort will be able to right the ship. Has America already reached the point where the ship can no longer be righted? Can America be saved from the impending catastrophe? Only time will tell.

Keith Hoar

Chapter Four: A Battle For Truth

The ship of Democracy, which has weathered all storms, may sink through the mutiny of those aboard.

Grover Cleveland

A Battle

> If a lie is only printed often enough, it becomes a quasi-truth, and if such a truth is repeated often enough, it becomes an article of belief, a dogma, and men will die for it.
>
> Isa Blagden
> The Crown Of Life, Vol. III, 1869, p. 155

For Truth

The Deception Worsens

As the final words of the preceding chapter were read and reviewed, one additional, crucial question presented itself. *"Is America's moral condition improving, staying the same, or is it getting worse?"*

As America nears the end of the second decade of the twenty-first century, upheaval, anger, unrest, distrust, disillusionment, and violence saturate the newspapers and television newscasts on a daily basis.

Considering the premise of this book, does *historical revisionism* directly or indirectly add to or influence the decreasing morality in America? Is there a *'deception'* being perpetrated upon America? The answer to that question is a resounding yes! Historical revisionism, and its underlying deception, absolutely does have an impact on America's morality. It has a direct impact on the weakening of America's foundation. The word *'foundation'* refers to those things upon which a society rests,

or those things by which social order is maintained. Another definition is: the great principles of truth and righteousness upon which American society once rested.

The destruction of America's foundation can be found in any of the following:

- When truth is no longer cherished
- When *true* justice is no longer practiced
- When deceit takes the place of honesty
- When scorn takes the place of honor
- When dishonesty prevails
- When integrity and virtue are considered old-fashioned and are no longer valued
- When living by standards or morality is sneered at and ridiculed

Some historical revisionists admit they deliberately dismiss the theological meditations of the colonists and founders. The revisionists (some deliberately and some driven by their own prejudices and anti-Christian biases) write their histories to deceive the American people into believing that America was not founded as a Christian nation, that America did not have a Christian heritage, and that the *Founding Fathers* intended that there be an impenetrable wall between church and state. The United States Supreme Court, quoting only cases or other justices that agreed with that desired position, have thereby instructed multiple generations of school children that God and the Bible do not belong in the public education system, in government, or in the work place.

Numerous generations have grown to adulthood being taught from altered histories that declare America is not a Christian nation and what is moral or immoral is determined only by individual circumstance. They have been taught the *Theory of Evolution* (more accurately it should be labeled a supposition) which contends all of creation is the result of a giant cosmic accident. Is it any wonder that generations of Americans begin to resemble the 'graduate beasts' as defined in one of the major premises of Communism. Without any moral absolutes to believe in or to be guided by, what else could have been expected.

To validate the claim that Americans are becoming like 'graduate beasts', recent research shows that even the church has been affected by historical revisionism.

In July 2015 Barna Group conducted a survey of America's general population to determine American views on morality (specifics will be presented later). The survey results are quite distressing to put it mildly. Overall, the survey found that eight in ten Americans *"expressed concern about the nation's moral condition"*. People of all ages, backgrounds, and religious beliefs seem to recognize, and admit, that America has a problem. What is even more disturbing is that those same people are divided on who or what determines morality. According to the survey, two-thirds of American adults admit they believe morality is relative to the circumstances.

It is interesting to note that those surveyed are concerned about America's moral condition yet many believe morality is simply relative. The question that must be asked is: *relative to what exactly?* If they believe morality is relative, they believe each individual must be allowed to decide their own morality. So what are they concerned about? If morality *is* relative, one individual's morality is no more right or wrong than any other individual's morality.

Sadly, this modernistic, evolutionary thinking affects not only people outside the church but also affects those within the church. The 2015 Barna Group research study mentioned earlier found that 41% of practicing Christians either somewhat or strongly agreed with the statement: *"Whatever is right for your life or works best for you is the only truth you can know"*.[1] This is in exact agreement with the old "values clarification" and "situational ethics" mantras of the 1980's and 1990's.

Over half of all Americans, and three-quarters of millennials, agree with the above statement and, therefore, believe morality is relative. A staggering four out of ten *practicing* Christians agree with the concept of relativistic morality. That is exactly the same kind of destructive thinking that afflicted Israel in the Old Testament. *"In those days there was no king in Israel: every man did that which was right in his own eyes."*, Judges 21:25. That is the sad state in which America finds itself. Everybody decides for *themselves* what is right *in their own eyes* no matter what consequences it has for them, for their families, or for society.

To demonstrate how deeply this new morality of self-fulfillment has crept into the 'Church', see the six survey questions and their responses shown below. David Kinnaman, President of Barna Group, argues in his book, *Good Faith*, that the new morality has all but replaced Christianity as the culture's new moral norm. The six guiding principles of self-fulfillment are (the percentages shown are for the respondents that *somewhat* or *strongly agreed* with the statement):

- The best way to find yourself is by looking within yourself. US Adults 91%; Practicing Christians 76%

[1] Barna Research Group, *"The End of Absolutes: America's New Moral Code"*, May 25, 2016, https://www.barna.com/research/the-end-of-absolutes-americas-new-moral-code/ (accessed 12/9/2017).

- People should not criticize someone else's life choices.
  US Adults 89%; Practicing Christians 67%
- To be fulfilled in life, you should pursue the things you desire most.
  US Adults 86%; Practicing Christians 72%
- The highest goal of life is to enjoy it as much as possible.
  US Adults 84%; Practicing Christians 67%
- People can believe whatever they want, as long as those beliefs don't affect society.
  US Adults 79%; Practicing Christians 61%
- Any kind of sexual expression between two consenting adults is acceptable.
  US Adults 69%; Practicing Christians 40%[2]

The foregoing information should provide a wake-up call to Christians everywhere. Not a single one of the above mentioned concepts can be found anywhere in the Bible. Despite that fact, a majority of Christians believe five out of six represent acceptable behavior!

In another article describing the results of the 2015 survey, David Kinnaman said:

The highest good, according to our society, is 'finding yourself' and then living by 'what's right for you'. There is a tremendous amount of individualism in today's society, and that's reflected in the church too. Millions of Christians have grafted New Age dogma onto their spiritual person..... While we wring our hands about secularism spreading through culture, a majority of churchgoing Christians have embraced corrupt, me-centered theology.

So, there appears to be a dichotomy at work among practicing Christians in America.... Such widespread cognitive dissonance—among both practicing Christians and Americans more generally—is another indicator of

[2] Barna Research Group, *Year in Review: Barna's 10 Most-Read Articles of 2016*, December 22, 2016, https://www.barna.com/research/year-review-barnas-10-read-articles-2016/ (accessed 12/9/2017).

the cultural flux Barna has identified through the past two decades.[3]

The word 'flux' in the quote above simply means instability. Instability could also mean shakiness or wavering. Americans are wavering in their basic convictions. They no longer hold to the absolutes of the past. That is exactly the result the communists that met at the University of California - Berkeley in 1992 advocated as one of their goals that would allow them to change society.

Some of you might be inclined to believe that Communism died following the breakup of the old Soviet Socialist Republic. Once again, you would be wrong. Communism is not dead nor is it dying. It never went anywhere. It is alive and well. The following pages will detail some of the views regarding Socialism/Communism from the younger generation called millennials."

A recent poll conducted in October 2017 by the Victims of Communism Memorial Foundation pointed out a disturbing drift toward Socialism and Communism among America's youth. The poll, conducted by the data firm YouGov, revealed that *half of millennials* responded that they would rather live in a socialist or communist country than a capitalist democracy. Yes, you read that statement correctly. A *staggering* 51% of millennials (defined as ages 21-29 in this survey) would prefer to live in a socialist or communist country than a capitalist democracy![4]

In a statement to Fox News, Marion Smith, executive director of the Victims of Communism Memorial Foundation, expressed deep concern regarding this trend, "Millennials now make up the largest generation in America, and we're seeing some deeply worrisome trends. Millennials are increasingly turning away from

---

[3] *The End of Absolutes: America's New Moral Code*, https://www. barna.com/research/the-end-of-absolutes-americas-new-moral-code/ (accessed 12/9/2017).

[4] Victims of Communism Memorial Foundation, *Annual Report on US Attitudes Toward Socialism*, October 2017, 13.

capitalism and toward socialism and even communism as a viable alternative."[5]

Oh, it gets even worse. The table below shows the percentage of millennials that viewed various communist leaders favorably:

- Karl Marx, the father of communism - 32%
- Che Guevara - 31%
- Vladimir Lenin - 23%
- Russian President Vladimir Putin - 21%
- Mao Tse-Tung - 19%
- Josef Stalin - 6%

A reality that is far more worrisome is that the survey revealed seven out of ten (72%) of millennials either did not know or misidentified the definition of communism.[6]

That disturbing fact speaks to a dangerous historical illiteracy that is sweeping through American society regarding Socialism and Communism. It also speaks to a systemic failure of the public education system to *truthfully* teach students about the brutality, hopelessness, and misery caused by Socialism and Communism; and also their abject failure in every place where they have been tried.

In an essay titled "*A Religion for a New Age*" published in *The Humanist* magazine's January-February 1983 issue, John J. Dunphy wrote, "I am convinced that the battle for humankind's future must be waged and won in the public school classroom by teachers who correctly perceive their role as the proselytizers of a new faith:…"[7] Be certain to read the end of the section "Education Today" in the Conclusion regarding how Socialist organizations

---

[5] Marion Smith, *Millennials think socialism would create a great safe space, study finds*, Fox News, November 3, 2017, http://www.foxnews.com/us/2017/11/03/millennials-think-socialism-would-create-great-safe-space-study-finds.html (accessed 12/11/2017).

[6] Victims of Communism Memorial Foundation, *Annual Report on US Attitudes Toward Socialism*, 15.

[7] John J. Dunphy, *The Book that Started It All*, Council for Secular Humanism, Secular Humanist Bulletin, vol 21 issue 4, https://www.secularhumanism.org/index.php/articles/3452 (accessed 12/11/2017).

are pushing their members to 'take jobs as teachers' in order to move teachers' unions in a more militant direction.

It appears that Mr. Dunphy has been proven correct. The battle to destroy America's Christian Heritage is being waged in the classroom. The sad fact is that not only is secular humanism winning but so is Socialism and Communism. The younger generations seem to believe that Socialism and Communism are good things and should be embraced. That attitude is likely because of public education teachers that possess socialist worldviews and endorse them in the classroom. Because of the staggering illiteracy with regard to Communism, today's public school students can rightfully wear the label *Useful Idiots*, a phrase generally attributed to Vladimir Lenin.[8]

The words of Ronald Reagan, given in his inaugural address on January 5, 1967, must be taken to heart now more than ever.

> "Freedom is a fragile thing and is never more than one generation away from extinction. It is not ours by inheritance; it must be fought for and defended constantly by each generation, for it comes only once to a people. Those who have known freedom and then lost it have never known it again."[9]

Now that you have been confronted with clear, irrefutable evidence of how the *historical revisionists* are rewriting history can you remain unconvinced and unmoved? Will you continue to allow the *historical revisionists* to toss America's precious Christian heritage into a *'memory hole'* like the one described in George Orwell's novel *1984*? Can you remain silent? Can you say and do nothing? Will you fall back into the same old rut, paralyzed by a towering mountain of apathy? America's future hangs in the balance. Will you not become educated on the issues, join the battle, and sound the alarm?

---

[8] An extensive search turned up no verifiable source(s) for this quote. It is simply offered as stated in many books and articles.
[9] Ronald Regan, Gubernatorial Inaugural Address, January 5, 1967, https://reaganlibrary. archives.gov/archives/speeches/govspeech/01051967a.htm (accessed 12/11/217).

Keith Hoar

A War Rages

There is a war raging in this country that threatens to destroy America's future. That war is plainly visible and increasing in influence. It is eating away at America's foundation.

The Supreme Court has said children cannot pray in school. The Supreme Court declares they cannot talk about God - well not the *real one* anyway. Use the name *Jesus* – no. Sing *Christmas* carols in school - absolutely not. Display a Bible verse at work - are you out of your mind? The Ten Commandments, the bedrock of America's morality and law, are being or have already been removed from classrooms, public buildings, and courtrooms all across the country. What is it that those who hate God and the Ten Commandments really fear? Are they afraid someone might read the Ten Commandments and actually obey them? Yes, but the root of the problem is much deeper and more basic than that. There is an anti-Christian bias that is permeating all facets of life in America.

The root of this anti-Christian bias is as old as the first sin itself. It begins with a questioning of truth. It first began when Satan asked Eve in the Garden, "...*Yea, hath God said*," (Genesis 3:1).[10] At the root of anti-Christian bias, there is a hatred of and refusal to acknowledge truth. Because God defines truth, hatred of truth is therefore hatred of God. Hate truth – hate God. Hate God – hate truth. Those two pronouncements are inseparable.

America has reached a point in time when everything is being questioned. The Bible, religion, authority, integrity, history, and even right and wrong. All foundational truths are being challenged and redefined. Even America's Christian heritage is being relegated to the meaningless category of "irrelevant theological meditations" (more on this dangerous misrepresentation of history later, see page 114). Christians have long and often differed among themselves on issues of doctrine, but historically they had always been in agreement that there is an *absolute* truth that undergirds all laws and morals. However, that has all changed. Society today,

---

[10] All Scripture quotations are from the Authorized King James Version Bible, Pure Cambridge Edition, (Cambridge, United Kingdom: Cambridge University Press).

including Christians, is seeking to define itself using situational ethics, values clarification, or relativistic ideas of what truth is or is not. Today, not just the secular world, but Christians and pastors, are attacking even the suggestion that there is such a thing as *absolute* truth. Data contained in a survey conducted after the 9/11 terrorist attack indicated that sixty-eight percent of adults who attended conservative, non-mainline churches questioned whether absolute moral truth exists.[11]

Carefully consider the following question that bears critical and urgent importance. *Does America have a Christian founding and thereby possess a Christian heritage*? That question regarding the role religion, specifically Christianity, played in the discovery and founding of the Republic called America has been a source of intense controversy and bitter debate ever since this nation began. The answer to that question has far reaching implications concerning how America's founding is envisioned and it also determines how Americans view themselves. It defines America's laws. It defines America's motives. It defines America as a people. Ultimately, it defines America as a nation.

In most high schools, colleges, and universities, a large portion of America's history is considered irrelevant to current post-modernist thinking. Many American history curriculums now have only passing references to the *Founding Fathers* with some modern historians going so far as to admit they remove "theological meditations" from the actual historical accounts because they are irrelevant. Some state school boards have gone so far as to approve new curriculum guidelines that do not require teaching the first one hundred years of early American History (see the discussion of this matter in the conclusion, see page 185). How can you begin to understand a nation's history if you eliminate its first one hundred years? The answer is rather obvious. You cannot! The above mentioned facts demand an answer to each of the following two questions:

---

[11] George Barna,"*How America's Faith Has Changed Since 9/11*", https://www.barna.org/component/content/article/5-barna-update/45-barna-update-sp-657/63-how-americas-faith-has-changed-since-9-11#.V446m_nzUx4 (accessed 09/02/2017).

Keith Hoar

- **What are the true facts of history?**
- **Do they really matter?**

As dozens and dozens of books, articles, and websites were reviewed during the writing of this book, a number of authors were found who bemoaned the condition of America's Christianity and how it differs little from the world. Despite their concern, many of those authors stated that they did not want to be viewed as an alarmist. Well, America's Christian heritage is being threatened, perhaps even abolished. *Someone* needs to be an alarmist. *Someone* must be willing to sound the alarm.

Reading statements like that begs the question, "*If God was suddenly missing, would anyone notice? Even worse, would anyone care?*" For the sake of argument, say God just up and left. He was not there when some poor soul cried out for Him. He could not be found in the world, anywhere. Would anyone notice or acknowledge His absence? "That sounds crazy and farfetched", you say. Well, that is precisely what happened to Israel in the Old Testament. God's presence departed from the Temple and withdrew from Israel and no one noticed!

Stop and let that sink in. In the wilderness, the "Presence of God" *always* went before Israel. The Shekinah Glory of God was always present with Israel as they wandered in the wilderness. The Glory of God stood as a pillar of fire by night and as a pillar of smoke by day, Exodus 13:21-22. Later, when Moses constructed the Tabernacle, that Shekinah Glory filled the tent of meeting, eventually coming to rest as a pillar of fire and smoke on the Ark of the Covenant, Exodus 40:34-38. When Solomon built his temple, the Glory of the Presence of God came to rest upon the Ark of the Covenant once again, I Kings 8:10-11.

For eight centuries, the Presence of God abode within the temple and with His people. But when Israel and Judah became backslidden to such an abominable state that idol worship, temple prostitution, and infant sacrifice were incorporated into the religion of Israel, the Glory of God departed.

Can you imagine the horror and sense of loss Israel felt when that happened? Wait! There was no horror. There was no alarm. No one cried out. Not one single soul noticed. First, the Glory of

94

God went up from the cherub and stood over the threshold of the house, Ezekiel 10:4. No one noticed. Then the Glory of God departed from off the threshold of the house and stood over the cherubim, Ezekiel 10:18. No one noticed. Then the Glory of God went up from the midst of the city and stood upon the mountain on the east side of the city, Ezekiel 11:23. And still no one noticed. No pillar of fire! No pillar of smoke! Gone! The Glory of God was gone and absolutely no one had noticed or sounded an alarm!

Why is that important and how does it relate to the topic being discussed here? It is *vitally* important because that same tragedy is happening again and again and again in churches all across America. The Holy Spirit, Jesus Christ's presence with the church, is departing. Why is that? Could it be due to the fact that He is no longer preeminent in Christians' lives? America is busily scrubbing the last remnants of God from academic life, public life, and sadly, private life as well. America has begun to worship the god of culture and the god of science rather than the God of Heaven.

A major battle in the war against Christianity is destroying America's Christian heritage. If the world is successful in convincing America that it is not a Christian nation and it has no Christian heritage, America's foundation will be destroyed. Consider King David's words, *"If the foundations be destroyed, what can the righteous do?"* (Psalm 11:3). The word foundation in that verse can be taken to mean that which is good, right, and just (piety, justice, fidelity, integrity, and mercy) which are the pillars or foundation of a people, a state, or a country. If America's moral foundations are destroyed, the condition of all righteous men will be desperate indeed. If you destroy a people's foundation, if you can persuade people that their religious heritage is a sham and a lie, you destroy them and take away their hope.

The *true facts* of history will demonstrate that America's heritage is, in fact, Christian. The brave men that first settled this country and those great men that framed the Constitution will be allowed to speak for themselves and in their own words regarding the Christian heritage of America. History will then show how the early pioneers built upon that foundation and how Christianity thrived. Following that, consideration must also be given to the evidence that demonstrates how Christianity is waning and turning to worldly methods and is losing the battle for its children. Finally, indisputable facts, gleaned from numerous official government sources, will reveal decades of declining morality that can be linked to America's refusal to acknowledge its Christian heritage.

America has reached a perilous point in its history. The German philosopher Georg Friedrich Hegel is often quoted as saying, "The only thing we learn from history is that we learn nothing from history."[12] That certainly seems true in regard to America's Christian heritage. However, it is even far more serious than simply forgetting or not learning. As will be documented on the pages that follow, there is a concerted effort by some, not just to revise history, but to eradicate any mention of America's Christian heritage. George Orwell, in his dystopian novel, *Nineteen Eighty-Four*, foretold of the danger of such an approach to history. In that novel, he wrote of an insidious place called the '*memory hole*'. In the novel, government censors, 'The Ministry of Truth', erased all traces of news articles embarrassing or unacceptable to Big Brother by sending them down an incineration chute called the '*memory hole*', thereby giving everyone the impression the offensive truth never existed.

There is a great, and often unconsidered, danger associated with the increasing reliance on the vast electronic storage systems in use today. A government, or court, or data storage provider, or search engine can arbitrarily rule certain information is unacceptable and may no longer be viewed. It could be an electronic book, an electronic newspaper article, or historical information considered irrelevant, unacceptable, or offensive. The unacceptable information is simply dropped into the '*memory hole*'. In an instant, the information no longer exists and history is changed.

Orwell's tale is fiction, but what is happening today is not fiction. You do not have to go to a communist country to find individuals rewriting history books. In America, most history texts written after 1932 suffer from varying degrees of *deliberate* alteration by revisionists (more on this wrongdoing later).

---

[12] An extensive search turned up no verifiable source(s) for this quote. It is simply offered as stated in numerous books and articles.

If you dare to acknowledge that the truth of America's Christian heritage can be hidden, altered, or perhaps even eliminated by scholars, academics, or revisionist historians with anti-Christian biases, you must face another real and distasteful truth. If the revisionists can silence the truth of history, they will also attempt to silence the Truth of the Gospel.

We must then ask, "What is truth?" Nearly two thousand years ago Pilate asked Jesus that same question, John 18:38. It is a question that has echoed throughout history to the present time. Was Pilate's question a true desire to know what truth was, a sarcastic insult, or perhaps just an apathetic reply to avoid an answer he knew he would not like? Truth is simply *telling it like it is*. Truth is the way things *really* are or were. Any other perception or view is wrong no matter what the motivation may be.

> **Truth**
> 1. Conformity to fact or reality; exact accordance with that which is, or has been, or shall be.
> 2. True state of facts or things.
>
> Noah Webster
> 1828 Dictionary

The Greek word Pilate used for 'truth' was *aletheia*, which literally means: 'true, or hiding nothing'. Therefore, it is the duty of historians to report the true facts of history *as they were, hiding nothing* and not as a *revised history* based on their dislikes, desires, or biases.

In a modernistic world that vehemently denies absolute truth can be known, the question, "*What is truth*", becomes more important than ever to answer. Consider the following quotes:

- "History is always written by the victor."[13]
- "History is a set of lies agreed upon."
- "History is the version of past events that people have decided to agree upon."[14]

---

[13] This quote is often attributed to Winston Churchill or sometimes to German philosopher Walter Benjamin. No verifiable source(s) could be found. It is simply offered as stated in numerous books and articles.
[14] These last two quotes are generally attributed to Napoleon Bonaparte. In several places as Napoleon quoting Fontanelle. No verifiable source(s) could be found for either quote. They are simply offered as stated.

It seems that Plato was correct when he philosophized: *"we are all blind to the true reality around us, that all we know is nothing more than a dim and hazy shadow on a cave wall"*?[15]

Historical revisionists seem to think history is nothing more than a matter of interpretation. They, the revisionists, along with modernists, believe actual, absolute, factual truth is beyond reach. If historians approach the writing of history texts driven by those kinds of biases, the history they produce will most certainly not resemble the true facts of history. It will be their interpretation of history. As Plato philosophized long centuries ago - *it will be a mere shadow of what actually happened.*

As America's citizens become less and less aware of, or interested in, true history, it seems that Plato's philosophy really is true. America is becoming blind to the true reality of history!

---

[15] Plato, *The Republic of Plato*, 380 B.C., 373.

Chapter Five: Discovering America's Christian Heritage

They knew they were pilgrims.

William Bradford
Of Plymouth Plantation
Ch. 7, pg. 47

Discovering America's

> Being thus arrived in a good harbor, and brought safe to land, they fell upon their knees and blessed the God of Heaven who had brought them over the vast and furious ocean, and delivered them from all the perils and miseries thereof, again to set their feet on the firm and stable earth, their proper element.
>
> William Bradford
> Of Plymouth Plantation
> Ch. 9, pg. 59

Christian Heritage

Most people, especially those in the younger generations, pay little, if any, attention to modern history and even less to the early history of America's beginning. The great peril that results from ignoring history is that you do not know where you came from, what you stand for, and almost certainly, where you are headed. Woodrow Wilson, a man who despised the Constitution according to August Heckscher's book, *The Politics of Woodrow Wilson*,[1] during a speech delivered at the University of North Carolina on January 19, 1909, stated, "A nation which does not remember what it was yesterday, does not know what it is today, nor what it is trying to do. We are trying to do a futile thing if we don't know where we have come from, or what we have been about".[2]

America is sliding down a path towards European style socialism. That is because Americans have either forgotten, or perhaps, simply refuse to acknowledge America's Christian heritage. The current generation does not understand nor does it value the role the Bible and Christianity played in the founding of America. According to George Barna, of Barna Group Ltd., the current generation is the most biblically illiterate generation in history. Mr. Barna says, "What used to be basic, universally-known truths about Christianity are now unknown mysteries to a large and growing share of Americans - especially young adults."[3]

Without an understanding of America's Christian heritage not only in the development but also in the discovery and founding of America, it is impossible to determine what is real history and what is revisionist history. Revisionist history is defined as: a false history fabricated by those whose sole aim is to re-write American History from their modernist viewpoint. For this book *historical revisionism* is defined as follows: *Historical revisionism: a phrase*

[1] August Heckscher editor, *The Politics of Woodrow Wilson*, (New York, New York: Harper & Brothers, 1956), 41–48.
[2] Woodrow Wilson, *The Papers of Woodrow Wilson*, Volume 18: 1908-1909, Arthur S. Link editor, (Princeton, New Jersey: Princeton University Press, 1974), 631-45.
[3] Barna Group, *Six Megathemes Emerge from Barna Group Research in 2010*, The Barna Group Ltd., December 13, 2010, pgs. 1-2; https://www.barna.org/barna-update/culture/462-six-megathemes-emerge-from-2010#.V4-9x_nzUx4 (accessed July 20, 2016).

that describes the process that attempts to rewrite history by minimizing, denying, altering, or simply ignoring essential facts."[4]

David Barton writing on the subject of *Original Intent* of the Constitution of the United States makes this statement regarding the proponents of historical revisionism:

> The courts are not the only force reshaping American culture; a second major influence is revisionists. This group promulgates a message of radical moral and social change through its use of 'historical revisionism' - a process by which historical fact is intentionally ignored, distorted, or misportrayed in order to maneuver public opinion toward a specific political agenda or philosophy.[5]

A desire to *revise* history to agree with a particular ideology or to formulate political correctness has led some historians to strike directly at the heart of America's founding. For example:

> "Just in time for Columbus Day, the purveyors of political correctness are preparing to unleash a barrage of historical revision and misrepresentation here in our backyard.
> On Saturday (09/26/2015, [date added]), the Eiteljorg Museum in Indianapolis will use grants financed by your tax dollars to present, '*A Symposium for Educators: Truth be Told: Alternative Narratives for Teaching about Columbus Day and Thanksgiving.*' This event will not only misinform those unfortunate enough to attend, but will also train your children's teachers to perpetuate the propaganda in their classrooms."[6]

Contradicting the character and purpose of Columbus's voyage to the Indies and eventual discovery of America

---

[4] G. I. Williamson, *Historical Revisionism*, http://reformed.org/misc/HistoricalRevisionism.pdf (accessed 09/06/2018).

[5] David Barton, *Original Intent: The Courts, the Constitution, & Religion*, (Aledo, Texas: Wallbuilder Press, 1996), 285.

[6] Peter Heck, Heck: *Revisionism about Columbus misleads students* http://www.indystar.com/story/opinion/2015/09/24/heck-revisionism-columbus-misleads-students/72735766/ (accessed 09/06/2018).

undermines the essence of America's Christian heritage. An exhibit on the Library of Congress website contains the following statement, "After five centuries, Columbus remains a *mysterious* [emphasis added] and controversial figure who has been variously described as one of the greatest mariners in history, a visionary genius, a mystic, a national hero, a failed administrator, a naive entrepreneur, and a ruthless and *greedy imperialist* [emphasis added]."[7] If educational elitists are allowed to have their way, schoolchildren will not know about the Christianity of the founders of this country. Consider the example below:

> California's state list of recommended books for students excludes American heroes and founders. While many great literary works appear on the 2,700-title list, books about Washington, Jefferson, Paine, and John Paul Jones are missing, as is the Bible, stories about America's war heroes, inventors, and the taming of the American west. Christopher Columbus is represented in only one book as an *exploiter of native Americans* [emphasis added].[8]

Columbus was not mysterious. He was not a greedy imperialist. And neither was he an exploiter of native Americans. Evidence will be presented in the following section to contradict the foregoing statements and to examine the true motive underlying Columbus's desire to sail westward to the Indies.

Christian Identity

The Oxford Dictionary lists an archaic definition of *heritage* as: "a special or individual possession; an allotted portion. God's chosen

---

[7] Library of Congress, *"1492: An Ongoing Voyage"*, http://www.loc.gov/exhibits/1492/columbus.html (accessed 09/06/2018).
[8] "Education Briefs", Education Reporter, (Washington, D.C." EagleForum, November 2002), http://www.eagleforum.org/educate/2002/nov02/er_nov02.shtml (accessed 07/21/2016).

people (the people of Israel, or the Christian Church)."[9] Using that definition, it is then fair to say a person's, a group's, or a country's heritage is what defines it. It is that characteristic or origin which gives it identity and purpose.

There are many books and articles that attempt to deny America has a Christian identity, or heritage, of any kind. The first question that must be asked is, *"Are those books and articles accurate and do they provide adequate proofs for their claims?"* The many articles researched generally followed the pattern revealed by Peter Lillback, author of the master work, *George Washington's Sacred Fire*. Mr. Lillback says, "Pick up books and articles on Washington from 1932 or earlier, and generally, with a few exceptions, you will read about George Washington the Christian. That began to change with the iconoclastic scholarship of the mid-twentieth century that sought to tear down the traditional understanding of our nation and its origin."[10]

Paul Heffron commenting on a book by Michael Farris, titled *From Tyndale to Madison*, said this, "The subtitle, ["How the Death of an English Martyr Led to the American Bill of Rights", was not cited in the original article.] suggesting a Christian origin for the Bill of Rights, caught my eye because I suspected this book was another of the Christian Nation revisions of American history. How extensive is the Religious Right's attempt at revising history? *I haven't researched that subject enough to give a well informed answer* [italics added], but it appears to me that there is a growing cottage industry of Christian revisionist books, tapes, etc., which dominate the curricula of many home schools and private Christian academies."[11] By Mr. Heffron's own admission he has not researched the subject well enough to give an informed answer. In addition, Mr. Heffron's article does not reference any source

[9] Oxford Dictionaries, Online, "https://en.oxforddictionaries.com/definition/heritage, (Accessed 09/06/2018).

[10] Peter A. Lillback, *George Washington's Sacred Fire*, (Bryn Mawr, Pennsylvania: 2006), 27-28.

[11] Paul Heffron, *"The Religious Right's Revision of American History"*, American Humanist Association, http://www.americanhumanist.org/HNN/details/2011-06-the-religious-rights-revision-of-american-history (accessed 07/22/2016).

material whatsoever to support his conclusions. Well, so much for Mr. Heffron's qualification and authority to speak on the subject.

The article "America's Christian Identity Myth", on *The Lloyd Thomas Pages* website, uses Article XI from an old document, *'The Treaty of Tripoli'*, as support for his statement, "The non-conformist religious origin of many of America's early settlers, such as the 41 Pilgrim Fathers who signed the Mayflower Compact, the Quaker religious background to the founding of Pennsylvania, the Calvinism of Massachusetts, etc. have been material used in the development of this myth. Sentiment aside however, the eventual formation of the United States of America and its founding leaders held a very different position."[12] That article lists no author and does not identify even one source to support its conclusions. Not only does the article lack any source material support, it is wrong in its conclusion regarding the *'Treaty of Tripoli'*. David Barton of Wallbuilders says this regarding the common misuse of the *'Treaty of Tripoli'*:

> The 1797 Treaty of Tripoli, specifically article XI, is commonly misused in editorial columns, articles, as well as in other areas of the media, both Christian and secular. We have received numerous questions from people who have been misled by the claims that are being made, namely, that America was not founded as a Christian nation. Advocates of this idea use the Treaty of Tripoli as the foundation of their entire argument, and we believe you deserve to know the truth regarding this often misused document.[13]

Mr. Barton, in support of his position, lists thirty-three primary sources to substantiate that the Barbary Powers Conflict was *always* viewed as a conflict between Christian America and Muslim nations.

---

[12] *"America's Christian Identity Myth"*, http://www.lloydthomas.org/5-SpecialStudies/USA.html (Accessed 09/06/2018).
[13] David Barton, *"Treaty of Tripoli"*, Wallbuilders.com, http://www.wallbuilders.com/LIBissuesArticles.asp?id=125 (accessed 09/06/2018).

Many more articles could be offered that demonstrate a similar lack of acceptable scholarship. Those articles say the same things, use the same faulty or weak scholarship, and come to the same unsupported and erroneous conclusions.

Scholarship that has as its ultimate purpose the tearing down of the traditional understanding of America's Christian origin has caused great damage. As evidence of that damage, Mr. Lillback says, "The impact of this approach to history can perhaps be seen in a recent Washington College Poll. It found that more Americans had a higher respect for Bill Clinton's job performance as the nation's forty-second president than they did George Washington's."[14] The Washington College Poll asked this question, "Thinking about all the presidents of the United States throughout history to the present, who would you say was America's greatest president?" The Washington College Poll results are presented below in their entirety:

1	Abraham Lincoln	20%
2	Ronald Reagan	15%
3	Franklin D. Roosevelt	12%
4	John F. Kennedy	11%
5	Bill Clinton	10%
6	Other/Don't Know	9%
7	George W. Bush	8%
8	George Washington	6%
9	Theodore Roosevelt	3%
10	Dwight Eisenhower	3%
11	Jimmy Carter	2%
12	Thomas Jefferson	2%
13	Richard Nixon	1%
14	John Adams	<1%
15	Andrew Jackson	<1%
16	Lyndon Johnson	<1%

Figure 7 - Washington College Poll

---

[14] Britt Hume, *"The Political Grapevine"*, February 22, 2005, Fox News, Quoted in Peter A. Lillback, *George Washington's Sacred Fire*, (Bryn Mawr, Pennsylvania: 2006), 27.

February 11, 2005

At this point, the two questions posed in the previous chapter must be restated:

- **What are the true facts of history?**
- **Do they really matter?**

The first question, as it pertains to this discussion, will be answered later. As to the second question: Do the facts of history really matter? Yes, they matter very much!

Peter Lillback asks the question, "Can an historic national hero become irrelevant?"[15] Yes, without a doubt an historic national hero can become irrelevant. Mr. Lillback said that the founding fathers have become *politically incorrect*. He answers his question with the following statement, "In fact, many of our founders - despite all their sacrifices to establish our great country with unparalleled freedoms - have been denigrated to the category of 'dead white guys'."[16] The *Washington Times* reported:

George Washington, Thomas Jefferson, and Benjamin Franklin are not included in the revised version of the New Jersey Department of Education history standards - a move some critics view as political correctness at its worst. The Pilgrims and the Mayflower also are excluded, as well as the word "war," which has been replaced with "conflict" in lessons about the early settlers, colonization and expansion. .....

'This is what you call a historical irresponsibility,' said David Saxe, a Penn State University education professor who reviews state history standards nationwide for the Thomas B. Fordham Foundation in Washington.[17]

---

[15] Lillback, *George Washington's Sacred Fire*, 27.
[16] Ibid.
[17] Ellen Sorokin, *"No Founding Fathers? That's our new history"*, Washington Times, January 28, 2002, http://www.washingtontimes.com/news/2002/jan/28/20020128-035145-4351r/, (Accessed 09/06/2018).

Sadly, the situation is becoming even more desperate than that. Not only are the national founding heroes becoming irrelevant, but so is America's Christian heritage. America's identity is becoming unimportant.

There is a dangerous tendency in many current history books on the *Founding Fathers*, confirmed in their concluding bibliographies, to cite only contemporary 'authorities' when speaking about the *Founders*.[18] So, must those revisionist histories simply be accepted unchallenged? No, absolutely not. In order to acquire an accurate and true history of the founding of America, the men that were there must be allowed to speak for themselves. You must listen to *them* and hear *their* words.

Genuine history proves there is a Christian identity that long predates the men called the *Founding Fathers*, those men that framed the Declaration of Independence. Was the New World discovered merely by accident while Columbus was seeking a trade route to the Indies as has been taught for so many years? Turn the clock back nearly three centuries and hear in *Christopher Columbus's own words* what he said about why he sailed westward to the Indies, eventually discovering America:

> It was the Lord who put into my mind (I could feel his hand upon me) the fact that it would be possible to sail from here to the Indies. All who heard of my project rejected it with laughter, ridiculing me. There is no question that the inspiration was from the Holy Spirit, because He comforted me with rays of marvelous inspiration from the Holy Scriptures.
>
> I am a most unworthy sinner, but I have cried out to the Lord for grace and mercy, and they have covered me completely. I have found the sweetest consolation since I made it my whole purpose to enjoy His marvelous presence. For the execution of my journey to the Indies, I did not make use of intelligence, mathematics, or maps. It is simply the fulfilling of what Isaiah had prophesied. . . .
>
> No one should fear to undertake any task in the name of our Savior, if it is just and if the intention is purely for

---

[18] David Barton, *Original Intent*, 5

His holy service. The working out of all things has been assigned to each person by our Lord, but it all happens according to His sovereign will, even though He gives advice. He lacks nothing that it is in the power of men to give Him. Oh, what a gracious Lord, who desires that people should perform for Him those things for which He holds Himself responsible! Day and night, moment by moment, everyone should express their most devoted gratitude to Him.[19]

Does not the passage cited above produce shock and astonishment? In the public school system during the last half of the twentieth century *never* was there any mention made of Columbus's faith, let alone that he had been given that mission by God Himself. Even more incredulous is the fact that he acknowledged his journey was a fulfillment of Scripture and that he was guided by the Holy Spirit. Take note that this is not the ranting of some zealous fundamentalist attempting to rewrite history. *These are Columbus's own words*! But why was that fact never taught? Extensive research revealed that until sometime after 1971, Columbus's *Libro de las Profecias of Book of Prophecies*, a compilation of all the teachings and prophecies of the Bible on the subject of the Earth, distant lands, population movements, and undiscovered tribes, was available only in Spanish and had never been published in this country. Much of that book was translated by August J. Kling who quoted several excerpts in an article in *The Presbyterian Layman* in October 1971.[20]

In the article referenced above Mr. Kling wrote "...after considerable research, we found a scholarly edition of the full text in the *Raccolata di documenti e studi* published in 1894 by a special commission of the Italian Ministry of Public Education."[21] At the time Mr. Kling wrote the article, he also stated, "To our

[19] Christopher Columbus, Roberto Rusconi translator, *Book of Prophesies*, (Berkeley, California: University of California Press, 1997), 67, 75.
[20] Peter J. Marshal, Jr. and David B. Manuel, Jr., *The Light And The Glory*, (Grand Rapids, Michigan: Baker Book House, 1977), 360.
[21] August J. Kling, "*Columbus – A Layman 'Christ-bearer' to Uncharted Isles*", *The Presbyterian Layman*, October 1971, 4.

knowledge, . . . *Book of Prophecies* has never been translated into English from the original Latin and Spanish, nor has it ever been printed in this country."[22] Extensive research within the Worldcat Library database system revealed not one single translation exists of Columbus's *Book Of Prophecies* dated earlier than a 1997 edition published by the University of California Press in Berkeley, California. That would certainly explain why there was no mention in the public school system of the Christian intentions behind Columbus's voyage.

Mr. Kling made several other noteworthy statements near the beginning of his article about Christopher Columbus's intentions. Mr. Kling wrote:

> Columbus's use of the Bible is one of the best documented facts of his remarkable career, but it is one of the least known to the general public.
> . . . All of Columbus's sailing journals and most of his private letters give evidence of his biblical knowledge and his devout love for Jesus Christ.
> . . . .Columbus believed that his own name, given to him in holy baptism, was a special sign that God had predestinated him to be the evangelist (Christophoros = Christ-bearer) who would open up the un-reached tribes of the "distant isles" to the saving knowledge of the Gospel of the Lord Jesus Christ."[23]

Ample evidence has been provided to completely refute the revisionists' claim that America was not founded as a Christian country. It certainly seems obvious from Columbus's writings that his discovery of the Americas was certainly not an accident. God planted an insatiable desire within Columbus's soul. A desire that would drive him to overcome the ridicule and rejection of those that mocked him. It seems undeniable that God's hand played a pivotal role not only in America's discovery but also in its eventual founding as well. It is safe to conclude that God's hand was at

---

[22] Ibid.
[23] Ibid.

work establishing America's Christian identity long before the Pilgrims landed at Plymouth Harbor, Massachusetts.

In the following section America's early beginning will be considered as the first settlers and eventually those called the *Founding Fathers* continued the Christian heritage Christopher Columbus began.

Christian Beginnings

The sixteenth century saw more and more vessels sailing toward the New World, their sails stretched taut against the bright blue sky. Some of those ships were Portuguese, but most were Spanish bound for conquest and colonization and the lure of bright, yellow gold. Most of those "explorers" were not really explorers. They were conquerors, looting and plundering the newly discovered lands and peoples of their gold and silver. In addition, the inhabitants of those lands had no immunity to the white man's diseases and the resulting loss of life was decimating. Could it be that God's plan for America would be doomed even before it began? No, absolutely not. God's plan can never be thwarted by what man chooses to do or the lies he tells, no matter how evil his actions and/or intentions.

From the time of Columbus's voyage to the early seventeenth century, a nearly endless stream of large, three-masted ships, brightly colored pennants flying above their billowing sails, sailed back and forth across the Atlantic. They sailed from Spain loaded with eager adventurers and returned with their holds full to the brim with riches plundered from the new world.

From 1600-1610 attempts were made to establish settlements at Jamestown and at Virginia Colony. Jamestown was abandoned and the colonists at Virginia Colony would have starved except for the providence of God. The extraordinary timing of their salvation was described by William Crashaw, "If God had not sent Sir Thomas Gates from the Bermudas, within four days they had all been famished. . . . . this was the arm of the Lord of Hosts."[24] Without a doubt, God moved to save Virginia and conditions slowly improved. James Blair, soon to be president of William and Mary College, applied to England's Attorney General Edward Seymore for a charter to be granted by Their Majesties.[25] James Blair pointed out that the colonists of Virginia had souls that needed to be saved. However, General Seymore thought the college a waste of good money and quite plainly said so, "Souls? Damn your souls! Make tobacco."[26] It seems quite sad that Virginia was to be saved by a smelly weed that would become one the leading causes of death in America.

The people who set sail from England had such high hopes. What went wrong in Virginia? They began with noble sentiments and good intentions, but those intentions were soon ignored when hard times fell upon them. The next settlers, a group of separatists, to cross the Atlantic came knowing they had no choice but to put all their trust in God.

Other explorers soon followed. Each subsequent group of explorers was required to beseech their own monarchs for a land charter. If granted, the charter would set forth the reason for that group's endeavor. Those charters stated in the colonist's own words their intentions. For example, the 1606 charter for a colony in Virginia declared, "To make habitation . . . and to deduce a colony of sundry of our people into that part of America commonly called Virginia . . . in propagating of Christian religion to such people as yet live in darkness."[27] Three years later in 1609 another charter for Virginia stated, "The principle effect which we can desire or expect of this action is the conversion . . . of the people in those parts unto the true worship of God and Christian religion."[28]

---

[24] George F. Willison, *Behold Virginia*, (New York, New York: Harcourt, Brace, 1951), 120.

[25] Marshall, *The Light and The Glory*, 103-104.

[26] Willison, *Behold Virginia*, 345.

[27] *Historical Collections: Consisting of State Papers and other Authentic Documents: Intended as Material for an History of the United States of America*, Ebenezer Hazard, editor (Philadelphia, Pennsylvania: T. Dobson, 1792), Vol. I, 50-51.

[28] Hazard, *Historical Collections*, Vol. I, 72.

In 1619 a group of English Christians called Separatists were being persecuted by the Church of England. The Separatists believed that the church could only fall under the headship of Jesus Christ and that no one, not even the Queen of England, could assume the title 'Head of the Church'. Because of this they chose to separate from the church and conduct their own worship services, thus earning the name Separatists. The increasing persecution drove them to seek religious asylum in Holland. More and more, the Separatists came to believe that America was the place to which God intended them to go. None of the horrors of which they heard: the starving in Virginia, Jamestown's death rate that exceeded fifty percent, or the brutality of the Indians; nothing could dissuade them.

On August 5, 1620, two ships, the *Mayflower* and the *Speedwell*, set sail for the New World. Twice they were forced to turn back. The first time after only three days and the second after only a week, both times due to cracks in *Speedwell's* seams. Given little choice, the passengers decided to sell the *Speedwell* and combine the passengers and cargo onto the *Mayflower* and continue their journey. The voyage was long and extremely difficult. They had to endure lack of food, violent storms, and harassment from the sailors. After many weeks of miserable conditions, the *Mayflower* set anchor in the natural harbor of Cape Cod in November 1620.

The *Mayflower's* passengers were deeply concerned. If they settled in Massachusetts, they would no longer be under the authority of the Virginia Company and they had no charter with the New England Company. In that location, the settlers would be under the control of no one. To prevent the threat of mutiny, they drew up an agreement, which came to be known as the Mayflower Compact. Their leaders signed the *Mayflower Compact* on November 11, 1620, before setting foot on dry land. The opening lines of that compact appear below:

> In the name of God, Amen. We whose names are under-written, the loyal subjects of our dread sovereign Lord, King James, by the grace of God, of Great Britain, France, and Ireland King, Defender of the Faith, etc.

> Having undertaken, for the glory of God, and advancement of the Christian faith, and honor of our King and Country, a voyage to plant the first colony in the northern parts of Virginia, do by these presents solemnly and mutually, in the presence of God, and one of another, covenant and combine ourselves together into a civil body politic, ...[29]

One of the men that made the voyage on the *Mayflower* was William Bradford, a young English farmer. Just one year later in 1621, William Bradford would soon be elected Governor of Plymouth Colony. He was reelected every year until his death in 1657, except for the five years in which he declined to serve. Mr. Bradford would later pen a history of what happened in Plymouth Colony. In regard to the intent behind their voyage, Mr. Bradford confirmed their purpose when he explained why the Pilgrims had come to the New World, "... a great hope and inward zeal they had of laying some good foundation, or at least to make some way thereunto, for the propagating and advancing the Gospel of the kingdom of Christ in those remote parts of the world."[30]

It is interesting and quite revealing to read the footnote in Peter Marshall's book, *The Light and the Glory*, where he comments on Mr. Bradford's book. Mr. Marshall wrote, "...anyone seriously interested should be sure to get an unexpurgated edition, for at least one modern version we know of has elected to leave out 'irrelevant theological meditations.'"[31] Irrelevant theological meditations? Irrelevant in whose mind and by what authority? Mr. Marshall's statement is a perfect example of *historical revisionism*. Certain authors decide, on their own authority, that an author's statements pertaining to or about God are irrelevant. Those decisions are based on their own bias and hostility toward God. The words and meditations of the Christian men and women who

---

[29] Kate Caffery, *The Mayflower*, (New York, New York: Stein and Day Publishers, 1974), 115.

[30] William Bradford, *Of Plymouth Plantation*, Harvey Wish, editor, (New York, New York: Capricorn Books, 1962), 40.

[31] Marshall, *The Light and The Glory*, 362

risked their lives to establish and further the Christian faith in America are not irrelevant.

The anti-Christian sentiment evidenced above and also found in many other places is certainly nothing new. It existed in England long before their voyage to the New World and it appears that it followed them across the Atlantic. In 1607 Mr. Bradford, describing the Pilgrims' covenant to establish their church, wrote, "Those reformers who saw the evil of these things, and whose hearts the Lord had touched with heavenly zeal for his truth, shook off this yoke of anti-Christian bondage, and as the Lord's free people, joined themselves by a covenant of the Lord into a church estate in the fellowship of the Gospel, to walk in his ways, made known unto them, according to their best endeavors, whatsoever it should cost them, the Lord assisting them."[32]

There are hundreds more similar quotes from the brave men that crossed the Atlantic or from the soul-stirring documents they penned that could be offered as evidence and support of America's Christian beginning. However, the quotes already exhibited provide more than ample evidence that from the early infancy of America, this country was considered a Christian country, founded to promote the Christian faith and to proclaim the Gospel of Jesus Christ.

With that in mind, it is appropriate and fitting to let Governor William Bradford's own words conclude this section, "Being thus arrived in a good harbor and brought safe to land, they fell upon their knees and blessed the God of heaven, who had brought them over the vast and furious ocean, and delivered them from all the perils and miseries thereof . . . ."[33]

How marvelous it would be if today's leaders would fall upon their knees and bless the God of Heaven for America's Christian beginning!

[32] William Bradford, *Bradford's History of the Plymouth Settlement 1608-1650*, Rendered into Modern English by Harold Paget, (New York, New York, E. P. Dutton & Company, 1920), 7.
[33] William Bradford, *Of Plymouth Plantation*, 59.

Christian Heritage Established

This section will jump forward in time approximately one hundred and fifty years, and beyond, to examine some of the quotes, writings, and documents attributed to those men that are called the *Founding Fathers*. Once the *Founders* have been allowed to speak for themselves, some quotes from official state, federal, and Supreme Court documents will be examined to see what they have to say on the subject of America's Christian heritage. Before turning to those quotes, consider the questions: *"What drove these men called Founders to stake their reputations, their fortunes, and their lives upon their belief in the absolute authority of the Bible? Why was it so important to them?"* It will be extremely beneficial to consider the words of the man whose invention was responsible for the printed word that is so routinely taken for granted today. Johannes Gutenberg (1400-1468) was the inventor of the movable type printing press. His invention allowed the rapid spread of ideas throughout Europe and eventually led to the Reformation. Significantly enough, the first book printed on that press was the Gutenberg Bible. Gutenberg, commenting on his printing press, said this:

> Yes, it is a press, certainly, but a press from which shall flow in inexhaustible streams the most abundant and most marvelous liquor that has ever flowed to relieve the thirst of men. Through it, God will spread His word; a spring of pure truth shall flow from it; like a new star it shall scatter the darkness of ignorance, and cause a light hithertofore unknown to shine among men.[34]

Those are extremely powerful words. Consider carefully the words Gutenberg chose: *"...the most abundant and marvelous liquor that has ever flowed..."* That phrase brings to mind the New Testament verse, *"He that believeth on me, as the scripture hath said, out of his belly shall flow rivers of living water."* (John 7:38).

---

[34] Stephen Abbott Northrop, D.D., *A Cloud of Witnesses*, (Portland, Oregon: American Heritage Ministries, 1987), 202.

What water (liquor) could possibly be more abundant, marvelous, or thirst-quenching than that?

Consider then the words: *"...scatter the darkness of ignorance, and cause a light ... to shine among men."* How could anyone help but remember the verse, *"For God, who commanded the light to shine out of darkness, hath shined in our hearts, to give the light of the knowledge of the glory of God in the face of Jesus Christ."* (II Corinthians 4:6). What could dispel darkness and ignorance more quickly and fully than that? Of a truth, ignorance flees when subjected to the glorious light of Jesus Christ! No wonder the founders of America held the Word of God in such high regard. It moved their souls to the core of their being. It defined who they were. It established their character. It motivated their actions. No wonder they were willing to stake their reputations and lives upon it. Let them speak in their own words on this matter, *"...with a firm reliance on the protection of Divine Providence, we mutually pledge to each other our lives, our fortunes and our sacred honor."*[35] Consideration will now be given to how those men built upon the Christian identity that was the discovery of the New World and upon the Christian beginnings of the early colonies. Proof will be given that by and through their efforts America was established as a free and Christian nation.

Where to begin? There are such numerous sources that could be examined that it seems nearly overwhelming. However, as you search for the moving of the Hand of God in America's early years, there seems to be a calm, a kind of doldrums that settled over America. This calm began sometime around the end of the Puritan era and ran until the first stirring of emotions that would lead America to declare its independence from Great Britain. It seemed that the congregations were growing indifferent to the messages of the Puritan ministers. Sunday after Sunday the ministers preached fiery messages from such Old Testament texts as:

Beware that thou forget not the LORD thy God, in not keeping his commandments, and his judgments, and his

---

[35] "Declaration of Independence", http://www.archives.gov/exhibits/charters/declaration_transcript.html (Accessed 09/01/2018).

statutes, . . . Lest when thou hast eaten and art full, and hast built goodly houses, and dwelt therein; And when thy herds and thy flocks multiply, and thy silver and thy gold is multiplied, and all that thou hast is multiplied; Then thine heart be lifted up, and thou forget the LORD thy God, . . . And thou say in thine heart, my power and the might of mine hand hath gotten me this wealth.", Deuteronomy 8:11-17.

Just one generation after the arrival of those first colonists upon the shores of Plymouth Colony *"true"* faith seemed to be slipping away. Cotton Mather, an American colonial clergyman, was regarded by many as the most brilliant man in New England. In 1702, Mr. Mather wrote *Magnalia Christi Americana, (The Great Achievement of Christ in America),* the most detailed history written about the first fifty years of New England. Observing the trend that was occurring in the colonies even after they had received such great blessings from the Hand of God, he wrote, "Religion begat prosperity, and the daughter devoured the mother."[36]

John Danforth preached to his congregation, " . . . to turn blessings into idols is the way to have them clapped under a blast. If the Lord loves His people, He will deliver their weapons out of their hands, that they are obstinately resolved to fight Him with. . . Better it is that Israel be saved and prosperity be lost, than that prosperity be saved and Israel be lost."[37]

Another alarming symptom of the spiritual indifference invading the colonies was the fact that the younger generation was not being converted. Quite revealing was the fact that sons were not coming to the same saving knowledge of Jesus Christ that their parents possessed. For that inexcusable tragedy, the parents bore responsibility. For they were the ones who eased up when the abundant blessing of God flowed and they no longer suffered the pangs of hunger and starvation. Their bellies were full, they no

---

[36] Cotton Mather, *Magnalia Christi Americana*, Stephen Foster, *Their Solitary Way, the Puritan social ethic in the first century of settlement in New England*, (New Haven, Connecticut: Yale University Press, 1971), 121.

[37] Peter Marshall, *The Light and the Glory*, 217.

longer felt the desperation of starvation, and so they laid down their cross. They refused to listen to the ministers and they ceased correcting and exhorting each other and their children. Rather than dependence on God, they chose greed, privacy, independence, and idolatry.[38]

Even as late as October 12, 1740, George Whitefield wrote:

Boston is a large populous place, very wealthy. Has the Form kept up; but has lost much of the Power of Religion. I have not heard of any remarkable Stir for the many Years. Ministers and People are obliged to confess, that the Love of many is waxed cold. Both, for the Generality, seem to be too conformed to the World . . . For I fear many rest in Head-Knowledge, are close Pharisees, and have only a Name to live. It must needs be so, when the Power of Godliness is dwindled away, where the Form only of religion is become fashionable amongst People...[39]

What was happening in America? Was the great faith that saw the settlers through those first dreadful winters dying out so soon? The colonists were learning that faith cannot be passed from generation to generation. It cannot be imparted by birth. It cannot be imparted by church membership. It cannot be imparted by baptism. Nor can it be imparted by the partaking of holy communion. Faith comes to no one simply because their parents possessed it. Faith is personal and can only spring from feelings of gratitude. The children knew nothing of the cold, sickness, persecution, and depravation that had forced their parents to depend upon God alone to provide. Therefore, they did not learn to put their trust solely in God. Rather, they learned to depend on their own efforts and to take the abundant blessings of God for granted. Thus the bright light of Christ began to fade from their

---

[38] Ibid., 220.

[39] George Whitefield, *A Continuation of Reverend Mr. Whitefield's Journal*, Seventh Journal Second Edition, (London, England, W. Strahan, March 11, 1741) , 44.

hearts. A similar, but far deeper, blight will be seen again many years in the future.

As stated earlier, both the seed of faith and the seed of anti-Christian sentiment crossed the Atlantic with the early settlers. Even though the strong commitment to faith exhibited signs of dying out with the passing of the Puritan era, there would come a re-awakening of that faith when America was bent to the breaking point under the unfair and intolerable dictates of Great Britain.

Move forward in time some forty-plus years from George Whitefield's quote of 1740 and consider some quotes from the framers of the constitution. Generally, those quotes will be considered chronologically and will be selected from the writings of various *Founders*. Only by examining the direct declarations and writings of the *Founders* can the true historical facts be learned. Their words, their conclusions, and especially their intent will become clear. Many of the quotes that follow are from books that contain literally hundreds of footnotes pointing to primary-source historical documents.

First, listen to an important figure from the American Revolution, Samuel Adams, who was considered to be the 'Father of the American Revolution'. He labored for over twenty years as an American patriot and leader. According to historians, he was the instigator of the Boston Tea Party. He was a signer of the Declaration of Independence. He called for the first Continental Congress and served as a member of Congress until 1781. Certainly his thoughts and writings are germane to this subject of America's Christian heritage. His pamphlet, *The Rights of the Colonists*, was widely circulated in 1772. In that report he stated, "I. The right to freedom being a gift of the Almighty, it is not in the power of man to alienate this gift and voluntarily become a slave. II. The rights of the colonists as Christians - These may be best understood by reading and carefully studying the institution of The Great Law Giver and Head of the Christian Church, which are to be found clearly written and promulgated in the New Testament."[40]

---

[40] Samuel Adams, *Old South Leaflets No. 173 The Rights of the Colonists*, Nov. 20, 1772, 3.

Benjamin Rush, a physician and signer of the Declaration of Independence, considered to be the 'father of public schools', wrote in a letter to Elias Boudinot in July, of 1788 regarding the formation of the Union of States, "I do not believe that the Constitution was the offspring of inspiration, but I am perfectly satisfied that the Union of States in its form and adoption is as much the work of Divine Providence as any of the miracles recorded in the Old and New Testament were the effects of a divine power."[41]

One year later, Fisher Ames, a Congressman from Massachusetts in the First Session of the Congress of the United States, suggested the wording for the Fourth Amendment to the Constitution which was adopted by the House on August 20, 1789, "Congress shall make no law establishing religion, or to prevent the free exercise thereof, or to infringe the rights of conscience."[42]

The fourth amendment has often been dreadfully and erroneously misused to exclude religion from government and schools. Considering the fact that Mr. Ames was the author of that amendment, it is quite interesting to hear what he had to say about religion in the school system. "Should not the Bible regain the place it once held as a schoolbook? Its morals are pure, its examples are captivating and noble. The reverence for the sacred book that is thus early impressed lasts long;"[43]

If, as it seems obvious, Mr. Ames did *not* espouse the notion of 'separation of church and state', where did that concept come from? On January 1, 1802, Thomas Jefferson wrote to the Danbury Baptist Association to calm their fears that Congress was in the process of choosing any one single Christian denomination to be the '*state*' religion. In that letter, Jefferson borrowed a phrase from the famous Baptist minister Roger Williams. Here is an excerpt of what Mr. Williams wrote, ". . . . the hedge or wall of separation

---

[41] Benjamin Rush, *Letters of Benjamin Rush*, L. H. Butterfield, editor (Princeton, New Jersey: American Philosophical Society, 1951), Vol. I, 475, to Elias Boudinot, July 9, 1788.

[42] Joseph Gales, *The Debates and Proceedings in the Congress of the United States, First Congress, First Session, 1789-1791, Volume 1,* (Washington, D.C.: Gales & Seaton, 1843), 795.

[43] Fisher Ames, *The Works of Fisher Ames*, (Boston, Massachusetts: T. B. Wait & Co., 1809), 134-135.

between the garden of the church and the wilderness of the world, God hath ever broke down the wall. . . ."[44] Here is a portion of Jefferson's letter in which he included the phrase he borrowed from Mr. Williams:

> ... Believing with you that religion is a matter which lies solely between man and His God, that he owes account to none other for faith or his worship, that the legislative powers of government reach actions only, and not opinions, I contemplate with solemn reverence that act of the whole American people which declared that their legislature should "make no law respecting an establishment of religion, or prohibiting the free exercise thereof," thus building a wall of separation between Church and state.[45]

Thomas Jefferson did *not* sign the Constitution and he was *not* present at the Constitutional Convention of 1878. In addition, he also was *not* present when the First Amendment and religious freedom were debated in the first session of Congress in 1789 because he was out of the country as U. S. Minister to France. Therefore, Thomas Jefferson had no first-hand knowledge of any of the comments or debate that transpired during that first session. A personal letter using *borrowed phraseology* on a completely different subject *written thirteen years after* the First Amendment and *based solely on second-hand information* cannot possibly be used to establish the intent of the constitutional delegates. In spite of that, Jefferson's opinion, for that is all it was, is still being misused to suppress the role of religion in all areas of public life.

Several of the questions David Barton raised in the foreword to his book, *Original Intent*, are quite appropriate regarding the frequent misuse of the *Founder's* writings:

---

[44] Lynn R. Buzzard and Samuel Ericsson, *The Battle for Religious Liberty*, (Elgin, Illinois: David C. Cook, 1982), 51.

[45] Library of Congress, *Jefferson's Letter to the Danbury Baptist*, The Final Letter as Sent, http://www.loc.gov/loc/lcib/9806/danpre.html, (Accessed 08/28/2018).

- Although there were fifty-five Founders who drafted the Constitution, and ninety more who drafted the Bill of rights, why does the current Court invoke only Thomas Jefferson and James Madison as its spokesmen? Are there no constitutional authorities among the other one-hundred-plus who framed those documents? Or, is it possible that their words would directly contradict the current Court's conclusions?

- Since Jefferson has over sixty volumes of written works and Madison has over twenty, why does the Court continually invoke only one or two select sentences from these exhaustive works? Is it perhaps that the rest of the statements made by Madison and Jefferson reveal the Court's intentional misportrayal of their intent?

- Since several signers of the Constitution were also Justices on the U.S. Supreme Court, why does the current Court avoid citing the declarations of those Justices on today's issues? Is it perhaps that the concise rulings of those who clearly understood constitutional intent would contradict and thus embarrass the Court for its current positions?[46]

Very interesting and thought provoking questions indeed. The raging controversy and debate that still swirls around this single issue could fill volumes.

Gouverneur Morris was the writer of the final draft of the Constitution of the United States. He was head of the Committee on Style and originator of the phrase, "We the people of the United States." He spoke one hundred seventy-three times during the Constitutional debates (more than any other delegate). Mr. Morris offered his expertise in *Notes on the Form of a Constitution for France* delivered to France as they were establishing a new form of government. In that work, Mr. Morris stated, "Religion is the

---

[46] David Barton, *Original Intent*, 6.

only solid basis of good morals; therefore education should teach the precepts of religion, and the duties of man toward God."[47]

Benjamin Rush, quoted earlier regarding the forming of the Union of States, said this after the adoption of the Constitution, "...the only foundation for a useful education in a republic is to be laid in RELIGION. Without this there can be no virtue, and without virtue there can be no liberty, and liberty is the object and life of all republican governments."[48] The religion Mr. Rush spoke of was Christianity. In his work, *Essays, Literary, Moral, and Philosophical*, published in the same year as the quote above, Mr. Morris said this:

I know there is an objection among many people to teaching children doctrines of any kind, because they are liable to be controverted. But let us not be wiser than our Maker. If moral precepts alone could have reformed mankind, the mission of the Son of God into all the world would have been unnecessary. The perfect morality on the Gospel rests upon the doctrine which, though often controverted has never been refuted: I mean the vicarious life and death of the Son of God.[49]

After reading the quote above there certainly can be no doubt that Mr. Rush was speaking of Christianity when he wrote about the foundation of government.

John Jay, Chief Justice of the United States Supreme Court, *Founding Father*, member of the First and Second Continental Congresses, Governor of the State of New York, and author of *The Federalist Papers* on October 12, 1816, in a letter to John Murray wrote the following: "Providence has given to our people the choice of their rulers, and it is the duty, as well as the privilege and

---

[47] Benjamin Franklin Morris, "Notes on the Form for the King of France", 1792, Jared Sparks, editor, *The Life of Gouverner Morris, with Selections from His Correspondence and Miscellaneous Papers*, Vol. III., (Boston, Massachusetts: Gray and Bowen, 1832), 483.

[48] Benjamin Rush, 1786 in "Thoughts upon the Mode of Education Proper in a Republic", *Essays on Education in the Early Republic*, Fredrick Rudolph, editor, (Cambridge, Massachusetts: Harvard University Press, 1965), 10.

[49] Ibid., 543-544.

interest of our Christian Nation to select and prefer Christians for our rulers."[50]

In crystal clear words that absolutely cannot be interpreted otherwise, the first Chief Justice of the United States Supreme Court stated that this *is* a Christian nation and that America should select and prefer Christians as rulers. Repeating the question Mr. David Barton asked (quoted earlier), "Why doesn't the current Supreme Court quote the early Court Justices such as Justice John Jay?" Historians confirm that John Jay was instrumental in causing the Constitution to be ratified. It must be concluded then that Chief Justice Jay was thoroughly familiar with the arguments and debates that formed the Constitution. Should not then Chief Justice Jay's words carry far greater authority than those possessing obvious anti-Christian sentiments that populate the current Court? The answer is a resounding and unequivocal yes they should.

Alexis de Tocqueville, French diplomat and political scientist, traveled widely in the United States and took extensive notes regarding his observations of democracy in America. In his book *Democracy in America*, de Tocqueville wrote the following regarding the influence of Christianity in America:

> It may be believed without unfairness, that a certain number of Americans pursue a peculiar form of worship, from habit more than from conviction. In the United States the sovereign authority is religious, and consequently hypocrisy must be common; but there is no country in the whole world in which the Christian religion retains a greater influence over the souls of men than in America; and there can be no greater proof of its utility, and of its conformity to human nature, than that its influence is most powerfully felt over the most enlightened and free nation of the earth.[51]

---

[50] John Jay, Letter to John Murray dated October 12, 1816 in *The correspondence and Public Papers of John Jay*, Henry P. Johnston, editor, (New York, New York: Burt Franklin, 1970), Vol. IV, 393.

[51] Alexis de Tocqueville, *Democracy in America* Third Edition, (New York: George Adlard, 1839), 303.

A few pages later de Tocqueville wrote of the importance of religion in regard to the maintenance of government:

> I do not know whether all the Americans have a sincere faith in their religion; for who can search the human heart? But I am certain that they hold it to be indispensable to the maintenance of republican institutions. This opinion is not peculiar to a class of citizens or to a party, but it belongs to the whole nation, and to every rank of society.[52]

Later in the development of America, William Henry Seward, Governor of the State of New York, a U.S. Senator, and Secretary of State under President Abraham Lincoln, was responsible for the great Alaska land purchase mockingly known as "Seward's Folly". In 1836, three years before becoming Governor of New York, Mr. Seward said, "I know not how long a republican government can flourish among a great people who have not the Bible; the experiment has never been tried; but this I do know: that the existing government could never have had existence but for the Bible."[53]

The noted historian Benjamin Franklin Morris who authored the book, *The Christian Life and Character of the Civil Institutions of the Unites States*, said:

> This is a Christian nation, first in name, and secondly because of the many and mighty elements of a pure Christianity which have given it character and shaped its destiny from the beginning. It is pre-eminently the land of the Bible, of the Christian Church, and of the Christian Sabbath.... The chief security and glory of the United

---

[52] Ibid., 305.
[53] William Henry Seward, 1836, Address as Vice-President of the American Bible Society, "Life of William Henry Seward", Stephen A. Northrop, *A Cloud Of Witnesses*, (Portland, Oregon: American Heritage Ministries, 1987), 404.

States of America has been, is now, and will be forever, the prevalence and domination of the Christian Faith.[54]

Numerous other quotes from state, federal, and Supreme Court documents will add additional clarity to the issue of America's Christian heritage. The first quote comes from the Supreme Court of the State of South Carolina in 1846 in the case of *City of Charleston v. S. A. Benjamin,* which cites an individual who willfully broke the statute against the sale of merchandise on the Lord's day:

> Christianity is part of the common law of the land, with liberty of conscience to all. It has always been so recognized....If Christianity is a part of the common law, its disturbance is punishable at common law. The U.S. Constitution allows it as a part of the common law....Christianity has reference to the principles of right and wrong....it is the foundation of those morals and manners upon which our society is formed; it is their basis. Remove this and they would fall....[Morality] has grown upon the basis of Christianity.[55]

In the case of the Church of the Holy Trinity v. United States, *1892*, the issue was over the suit brought by the U.S. Attorney's office against a church in New York for hiring a clergyman from England. The U.S. Attorney's office used an 1885 federal immigration law that declared it was unlawful for any person, company, or corporation to assist or encourage importation of any alien or foreigners into the United States. The United States Supreme Court concluded that the suit was an absurd application of the law in an attempt to prosecute the church. After vindicating the church, the United States Supreme Court spent the remainder

---

[54] Benjamin Franklin Morris, *The Christian Life and Character of the Civil Institutions of the Unites States, The Official and Historical Annals of the Republic* (Philadelphia, Pennsylvania: George W. Childs; Cincinnati: Rickey & Carroll, 1864), 11.

[55] Supreme Court of South Carolina, 1846, *City of Charleston v. S. A. Benjamin*, 2 Strob. 518-520 (1846). David Baron, *The Myth of Separation*, 73.

of the case stating why it would be wrong to hinder in any way the propagation of Christianity. The United States Supreme Court wrote: "[No] purpose of action against religion can be imputed to any legislation, State or national, because this is a religious people. This is historically true... These, and many other matters which might be noticed, add a volume of unofficial declarations to the mass of organic utterances that this is a Christian nation."[56]

In the case of *Zorach v. Clauson, 1952*, The United States Supreme Court upheld the constitutionality of students receiving religious instruction during the school day. However, the case represented a major departure from historical precedent in that the court ruled that the religious instruction must take place off school grounds. The Supreme Court's ruling declared:

> The first Amendment, however, does not say that in every and all respects there shall be a separation of Church and State...Otherwise the State and religion would be aliens to each other - hostile, suspicious, and even unfriendly...
> We are a religious people whose institutions presuppose a Supreme Being...When the State encourages religious instruction or cooperates with religious authorities by adjusting the schedule of public events to sectarian needs, it follows the best of our traditions...To hold that it may not would be to find in the Constitution a requirement that the government show a callous indifference to religious groups. That would be preferring those who believe in no religion over those who do believe...[W]e find no constitutional requirement which makes it necessary to be hostile to religion...We cannot read into the Bill of Rights such a philosophy of hostility to religion.[57]

The Supreme Court again stated that history and government are inseparable from religion. In the case of *Stone v. Graham,*

---

[56] *Church of the Holy Trinity v. United States*, Supreme Court of The United States, 143 U.S. 557 (1892), 465, 471, https://supreme.justia.com/cases/federal/us/143/457/case.html, (Accessed 08/01/2018).

[57] *Zorach v. Clauson*, 343, U.S. 306 (1952), 312-315, Supreme Court of The United States, https://supreme.justia.com/cases/federal/us/343/306/case.html, (accessed 08/01/2018).

1980, the Court ruled, "The Establishment Clause does not require that the public sector be insulated from all things which may have a religious significance or origin. This Court has recognized that "religion has been closely identified with our history and government," *Abington School District*, supra at 374 U. S. 212, and that "[t]he history of man is inseparable from the history of religion," *Engel v. Vitale*, 370 U. S. 421, 370 U. S. 434 (1962)."[58]

Consider one final quote which comes from an Executive Proclamation issued by the State of Idaho on October 16, 2011, declaring October 16-22, 2011, as "Christian Heritage Week". In part the proclamation read:

> WHEREAS, the Preamble to the Constitution of the State of Idaho states that, " We, the people of the State of Idaho, grateful to Almighty God for our freedom, to secure its blessings and promote our common welfare do establish this Constitution"; and
>
> WHEREAS, George Washington enunciated: "animated alone by the pure spirit of Christianity, and conducting ourselves as the faithful subjects of our free government, we may enjoy every temporal and spiritual felicity"; and
>
> WHEREAS, James Madison, father of the U.S. Constitution, advocated "the diffusion of the light of Christianity in our nation" in his Memorial and Remonstrance; and
>
> WHEREAS, learning about the importance of Christian heritage to our institutions, values and vision is invaluable, and teaching future generations about the important role of Christian heritage is meaningful to peoples of all faiths, just as learning about the heritage of other faiths is meaningful to Christians;

---

[58] *Stone v. Graham*, 1980, 449, U.S. 39 (1980), 45-46, Supreme Court of The United States, https://supreme.justia.com/cases/federal/us/449/39/case.html, (accessed 08/01/2018).

NOW, THEREFORE, I, C.L. "BUTCH" OTTER, Governor of the State of Idaho, do hereby proclaim October 16-22, 2011 to be Christian Heritage Week.[59]

It is richly evident from the many quotes of the *Founders* of this country, along with excerpts from various state, federal, and United States Supreme Court documents, that the current Court has abundant legal precedents upon which they may rely to declare that America is, in fact, a Christian Nation. The Court may further declare that there is no such thing as 'separation of Church and State' in the Constitution or in the Fourth Amendment. However, the sad, and inexcusable, fact is that this great wealth of precedents is simply being ignored.

No matter what position the *modern* United States Supreme Court has taken, by considering the evidence cited in this chapter, it can safely be declared that America's discovery and her identity was, and is, Christian. It can further be declared that the early colonists built upon that Christian identity and thus America's early beginning was also Christian. And finally, it can be declared that the *Founders* built upon that identity and beginning and established a nation that is Christian in name, in character, in philosophy, and in faith.

---

[59] State of Idaho, October 16, 2011, Executive Proclamation, signed by Governor C. L. "Butch" Otter and Secretary of State Ben Ysura, https://gov. idaho.gov/mediacenter/proc/2011/procOct11/10-16-2011%20Christian% 20Heritage%20Week.html (accessed 07/27/2018).

Chapter Six: Displaying America's Christian Heritage

Our greatest need is to regain confidence in our spiritual heritage.

John Foster Dulles
Time Magazine,
Apr. 24, 1950

Displaying America's

Let us with caution indulge the supposition that morality can be maintained without religion. Reason and experience both forbid us to expect that national morality can prevail in exclusion of religious principle.

George Washington
Farwell Address, September 17, 1796

Christian Heritage

Moving forward into the last half of the nineteenth century and into the twentieth century, consider what Christianity, in general, has added to the Christian heritage that those in earlier centuries struggled so hard to build. Before continuing, some clarification will be needed.

Christianity is a monotheistic religion based on the life and teachings of Jesus Christ as presented in the New Testament. Christianity encompasses numerous religious traditions that vary widely by culture and location. It includes many diverse beliefs, sects, and what some would call cults. Over the past two centuries, it has generally divided into four main branches:

- The Roman Catholic Church
- Eastern Christianity (Eastern Orthodox Church and old Oriental Churches)
- Protestantism (Anglican, Reformed, Lutheran, Episcopalians, Methodist, Evangelicals, Charismatics, Pentecostals, et.al.)
- Anabaptists

The Anabaptists are distinctly separate from Protestantism, with which they have often been mistakenly included. The name Anabaptist is derived from the Latin term *anabaptista*, or 'one who baptizes over again'. The Anabaptists practiced adult baptism, because, upon having a new faith, they baptized converts who had already been baptized as infants in the older, main-line Christian churches. Anabaptists required that candidates be able to testify of their own confessions of faith and so refused to accept the baptism of infants. As a result, Anabaptists were heavily persecuted during the sixteenth and seventeenth centuries by both Protestant and Roman Catholic churches.[1]

In the following sections of this chapter, the growth of Christianity in the last half of the nineteenth century and into the twentieth century will be examined in general terms. Because

---

[1] Online Etymological Dictionary, *"Anabaptist"*, © 2001-2010 Douglas Harper, http://www.etymonline.com/index.php?allowed_in_frame=0&search=Anabaptist&searchmode=none, (Accessed 09/06/2018).

Christianity will be defined and described in general terms, you will see ecumenicalism and secularism begin to raise their ugly heads.

Beyond this chapter, Christianity will be more closely defined to mean those individuals who are classified as traditional, fundamentalist, and/or Bible believers. Within this book, fundamentalism is defined as believing the following tenets:

- Jesus Christ is fully God and fully man.
- Salvation is by grace and not of good works.
- The Bible is infallible and inerrant.
- The Bible is the absolute and final authority for faith and practice.
- The local Church is autonomous and answers only to God.
- Separation from both unbelief and theological liberalism.

There are a number of other distinctives that could be used to describe fundamentalism, but those listed above are the most important. American fundamentalism began in the last quarter of the nineteenth century as American churches began to be assaulted by liberal affirmations and attitudes. Highly educated, but worldly, scholars and teachers brought Modernism from the academic world to the classrooms of bible colleges and universities. Young theology and ministerial students' minds, and eventually their churches, were poisoned with a philosophy that questioned absolutes and the foundations of what they believed. As a result, "Christian orthodoxy crashed with a resounding thud".[2]

In the later decades of the nineteenth century most Americans were considered to be conservatives because they believed in the historic, time-honored biblical truths. They believed those truths offered the most effective way to deal with the intellectual, social, and technological challenges of a modern world. Grant Wacker in his book, *Religion in Nineteenth Century America*, says this:

---

[2] George W. Dollar, *The Fight for Fundamentalism*, (Orlando, Florida: Daniels Publishing, 1983), 1.

Religious conservatives came in a bewildering variety of species. Some proved primarily interested in defending the authority and accuracy of the Bible. Others concerned themselves above all with strict standards of personal conduct. Some found their greatest joy in the biblical promise that Jesus Christ would soon return. Still others looked to the traditions of their own extended family or ethnic group for guidance. What they all held in common was a simple though powerful conviction that the past held the key to the future.[3]

The last sentence of the above quote is critically important. Mr. Wacker stated that nineteenth century Christians believed their past held the key to their future. Who and what they were was defined by their past - their history. History is just as important today as it was for nineteenth century Christians. America's history has been, and is being, rewritten by those who wish to eliminate any influence Christianity may hope to have on future generations.

Another form of liberal religious tradition planted itself early in America's history. The first Universalist – Unitarian congregation was planted in the last quarter of the eighteenth century and grew rapidly during the first few decades of the nineteenth century. The Universalist – Unitarian position was that conscience and reason were the only and final authority.[4] That position is confirmed in their own definition of their beliefs:

In Unitarian Universalism, you can bring your whole self: your full identity, your questioning mind, your expansive heart. Together, we create a force more powerful than one person or one belief system. As Unitarian Universalists, we do not have to check our personal background and beliefs at the door: we join together on a journey that honors everywhere we've been before. Our beliefs are diverse and inclusive. We have no shared creed. Our

---

[3] Grant Wacker, *Religion in Nineteenth Century America*, John Butler & Harry Stout eds., (New York, New York: Oxford University Press, 2000), 139.

[4] Timothy L. Hall, *Religion in America*, (New York, New York: Infobase Publishing, 2007), 143

shared covenant (our seven Principles) supports "the free and responsible search for truth and meaning." Though Unitarianism and Universalism were both liberal Christian traditions, this responsible search has led us to embrace diverse teachings from Eastern and Western religions and philosophies.[5]

Two extremely powerful, yet opposing forces, reason and revivalism, would often clash with each other during the coming decades. Even though revivalism would appear to be the stronger more dominate force, there would remain an undercurrent of the liberal philosophy that sought human reason above all else.

Age of Faith and Duty

By the middle of the nineteenth century the conflict over slavery pushed the nation toward war, and religious believers, churches, and institutions were swept up into a moral and political dispute that ultimately resulted in the Civil War. That horrible war ripped families apart, created denominational fractures, and split churches, producing long-lasting divisions. Those divisions and fractures remained long after the war ended.[6]

The years immediately after the Civil War saw an increase in revivalism. By some accounts the revivals spawned by the Second Great Awakening never totally died out but flowed across the decades into the nineteenth century.[7]

Baptist and Methodist congregations began to spread rapidly beginning at the second half of the eighteenth century because they were not hesitant to preach the Christian Gospel to the blacks, both free and slave. The Baptist and Methodist preaching emphasized the equality of all sinners in need of God's saving grace. This religious enthusiasm and zeal was characteristic of both the eighteenth and nineteenth century awakenings. This sharing of the

---

[5] *"Unitarian Universalist Beliefs"*, http://www.uua.org/beliefs/what-we-believe (Accessed 08/01/2018).

[6] Hall, *Religion in America*, 165.

[7] Ibid., 189.

Gospel encouraged the conversion of many slaves to evangelical Christianity and quickly swelled the membership of those churches.[8]

The twentieth century opened with the Ecumenical Missionary Conference, held in New York City on April 21 through May 1, 1900. Carnegie Hall served as the conference headquarters and location of in-depth addresses for the more than sixty sessions that also filled nearby churches and meeting places. Estimates placed total attendance at 160,000 to 200,000 for the ten-day event. Simply stated, it was the largest sustained formal religious event in the history of the Republic to that date and the best-attended international missionary conference in history.[9]

The "Church" was beginning to see and understand its duty in the evangelization of the lost. On the surface the conference was intended to "mobilize congregations and Christian public opinion toward greater missions commitment, financial support, and increased numbers of missionary recruits."[10] However, the actual result was an ecumenical joining together of many diverse religious groups. How could these groups join together in religious efforts when they held such vastly different theological views? "Ecumenism" became the watchword of the day. Webster defines ecumenism as "a movement that promotes cooperation and better understanding among different religious denominations, aimed at universal Christian unity."[11] The conference's stated goal was unity among different religious denominations. How is that possible? There was only one way for such diverse religious groups to attain unity and that was to set aside and ignore biblical doctrine for the sake of unity.

The twentieth century ecumenism that was born in the New York Missionary Conference continued to flourish and was further advanced by the Edinburgh Missionary Conference of June 14 through 23, 1910. The Global Ministries of the Methodist Church

---

[8] Ibid., 150, 151.

[9] *"The New York 1900 Ecumenical Missionary Conference"*, Highbeam Research, http://www.highbeam.com/doc/1G1-68157992.html, (Accessed 08/20/2018).

[10] Ibid.

[11] Webster's Dictionary, http://www.webster-dictionary.org/definition/ecumenism, (Accessed 8/28/2018).

on their web site describes Methodist layman, John R. Mott's call to assemble all the missionary societies and agencies of his time. He said, "The purpose was to hold what became known as the first World Missionary Conference, taking place in Edinburgh, Scotland, in 1910. To many, this landmark conference was considered the beginning of the modern ecumenical movement, …"[12] That conference gave rise to a council that thirty-eight years later would become a constituting part of the World Council of Churches.

The word *ecumenical* is derived from the Greek word *oikumene*, which means "the whole of the inhabited world". (see Acts 17.6; Mt. 24.14; Heb. 2.5). In traditional Catholic usage it means "a general or universal council of the Church". In the twentieth century, the word ecumenical has come to designate a movement that seeks to overcome divisions due to doctrine and achieve unity among all Christians. Since the early beginnings of the New Testament Church there have been various heresies and schisms. During the first half of the twentieth century, the main impetus behind the ecumenical movement came from Protestant church leaders. At the Edinburgh Missionary Conference of 1910, regarded as the birth of the twentieth century Ecumenical Movement, Anglican and Protestant missionaries became deeply convinced that divisions among Christians were becoming a powerful obstacle to the spread of Christianity.

It seems that the missionary movement somehow believed that "the glorious Gospel of Jesus Christ" was independent and free of all doctrinal tenets and was a common ground on which they could all gather.[13]

---

[12] S. Wesley Ariarajah, "*A Turning Point in Interfaith Relations*", Global Ministries The United Methodist Church, http://www.umcmission.org/Find-Resources/New-World-Outlook-Magazine/New-World-Outlook-Archives/2013/November-December-2013/1106-A-Turning-Point-in-Interfaith-Relations (Accessed 08/02/2018).

[13] "*The Ecumenical Movement*", Encyclopedia.com, http://www.encyclopedia.com/article-1G2-3407703543/ecumenical-movement.html (accessed 08/02/2018).

Growth of Christianity

There are many who suggest that the success or failure of churches can only be understood by studying business and marketing models. They suggest that religious economies as well as commercial economies exist. Proponents of that theory hold that this theory offers a framework for understanding past cycles of church growth and decline. Finke and Stark maintain that there are four factors essential to both commercial and religious economies:

- Organization (Church Polity)
- Sales Representatives (Clergy)
- Product (Religious Doctrine and Life)
- Marketing Techniques (Evangelism and Church Growth)[14]

They used this thesis to explain the changes that have occurred in the religious landscape. A significant change can be noted in the number of people that claim church membership and also in their distribution amongst the various religious denominations from the start of the Revolutionary War until the middle of the nineteenth century. After the Revolutionary War there was a demand for revival and increased individual freedoms. This caused a major transformation of the old established churches. What followed was a lack of religious unity and an ever increasing demand for religious freedom. Below is a table showing the change in church membership from the beginning of the Revolutionary War until the middle of the nineteenth century.

Denomination	1776	1850
Sum of Congregationalists, Episcopalians, and Presbyterians	55.0%	19.1%
Congregationalists	20.4%	4.0%
Episcopalians	15.7%	3.5%
Presbyterians	19.0%	11.6%

---

[14] Roger Fink and Roger Stark, *The Churching of America: Winners and Losers in Our Religious Economy,* (New Brunswick, New Jersey: Rutgers University Press, 1992), 17.

Baptists	16.9%	20.5%
Methodists	2.5%	34.2%
Those claiming church membership	17.0%	34.0%

Figure 8 - Change in Church Membership
1776-1850[15]

As can be seen from the table above, there were significant losses in the mainline denominational churches. Those losses are further emphasized by the fact that the total number of citizens claiming church membership doubled during the same time period that the denominational churches were losing members. Those sweeping changes in the religious landscape may have had as much to do with class as they did with theology. People began to have a taste for freedom in their political lives which created a similar desire for freedom in their religious lives. Popular church movements, including Baptists, Methodists, Mormons, and others, grew significantly because the message of their preaching was practical, down to earth, and, most importantly, effective in reaching people.

In the final decades of the nineteenth century and the beginning decades of the twentieth century, two intellectual developments posed serious challenges to fundamental Christian faith. The first was the growth and overwhelming acceptance of the scientific hypothesis (more accurately labeled a supposition) known as Darwinism. The second was the introduction of German critical theories regarding the interpretation of biblical texts into American schools of religion.[16] Both of the above stated challenges were the results of German Protestantism. James Nichols, describing the influence of German idealism, said, "Although German Protestantism was generally uncreative in its corporate life and social ethics, it is quite another story in the intellectual sphere... German Protestantism alone embarked on a bold effort to

---

[15] David F. Wells, *God In The Wasteland: the reality of truth in a world of fading dreams*, (Grand Rapids, Michigan: William B. Erdman Publishing Company, 1994), 63.

[16] Hall, *Religion in America*, 238.

achieve one coherent *intellectual* [emphasis added] world for the modern Christian."[17]

The revivalism that began in the late nineteenth century could and did inspire tangible actions in society, but those actions were focused on the individual rather than on society as a whole. In addition, the industrial revolution that began in the last half of the nineteenth century also redefined how Americans viewed society. Many religious commentators of that day began to cast doubt on whether the church's individual focus was sufficient to address the contemporary conditions of an industrial society. They declared that revivals would not cure unsanitary conditions in urban slums or resolve labor disputes between workers and employers. The new, modernized religious thinking demanded that the sources of power and wealth had to be confronted. As industrialization and urbanization accelerated, some Protestant clergy leaders insisted that Christians had a responsibility to ensure social justice for the masses. Thus began the Social Gospel Movement in America.[18]

A young, German theologian, Dietrich Bonhoeffer, arrived in New York in 1930 during a time of incredible energy and economic growth. The Chrysler Building, the tallest man-made structure on planet Earth, had just been completed. In just a few months it would be eclipsed by the Empire State Building. The George Washington Bridge, under construction, would become the longest bridge in the world, by nearly a factor of two. Yes, America seemed to be bursting at the seams with prosperity. While America was experiencing unparalleled economic growth, the theological condition Bonheoffer found at Union Theological Seminary was quite the opposite.

Bonhoeffer, already holding a Doctorate from Berlin University, was in New York to spend a year as an exchange student at Union Theological Seminary. Finding the theological condition much worse than expected, he wrote this to his superintendent:

---

[17] James H. Nichols, *History of Christianity 1650-1950*, (New York, New York: The Ronald Press Company, 1956), 163.

[18] Hall, *Religion in America*, 214-215.

There is no theology here. . . They talk a blue streak without the slightest substantive foundation and with no evidence of any criteria. The students - on the average twenty-five to thirty years old - are completely clueless with respect to what dogmatics is really about. They are unfamiliar with even the most basic questions. They become intoxicated with liberal and humanistic phrases, laugh at the fundamentalists, and yet basically are not even up to their level.[19]

Bonhoeffer literally had no idea what he was in for at Union. The battle between liberals and fundamentalists was already well underway. Leading the charge for theological liberalism was America's most famous *liberal* preacher, Harry Emerson Fosdick.

In an attempt to eliminate fundamentalism, the Rockefeller Foundation funded the construction of the opulent Riverside Church that would serve as platform for Fosdick's *'progressive'*, modernist views.[20] The *modern* church was rapidly moving away from the old-fashioned Gospel. The *modern* church abandoned its search for souls and began a steady craving for money, power, and respectability.

Bonhoeffer was quite explicit in describing the weaknesses he observed at Union and in churches in New York City. He wrote this scathing comment in regard to the theological atmosphere at Union which he felt was accelerating the secularization of Christianity in America:

A seminary in which it can come about that a large number of students laugh out loud in a public lecture at the quoting of a passage from Luther's *De servio arbitrio* on sin and forgiveness because it seems to them to be comic has evidently completely forgotten what Christian theology by its very nature stands for.[21]

---

[19] Eric Metaxas, *BONHOEFFER: Pastor, Martyr, Prophet, Spy*, (Nashville: Thomas Nelson, Inc., 2010), 101.

[20] Ibid., 102.

[21] Ibid., 105.

Sadly, the theological drift toward modernism and disbelief Bonhoeffer experienced in New York City would soon spread to other churches in America. The relentless march toward modernism, progressivism, and ultimately, socialism would only increase over time.

Even though the outward manifestation of churches in America would give the appearance of growth, true Christianity was on the verge of entering a period of decline. Timothy Hall, in the introduction to his book *Religion in America*, commenting on this particular time period, made this statement, "Champions of modernity have frequently predicted that religious faith and practice must inevitably decline. Toward the dawn of the twentieth century, some influential social observers began to announce the expected demise of religious faith."[22]

Beginning in the 1930s, rather than view the modernization and secularization of the church with skepticism, '*enlightened*' Americans refused to acknowledge the danger and welcomed the changes as progress. Mr. Dietrich Bonhoeffer was virtually alone is his appraisal of the impending demise of the church. Regarding what he observed in New York, he said:

> In New York they preach about virtually everything; only one thing is not addressed, or it is addressed so rarely that I have as yet been unable to hear it, namely, the gospel of Jesus Christ, the cross, sin and forgiveness, death and life.[23]

Just as Mr. Hall predicted, Christianity in America was beginning to decline. James Nichols, Professor of Church History at the University of Chicago, in his book, *History of Christianity 1650-1950*, writing on the institutional consolidation of American evangelism said this regarding the perceived decline of Christianity:

> The decline of Christian influence generally in the national culture was not as marked as in European

---

[22] Hall, *Religion in America*, xi.
[23] Metaxas, *BONHOEFFER: Pastor, Martyr, Prophet, Spy*, 106.

countries or Great Britain, but it was still noticeable. In America it was concurrent with a continuing extension of church membership and nominal adherence. Commenting on American social trends in 1933 the Hoover Commission observed, "Church and family have lost many of their regulatory influences over behavior, while industry and government have assumed a large degree of control." . . . . The proportion of articles on Christianity in general magazines also declined noticeably, and the tone indicated a general decrease of respect as well as of interest. "The most fundamental change in the intellectual life of the United States", commented an analyst for the Hoover Commission, "is the apparent shift from biblical authority and religious sanctions to scientific and factual authority and sanctions."[24]

Mr. Nichols also noted that a similar decline was infecting the public school system:

A similar trend could be observed with regard to the curriculum and tone of public education. Secondary education in America had been pioneered by the Protestant churches. But in the first thirty of forty years of the twentieth century the Protestant churches retired almost completely from this field, whereas the public high schools multiplied ten times or more. In the curricula of these public schools, elementary as well as secondary, the Christian perspective steadily lost ground before that of scientific humanism. Even in higher education, although the churches still supported and controlled about a third of the whole enterprise at mid-century, the Protestants had come perilously close to losing any sense of distinctive direction. The great growth was in state universities, and here the significance of Christian faith was minimal. The American people were to be nearly illiterate religiously in the second half of the twentieth century.[25]

---

[24] Nichols, *History of Christianity 1650-1950*, 405.
[25] Ibid.

Mr. Nichols reveals two interesting and informative facts in the two quotes shown above. First, even though Christian influence was declining, church membership was expanding. Unfortunately, church membership was expanding by accepting only nominal adherence to doctrinal standards. Webster's dictionary defines nominal as "existing in name only; not real".[26] It seems that churches were increasing in numbers but the new adherents being added to church membership roles were counterfeits. They were Christians in name only. This was likely the beginning of the "growth at any cost and by any means" syndrome that would ultimately destroy many churches from the inside. Secondly, the church willingly abdicated its role in public education. Even worse was the fact that the church had little to no influence in higher education. The church had fallen victim to the misleading belief that a weekly half hour Sunday School session, conducted by mostly untrained volunteers, was somehow sufficient to overcome the eight hours per day of secular Humanism being disseminated in the public school system.

During the mid-twentieth century, the chasm, also called the wall of separation between church and state, grew even wider. Occasionally, the church did battle against the state's intrusion into the public school, but only half-heartedly. Mr. Nichols commenting on the debate over constitutional issues surrounding separation of church and state said this, "The jurists of the Supreme Court exhibited as much confusion as the common man as, in a series of postwar cases, they fumbled for an interpretation of the Constitution."[27] So began the progressive loss of Christian influence throughout all facets of American life.

In the following section, developments in the last half of the twentieth century will be examined to determine if Christianity's decline would continue.

---

[26] Merriam-Webster Dictionary, http://www.merriam-webster.com/dictionary/nominal, (Accessed 08/02/1018).

[27] Ibid., 419.

Boom or Bust

How would you choose to define America during the last decades of the twentieth century? Many would choose to define America as a secular republic. Others would adamantly define America as a Christian republic. Still others would say it was a secular country but it *should* be a Christian country and that is what they are striving to achieve. The sad truth is that "true" biblical Christianity continues to decline and as a consequence, America is sliding deeper into secularism.

Although Donald McGavran had already formulated the main principles of church growth theory in the 1930s while serving as a missionary to India, it was not until the 1970s that his ideas moved beyond missionary circles and affected established churches.[28] These growth principles began to find wide acceptance in the evangelical world in the 1970s because it was a time when the theological character of evangelicalism began to fade, leaving the churches wide open to the intrusion of raw pragmatism.[29] This is an obvious continuation of the "growth at any price and by any means" method that was mentioned earlier.

George Barna, the well-known Christian researcher, asserts that the evangelical church in America is losing. There can certainly be no argument with that statement. However, Mr. Barna also advocates that the church must use aggressive marketing techniques to "sell" the church. In his book, *Marketing the Church*, Mr. Barna says:

> My contention, based on careful study of data and the activities of American churches, is that the major problem plaguing the Church is its failure to embrace a marketing orientation in what has become a marketing-driven environment". [30]

---

[28] David F. Wells, *God in the Wasteland*, (Grand Rapids, Michigan: William B. Erdmans Publishing Company, 1994), 69.

[29] Ibid., 71.

[30] George Barna, *Marketing the Church*, (Colorado Springs, Colorado: 1988), 23.

Mr. Barna stated that the first premise upon which his book rested was the fact the Church is a business and, "As such, the local church must be run with the same wisdom and savvy that characterizes any for profit business. As in the business world, every church must be managed with purpose and efficiency, moving toward its goals and objectives."[31]

Mr. Barna, in an earlier section, made an even more wildly erroneous statement, "Ultimately, many people do judge the pastor not on his capability to preach, teach, or counsel, but on his capacity to make the church run *smoothly and efficiently*. [emphasis added] In essence, he is judged as a businessman..."[32] Exactly where does Mr. Barna find that concept detailed in Scripture? The painful truth is that many churches are buying into Mr. Barna's marketing philosophy. Using that philosophy, pastors are forced to transform from being pastors to being C.E.Os. and from obtaining an M.Div. to obtaining an M.B.A. Mr. David Wells rightly dismisses Mr. Barna's philosophy when he says:

> Allowing the consumer to be sovereign in this way, in fact, sanctions a bad habit. It encourages us to indulge in constant internal inventory in the church no less than in the marketplace, to ask ourselves perpetually whether the "products" being offered meet our present "felt needs". In this sort of environment, market research has found that there is scarcely any consumer loyalty to particular products... And so it is that churches that have adopted the strategy of marketing themselves have effectively installed revolving doors. The pews are full, but never with the same people from week to week. People keep entering, lured by the church's attractions or just to check out the wares, but then they move on because they feel their needs, real, or otherwise, are not being met.[33]

Proponents of the Church Growth movement claim that "smallness" is a frame of mind. They say, "...it is a 'condition'

---

[31] Ibid, 26.
[32] Ibid, 14.
[33] Wells, *God in the Wasteland*, 75.

resulting from the inability to think beyond the traditional, an inability to make connections with contemporary people, and an inability to update routines, music, plans, expectations, and services. They attribute smallness to pinched and narrow thinking and accuse the traditional church of being addicted to smallness."[34]

The Church Growth movement, in their blind zeal for numbers, has become more and more liberal in their theology in order to attract the masses. By marketing the church as a "product" pastors have violated its character as a gathering place for worship and service to God. They have lost any desire for biblical truth. What they "push" as their "product" is no longer the truth about Christ and His saving grace but something entirely different. They have offered up a steady stream of programs, performances, pageants, and parades.

The 1950s saw a boom in the Evangelical church in America. The post–World War II prosperity experienced in the Unites States had a profound effect on the church. Church buildings were erected in large numbers, and the Evangelical church's activities and programs grew right along with their expansive physical growth.

Fundamentalism began as a movement that arose within British and American Protestantism in the late nineteenth and early twentieth centuries. It was mainly a reaction to modernism and the liberal Protestant groups that denied historic doctrines that were considered fundamental to Christianity. In spite of their denial of many fundamental Christian doctrines, they still called themselves "Christian." Those that were committed to upholding the historic Christian doctrines divided from the more liberal denominations and groups and over time became known as Fundamentalists. The term "fundamentalist" was first used in 1920 by Curtis Lee Laws to describe the "Baptist party".[35]

Fundamentalism grew, at least in part, as a reaction to the liberal influences in the Church Growth movement. It also was organized to reject the radical influences of philosophical humanism that was beginning to dilute the Christian religion. Over

[34] Ibid., 77.
[35] George M. Marsden, *Fundamentalism and American Culture*, (New York, New York: Oxford University Press, Inc., 2006), 107.

time, the Fundamentalist Evangelical movement divided into two main groups, one retaining the label *Fundamentalist*, while those who were more moderate in their theology came to be known by the label *Evangelical*. The more liberal Evangelicals came to be known as neo-Evangelical not so much in terms of their stated theology, but rather because they were progressive in their civic, social, and scientific perspectives.

Liberal Christianity grew rapidly during the twentieth century and by the 1960s it infected the leadership of many of the mainline denominations. At the end of the twentieth century, even though secular society considered them the representatives and spokesmen of Christianity, the mainline churches were shrinking. This was likely due to a loss of evangelistic zeal, the loss of some of their membership to more conservative churches, and partly to the failure of one generation to pass on Christianity to the next.

So, having reached the end of the twentieth century, the following question must be asked, *"Is the growth that has been touted by the Church Growth movement and liberals really a boom or is it a bust?"* From surveys taken to measure changes in church attendance statistics, it must be concluded that it is a bust. Here is a statement made by Grant Wacker in his book, *Religion in Nineteenth Century America*, regarding the state of religion in America at the end of the twentieth century:

> At the end of the twentieth century, religion in the United States seemed to hold more questions than answers. If visitors from a distant country had arrived in Washington, D.C., toured the Supreme Court, and seen a session of Congress, then observed the classical Greek marble buildings lining the streets, they probably would have gained the impression that the United States was a wholly secular nation, without any references to God in its public life.[36]

Surveys reveal rather alarming trends regarding the religious landscape in America at the end of the twentieth century. Here is what one of those surveys revealed:

---

[36] Wacker, *Religion in Nineteenth Century America*, 171.

149

- The percentage of American adults who identify themselves as Christians dropped from 86% in 1990 to 77% in 2001, an unprecedented drop of nearly one percentage point per year.
- From 1992 to 2003, average attendance at a typical church service dropped by 13% while the population of America increased by 9%!
- Confidence in religious institutions hit an all-time low.
- At the present rates of change, Islam will become the dominant religion in the world before 2050 CE.
- Agnostics, Atheists, and secularists are growing rapidly.[37]

David Olson, in his book *The American Church in Crisis*, details his analysis of church attendance by region while factoring in the growth in population. Even though the South and West showed small growth in numeric church attendance, each region's total population grew by 25% and 29% respectively.

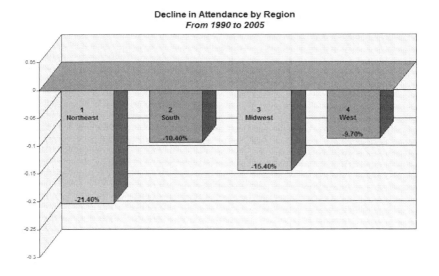

Figure 9 - Decline in Attendance Percentage by Region From 1990 to 2005[38]

---

[37] *"Trends Among Christians in the U.S."*, http://www.religious tolerance.org/chr_tren.htm (Accessed 08/20/2018).

When consideration is given to population growth, it is readily apparent that growth in church attendance did not even come close to keeping up with population growth. Population grew slower in the Northeast and Midwest while the percentage of church attendance declined even more.

Many more surveys could be cited that paint the same dismal picture of church attendance as the twentieth century closed. While there might have been some numeric gains in raw numbers, the "*real*" percentage growth of church population as a whole was actually decreasing significantly. Given the true attendance statistics, it would seem that the purported boom was not really a boom at all but rather a dismal bust. But what of the spiritual condition of religion during that time frame? A "bust" in the area of the "actual" spiritual condition of religion also occurred, especially after young people returned from secular state colleges and, sadly, from Christian colleges as well. One crystal clear example of that is the following recounting of a Christian young man's horrible experience when he went off to Bible College:

> The idea of Christian America came to me personally quite early: I was brought up in a fundamentalist household in Philadelphia and was sent to a fundamentalist school. . . . We had to memorize a chapter of the Bible every week, we were told that it would be sinful to vote for John Kennedy because he answered to the Pope, and we can't trust Catholics, let alone atheists, and that America was very much a Christian republic or ought to be. This was the unquestioned orthodoxy in my household.
>
> Then I went off to a Christian College [name withheld] and I had a new professor there named [name withheld]. And he in no uncertain terms proceeded to disabuse me of the notion that it's appropriate even to talk about Christian America. Such things bordered on idolatry rather than truth, he said.

---

[38] David T. Olson, *The American Church in Crisis*, (Grand Rapids, Michigan: Zondervan Publishing, 2008), 79.

On two fronts he disabused me of the idea of a Christian America. He did this first theologically, arguing that the idea of a covenanted society, ... simply didn't bear scrutiny. God's covenanting with nations stopped with Christ and ancient Israel; there was subsequently no such thing as nation-states . . . . . He said that's nonsense; these things simply don't exist. That was an eye-opener to me.

The other dimension was constitutional. [Name withheld] said America as a nation-state in fact did not begin in 1630; it began in 1776 and assumed constitutional shape in 1787, when church and state were *explicitly* [emphasis added] separated. This was, indeed, the genius of the Constitution - this radical idea of the separation of church and state, liberty of conscience without restraint.[39]

The experience recounted above would be expected from a secular college or university but certainly not from a Christian college. The remainder of the article indicated that the young man fell victim to the professor's attack and returned home with the false belief that America was not born as a Christian nation. Even worse was that he also accepted the *blatantly incorrect* position that the Constitution explicitly built a wall of separation between church and state. That untruth has already been debunked in chapters five and six of this book.

Sadly the story of a young Christian like the one above having his or her faith destroyed while attending a Christian college is repeated far too often. Apologist Ken Ham along with Greg Hall has written a book titled *Already Compromised*. Their book is a stunning revelation about America's Christian colleges! It is an eye-opening assessment of two hundred Christian colleges and universities from all across America. During the unprecedented 2010 study by Britt Beemer's America's Research Group, those colleges were polled regarding core faith questions. The results are

---

[39] "*In Search of Christian America*", Harry S. Stout, Yale Divinity School's Reflections, Fall 2007 edition, http://reflections.yale.edu/article/faith-and-citizenship-turbulent-times/search-christian-america (Accessed 08/15/2018).

truly revealing and shocking in the extreme! More will be offered on that issue in a later chapter.

From history, it appears that the supposed "boom in church growth" fails miserably on both fronts, in actual percentage attendance growth and, more importantly, in spiritual growth.

The overall numbers would seem to indicate that the number of people attending church on any given weekend has increased. However, when you take into consideration the total growth in population of the United States you get an entirely different picture. The percentage of people attending church has actually decreased. David Olson, in his book, *The American Church in Crisis,* describes survey data for church attendance for the years 1990 through 2005 for various church groups. That survey data is reproduced below in graphic form:

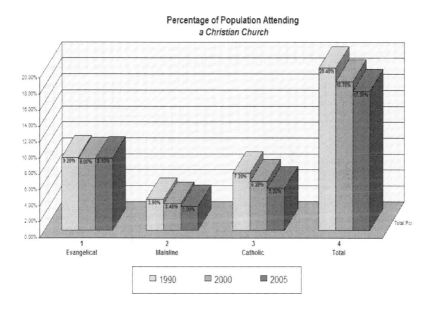

Figure 10 - Percentage of Population Attending Christian Churches, 1990 - 2005[40]

The only group to even hold nearly steady was evangelical churches which showed a 0.1% overall decrease during the fifteen

---

[40] Olson, *The American Church in Crisis*, 36.

year period. Considering all churches combined there was a 2.9 percent decrease in attendance. Mr. Olson also states, *"In no single state did church attendance keep up with population growth!"*[41]

More evidence that the *"supposed"* boom in church attendance was in actuality a horribly, disappointing bust.

---

[41] Ibid., 37.

Chapter Seven: Dismantling America's Christian Heritage

Democracy is a device that ensures we shall be governed no better than we deserve.

George Bernard Shaw

Dismantling
America's

> If the polls are right, our Judeo-Christian heritage
> is no longer the foundation of our values.
> We have become a post-Christian society.
>
> Charles Colson
> Imprimis, Vol. 22, No. 4

Christian
Heritage

This chapter is much more than a diatribe on the decaying morals in American society. It is also a spotlight cast with equal brightness upon the decaying morals within the church in general and within orthodox Christianity specifically. The decaying of morals in society and in Christianity is frequent fodder for many "talking heads" and cable news pundits. They rant and they rave. They wring their hands and cry, "*What are we going to do?*" Mr. David Wells in his book, *Losing our Virtue: Why the Church Must Recover its Moral Vision*, says he does not "wish to wave red flags before bulls and further provoke those who took offense at my earlier books."[1] There must be no such resistance to flag-waving or alarm-sounding. It is long past time for someone to raise the red flag and to sound the alarm. It matters not if you think "they" (the world and some *so-called* Christians) may get angry and shout insults. It is absolutely crucial to sound the alarm, to wave the flag, to publicly declare the truth, or whatever else might be required to get the attention of those who still have "*ears to hear*".

What follows is a discussion of the result of the battle between true Christianity (a Christian worldview) and worldly philosophy (a secular worldview). School children in America are now being educated using totally humanistic values in the public school system. For the most part, young people, especially those headed off to secular colleges and universities, have no idea what their worldview is or should be and they are woefully unprepared to defend their beliefs. It is of extreme importance that children and adults understand the different worldviews being taught. Worldly, secular philosophy, also called humanism, simply means a purely scientific way of looking at your "experience" in the world. It is a naturalistic explanation for "the way things are." The way you live in the world, how you evaluate your experiences in the world, and the way you teach your children are all entirely dependent on your worldview. The secular philosophy of the past half-century has caused many to reject any notion of absolute authority in life, public or private. Belief in the Absolute has become blurred to the

---

[1] David F. Wells, *Losing our Virtue: Why the Church Must Recover its Moral Vision*, (Grand Rapids, Michigan: 1998), 1.

point of obscurity. The proponents of secular philosophy call belief in an Absolute old-fashioned, narrow-minded, backward, silly, ridiculous, downright stupid, or any one of dozens of other insulting labels.

True religion (a Christian worldview) is essentially the act of faith in God as Creator of all that ever was, is, or will be. That *does not* mean faith in the fuzzy, clouded image of God that the world has imagined. It means faith in the one Absolute, Eternally-existing God. When the world speaks the word "God", it is almost always used in an epitaph of anger or vulgarity. Martin Buber in his book, *The Eclipse of God*, describes a conversation he had with an old man in his study regarding his speaking of God in the preface to that book. During that conversation the old man asked:

> How can you bring yourself to say 'God' time after time? How can you expect that your readers will take the word in the sense in which you wish it to be taken? What you mean by the name of God is something above all human grasp and comprehension, but in speaking about it you have lowered it to human conceptualization. What word of human speech is so misused, so defiled, so desecrated as this! All the innocent blood that has been shed for it has robbed it of its radiance. All the injustice that it has been used to cover has effaced its features. When I hear the highest called 'God' it sometimes seems almost blasphemous.[2]

Mr. Buber explained to the old man that was just the reason he must never abandon it. You should feel the same sense of duty to God as Mr. Buber. The fight to preserve an understanding, or reverence, for the awesome holiness of God must *never* be abandoned. In his book, Mr. Buber writes from the premise that scientific intellectualism has caused an eclipse of God, in a similar manner as when a celestial eclipse occurs. During a solar eclipse the moon passes between the sun and your eyes. Your vision of the sun may be reduced or, perhaps, it may even be totally obscured.

---

[2] Martin Buber, *The Eclipse of God*, (Westport Connecticut: Greenwood Press Publishers, 1977), 16.

Even though the image viewed of the Sun has changed; in fact, absolutely nothing has changed about the Sun itself. It is only that something has "come between" the Sun and the viewer. The *"Eclipse of God"* Mr. Buber describes can be viewed in exactly the same manner. Absolutely nothing about God has changed. In actuality, something has come between you and your view of God. The "something" that clouds and distorts a correct view of God is modernity, modernism, secularism, humanism, evolutionism, etc. – all the things that define a humanistic worldview. Modernism is a revolt against conservative values whereas modernity is simply the belief that the present is discontinuous with the past. Through a process of social and cultural change, life in the present is fundamentally different from life in the past. That definition of "modernity" encompasses all the other "ism's" listed above.

The cover of the April 8, 1966, edition of *Time Magazine* and the accompanying article described a movement in American theology known as the "God is Dead" movement. That movement came from a radical Christian theological school of thought, mainly Protestant, that arose in the United States during the 1960s. It elicited prolonged attention, controversy, and debate. Many varied viewpoints have been grouped under this radical school of thought. Common to nearly all of them is the idea that belief in God is impossible or meaningless in the modern world and that human fulfillment is to be found only in a secular lifestyle.[3]

Those words would be shocking enough coming from some professed atheist like Friedrich Nietzsche, Martin Heidegger, or Jean-Paul Sartre. However, those words were not written by a belligerent existentialist. Rather, and somewhat unbelievably, they were written by Thomas J. J. Altizer, associate professor of religion at Emory University, a Methodist school of theology.[4]

Does that mean that the liberal existentialists and liberal theologians have finally succeeded in killing God? No, certainly not. Their proclamations only mean that modern man has become

---

[3] *"Death of God Movement"*, Encyclopedia Britannica, http://www.britannica.com/EBchecked/topic/154552/Death-of-God-movement, (Accessed 08/04/2018).

[4] *"Theology: The God Is Dead Movement"*, Time Magazine, http://www.time.com/time/magazine/article/0,9171,941410,00.html, (Accessed 08/04/2018).

incapable of perceiving or apprehending the reality of God. A true understanding of God is not fashioned in the imagination of man. Man's capacity to understand the "divine" in his mind is born of the spirit through faith. That truth is something the unregenerate mind cannot even begin to fathom.

Anyone truthfully examining the cultural landscape in America today would readily concur that there has been an "*Eclipse of God*". Man's scientific intellectualism has obscured his ability to look upon the face of God. Man's vision of God has become faint and blurred. What modern man sees is filtered through the lens of many decades of humanistic, intellectual misinformation. What has led to this hideous chasm of doubt and unbelief? What follows in the next section is one theory to answer that question.

First Love Lost

The primary reason why modern Christianity has lost its first love can be summed up in one single word - presumption! Webster's dictionary defines presumption as "An overstepping of the bounds of reverence, respect, or courtesy; a taking of something for granted; arrogant behavior that you have no right to." Presumption is always destructive in human relationships, but it is especially damaging and destructive when it rears its ugly head in a person's relationship with God. In those times, God is taken for granted. The last definition above, "*arrogant behavior that you have no right to*", certainly describes liberal America and most of Christianity at the beginning of the twenty-first century.

Over the past six or seven decades it seems that orthodoxy (which Webster's Dictionary defines as - soundness of faith; a belief in the doctrines taught in the Scriptures) in virtually every aspect of life has been ignored and/or discarded. Whether in dress, conversation, entertainment, life, and even religion, what was once considered normal and good has been rejected and what was abnormal and bad has been accepted. As you look at American society you must ask the question, "*Has this departure advanced the quality of life in the United States?*" The answer to that question is an obvious, unequivocal, and emphatic NO! Read on for some examples of what the godless society is producing.

In a chapter titled "The Dumbing Down of America" from Dr. D. James Kennedy's book, *What If America Were A Christian Nation Again*, Mr. William J. Bennett, former United States Secretary of Education, expressed his concerns about what was happening to education in America. He is quoted as saying, "Truly, my friends, the situation has gone from deplorable to catastrophic."[5] Later in that same chapter, Dr. Kennedy described a 2001 television documentary that included an interview with serial killer Jeffery Dahmer.

> He [Jeffery Dahmer] said that evolution in school undermined his faith that human life had any value, and that when he accepted that view, it totally devalued his opinion of his fellow man, and, since it taught him there was no God to whom he would be accountable, it gave him permission to do as he pleased. His father confirmed this change in Jeffery's outlook from what he learned at school.[6]

At the close of that chapter Dr. Kennedy assures his readers that he does not believe that everyone who goes to public school will be overwhelmed by evil. However, he goes on to describe frequent counseling sessions he had with parents. During those counseling sessions, the distressed parents often expressed grief over what happened to their child after attending college. According to Dr. Kennedy, a typical session went like this:

> Parents come to me in tears. "I cannot understand it - little Johnny – I sent him off to college. All those years of

---

[5] D. James Kennedy, *What If America Were A Christian Nation Again*, (Nashville, Tennessee: 2003), 120.

[6] "Robert Ressler: *The Man Who Lives With Monsters*", Mugshots, Court TV, January 29, 2001. Quoted in Kennedy, *What If America Were A Christian Nation Again*, 122.

Sunday School, and he comes back an atheist. What did we do wrong?"

I'll tell you. These parents sent Johnny to an atheistic school where a bunch of professors with impressive degrees and tremendous influence and persuasiveness tore him apart. But Johnny had to go to that school, because he would get a much better job after he graduated from this prestigious college![7]

Dr. Kennedy did not mention the diverse forces that convince many Christian young people they must attend a secular college to be successful. America's view of what is important and what is to be sought after has changed dramatically. The attack on sound biblical doctrine is not coming from just those within secular academia.

Another cause of presumption could be the drift in beliefs and doctrine because of America's increasing modern affluence (more on this topic in the next section). Honor and respect for God wanes as beliefs drift. However, not all presumption can be blamed on careless drifting. Strong evidence shows that much of modern liberalism in religion was deliberately planned and executed. What is surprising is that the source is not who you might expect. William Hordern, in his book *A Layman's Guide to Protestant Theology*, referring to that deliberate intent to introduce liberalism wrote:

> The method of liberalism includes the attempt to modernize Christianity. The world, liberals argue, has changed radically since the early creeds of Christendom were formulated; this makes the creeds sound archaic and unreal to modern man. We have to rethink Christianity in thought forms which the modern world can comprehend. Harry Emerson Fosdick argued that we must express the essence of Christianity, its "abiding experiences," but that we must not identify these with the "changing categories" in which they have been expressed in the past. For example, says Fosdick, an abiding experience of

---

[7] Kennedy, *What If America Were A Christian Nation Again*, 135.

Christianity has been its conviction that God will triumph over evil. This has been traditionally pictured in the category of Christ's second coming on the clouds to destroy evil and set up good. We can no longer retain the outworn category, but we can still believe the truth which this ancient thought form was trying to express. We can continue to work in the faith that, through His devoted followers, God is now building His Kingdom and that there will be a renewing of life, individual and social, to bring it into conformity with the will of God. The essence of the faith is thus retained, argues Fosdick, while the thought form in which it was once clothed has been abandoned.[8]

Harry Emerson Fosdick was an American clergyman educated at Union Theological Seminary in 1904. He was ordained as a Baptist minister in 1903 and became the most prominent, albeit *liberal*, Baptist minister of the early 20th Century. As a minister and theologian, Mr. Fosdick would be expected to lead and protect the flock of God, not lead it astray with modernistic, liberal pronouncements.

On the same page, Mr. Hordern describes the second aspect of liberalism's deliberate attempt to move orthodox religion to a more modernist position:

A second aspect of the method of liberalism is its refusal to accept religious belief on authority alone. Instead, it insists that all beliefs must pass the bar of reason and experience. Man's mind is capable of thinking God's thoughts after Him. Man's intuitions and reason are the best clues that we have to the nature of God. The mind must be kept open to all truth regardless of from whence it comes. This means that the liberal must have an open mind; no questions are closed. New facts may change the convictions that have become hallowed by custom and time. The liberal will venture forth into the unknown,

---

[8] William Hordern, *A Layman's Guide to Protestant Theology*, (New York, New York: Macmillan, 1955), 74.

firmly believing that all truth must be God's truth. In this spirit, the liberal accepts the higher criticism of the Bible and the theory of evolution. He refuses to have a religion that is afraid of truth or that tries to protect itself from critical examination.[9]

That soul-damning, liberal philosophy is taught not only in secular colleges and universities, it has also invaded many Christian colleges to such a degree that many of them hardly deserve to have Christian in their names any longer. How does this happen? Once again, it comes down to presumption.

Presumption often goes like this: *"God is merciful. I am a sinner. Therefore, God is obligated to be merciful to me regardless of what I do."* That is spiritual presumption. God is merciful to forgive us. However, modern believers have come to expect it. Believing that, they behave as they please. They treat God as if He were nothing more than a "fire escape" or "get out of jail free card". He is no longer the Sovereign Creator to whom they owe total loyalty and obedience.

A good example of spiritual presumption is pictured in the story told by Historian Robert Hughes of a convict who was sentenced to life imprisonment on a maximum-security island off the coast of Australia.

One day, with no provocation, he turned on a fellow prisoner and beat him senseless. Authorities shipped the murderer back to the mainland to stand trial, whereupon he gave a straightforward, passionless account of the crime. He showed no sign of remorse and denied having held any grudge against the victim. "Why, then?" asked the bewildered judge. "What was your motive?" The prisoner replied that he was sick of life on the island, a notoriously brutal place, and saw no reason to keep on living. "Yes, yes, I understand all that," said the judge. "I can see why you might drown yourself in the ocean. But murder? Why murder?" "Well, I figure it's like this," said the prisoner. "I'm a Catholic. If I commit suicide I'll go

---

[9] Ibid.

straight to hell. But if I murder someone, I can come back here to Sydney and confess to a priest before my execution. That way, God will forgive me"[10]

It is doubtful that most Christians would ever be so bold as to freely admit an attitude such as is exhibited in the story above. But that is exactly how many Christians live. They live their lives as "*they*" want to. They seek after the things of the world. But when things go wrong and they begin to suffer the consequences of sin, they cry out to God for forgiveness. They presume upon God's great mercy and expect, perhaps, even demand, that He forgive them as He promised He would.

Loving God goes far beyond just following a creed or a set of rules. The opposite of presumption is humility, meekness, or servility. The last of those definitions can also mean bondage. The New Testament concept of servility or bondage is the Greek word "*doulos*" which means a bondslave, someone who willingly gives himself up to another's will or service. That is to be a Christian's attitude, a willing life of service to another. It is more than just "doing" something. The author of II Chronicles describes Amaziah's revenge upon the one that killed his father, the king. II Chronicles 25:2 says, "*And he did that which was right in the sight of the LORD, but not with a perfect heart.*" The English word *perfect* in that verse means whole or complete. The chronicler is saying that Amaziah did that which was right, but he did it half-heartedly. He went about serving the Lord in a perfunctory manner and with a half-hearted obedience. That is the first indication that you have lost your first love. You do the "right" things, half-heartedly. There is no joy or zeal in what you do. Soon, that lack of love in your heart leads to doing things that are not right. What God wants is wholehearted obedience. In Israel's early history, whenever a more numerous or powerful army threatened them, they looked to the Ark of the Covenant. Did they trust in the ark of God or did they trust in the God of the ark? A similar question might be asked of Christians today. Are they trusting in the God of the Bible or are they trusting in their religion to save and protect them?

---

[10] Phillip Yancey, *What's So Amazing About Grace*, 177.

In what ways do Christians exhibit a loss of their First Love? Listed below are several possibilities that describe that condition:

- When they inwardly strive for the acclaim of this world rather than the approval of the Lord.
- When they view the commands of Christ as restrictions to happiness rather than expressions of His love.
- When their thoughts during leisure moments do not reflect upon the Lord.
- When their delight in the Lord is no longer as great as their delight in someone or something else.
- When their soul does not long for times of rich fellowship in God's Word or in prayer.
- When they become complacent to sinful conditions around them.[11]

The last item in the list above is certainly one of the major weaknesses in many evangelical churches today. Modern churches have become complacent to the rampant sin that saturates American society in the twenty-first century and has, in many cases, crept into the churches themselves.

Christians presume upon God when they claim the assurance that His salvation offers but rarely serve the Lord and show little or no effect of His Word working in their lives. They presume upon God when they view His grace as an excuse for sin and do not view it as a cause to repent and turn from sin. They presume upon God when they continue in what they know is wrong behavior, or if they are guilty of Paul's warning, *"Or despisest thou the riches of his goodness and forbearance and longsuffering; not knowing that the goodness of God leadeth thee to repentance?"* (Romans 2:4). For the Christian, that is presumption. No wonder David prayed, *"Keep back thy servant also from presumptuous sins; let them not have dominion over me: then shall I be upright, and I shall be innocent from the great transgression."* (Psalm 19:13).

---

[11] *"Lost our First Love"*, Pulpit Helps, May 1992.

Suffering From Affluenza

One Sunday, during an adult Sunday School class, affluence was acknowledged as a major factor in America's turning away from God and becoming, at best, ambivalent toward His grace and mercy. That concept was made clear by an article describing Psychologist Oliver James's book *Affluenza*. Mr. James's book, part self-help, part political manifesto, is his account of why Americans are so miserable despite unimaginable levels of prosperity. It is also a scathing attack on a covetous and greedy society.[12] In that book he writes, "The great majority of people in English-speaking nations (Britain, America, Australia, Canada, Singapore) now define themselves through earnings, possessions, appearances, and celebrity..."[13] According to Mr. James the Affluenza virus is a set of values that make people vulnerable to emotional distress. It is an insatiable desire for money, fame, and power and a blind obsession to compete with and compare self to others or their possessions.

PBS aired a program titled "*Affluenza*" on Thursday, July 2, 1998. During that program they defined Affluenza as: Af-flu-en-za, noun, 1. The bloated, sluggish, and unfulfilled feeling that results from efforts to keep up with the Joneses; 2. An epidemic of stress, overwork, waste, and indebtedness caused by a dogged pursuit of the American Dream; 3. An unsustainable addiction to economic growth.[14] During that one-hour television special, they explored the high social and environmental costs of materialism and over-consumption, from a secular point of view. Christians readily recognize this affliction and label it "materialism". Materialism is placing your trust in money or the things it can buy. Those afflicted believe it will provide for them, protect them, and

---

[12] Guy Aitchison, "*Affluenza by Oliver James - the Blairite Virus*", openDemocracy Ltd, http://www.opendemocracy.net/ourkingdom/2008/01/17/affluenza-by-oliver-james-the-blairite-virus (Accessed 07/24/2018).

[13] Neil Powell, "*Money Has a Power Over Us*", http://www.afaithtoliveby.com/2011/02/24/money-has-a-power-over-us/ (accessed 07/24/2018).

[14] "*Affluenza*", Public Broadcast System, http://www.pbs.org/kcts/affluenza/ (accessed 07/24/2018).

make them happy. In return for those expectations and trust they are forced to serve it. The scriptural equivalent of materialism is mammonism. Jesus, teaching in Matthew chapter six, was crystal clear that man cannot serve two masters. For many people, including far too many Christians, the ultimate goal in life is the acquisition of greater wealth and power. They want and demand more and more wealth. It seems that no matter how much wealth they are able to obtain, it is never enough. Francois Marie Arouet, also known as Voltaire, was quoted as saying, "When it's a question of money, everybody is of the same religion."[15] Voltaire's thinking was that the "love of money" affects all people no matter what religion they claim. Similarly, the Affluenza virus is quite contagious and infects all people and all religions.

A preacher speaking on the subject of "the love of money" asked, "Are you pursuing God or goods?" Modern Christians have become so blinded by the glitz and glamour of the world that they have little room left for God. This horrible disease affects not only your body; it affects your soul. How often do you ask God to bless you so you can give more to His work, or are you tempted to lie like Ananias and Sapphira and to withhold that which rightly belongs to God?

American society is literally drowning in prosperity. Every day Americans throw away and waste more than some countries could exist upon for an entire month. And still they are not satisfied. *"More, more, give us more"*, society screams! American society cultivates and nurtures a never-ending drive to accumulate more and more of everything. But, sadly, as more and more is accumulated, satisfaction wanes and the ultimate result is that the sufferers of Affluenza are left feeling worthless, dissatisfied, empty, used, and unfulfilled.

The Affluenza virus also contributes to heart disease. It destroys the hearts of American society. As Americans become more and more affluent, they depend on God less and less. That negatively affects their involvement and support of the local church. A report by the Congressional Budget Office (CBO) finds that proposed changes to the tax code could reduce overall

---

[15] Francois Marie Arouet Voltaire. Quotes.net. STANDS4 LLC, 2011. 29 November. 2011. http://www.quotes.net/quote/18598 (accessed 08/04/2018).

charitable contributions. However, the CBO does not expect religious organizations to be affected because religious donors are less sensitive to the tax benefits of contributions. Instead, it is the charities favored by the rich (the arts, education, and healthcare) that are more likely to see lowered donations. The chart below shows how the percentage of charitable contributions given to religious organizations decreases with rising income.

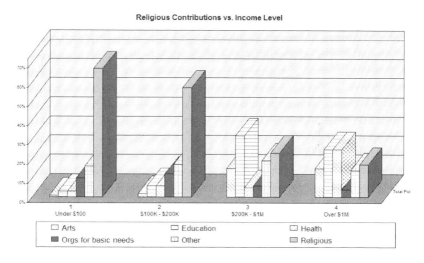

Figure 11 - Religious Contributions vs. Income Level[16]

From the table above you can see that those making between $200,000 and $1 Million per year give slightly less than one-quarter of their donations to religious groups while those making more than $1 million per year give approximately one-sixth of their contributions to religious groups. Those percentages vary significantly from those making $100,000 per year or less. Those individuals give two-thirds of their donations to religious groups. This certainly seems to be a solid confirmation of the Affluenza virus that is afflicting American society. The more money Americans make the less they feel the Hand of God in their lives.

---

[16] Frank J. Sammartino, *"Options for Changing the Tax Treatment of Charitable Giving"*, Congressional Budget Office, http://permanent. ccess.gpo.gov/gpo14068/10-18-charitableTestimony.pdf (Accessed 06/07/2018).

Americans are rich and do not think they need God. They believe they can take care of themselves. A verse of Scripture that has direct application to the contributions chart shown in Table 3.1 is, *"Because thou sayest, I am rich, and increased with goods, and have need of nothing; and knowest not that thou art wretched, and miserable, and poor, and blind, and naked:"* (Rev. 3:17). Those words were spoken to the Church of Laodicea because of their lukewarmness. Just like the Laodiceans, America is rich and increased with goods, and they "think" they have need of nothing. As expected, today's "modern church" has also become lukewarm and oblivious to the need of God in their lives.

Why has this lukewarmness settled upon the twenty-first century church? As stated earlier, it is at least partly because Christians in America have lost their first love. Today's worship services in most evangelical churches have been modernized to the point that they would be entirely unrecognizable to the church of one hundred years ago. Churches have become centered on the individual. Programs and activities are designed to entertain rather than instruct. Everything is energized by high-power appeal and is driven by modern marketing theory. The music in most evangelical churches would be far more appropriate in a tavern or saloon. All this is done to entice and entertain the modern church attendee. Where is the deep hungering and longing to study Him, to know Him, to understand who He is, that attribute which described the first settlers to arrive on the shores of New England or of the *Founders* who drafted the most incredible human document ever written? Sadly, it is gone or at least deeply hidden beneath an ocean of apathy and neglect.

The spiritual malaise and lukewarmness that is infecting an entire generation gives rise to the dangerous surrender described in the next section.

Slippery Slope to Compromise

The Merriam-Webster dictionary defines slippery slope as "a course of action that seems to lead inevitably from one action or result to another with unintended consequences."[17] Beyond any doubt, American secular society has stepped over the edge and onto the slippery slope and is plummeting toward disaster and decay. The bigger concern is that Christianity is only a half-step behind the world. Ken Ham in his book, *Already Compromised*, says there is an entropy (a measure of the disorder of a system) taking place on college campuses from what he calls "a moral and theological slippery slope"[18] which he says is taking higher learning in the wrong direction. Not only are the staff of institutions of higher learning being corrupted, but also the hearts and minds of naïve and gullible students are being corrupted right along with them.

The scorn and contempt for the Bible and God on secular college campuses is exactly what would be expected given the erroneous *"wall of separation"* that has been forced upon America's educational system. Some of you might be tempted to say, *"So what? We don't care what the world does. We send our kids to Christian schools."* Well, the secularization of public universities would be bad enough, but the exact same malady is infecting Christian colleges and universities, and not just liberal Christian colleges. It is also happening at schools still considered, by some at least, to be conservative. What follows is an examination of some of the signs, indicators, and results of the *"slide"* to secular liberalism in American society in general and then how that "slide" has also crept into Christianity.

The change was gradual and began many decades ago. Prosperity in America began to bloom and grow beginning with the end of World War II. Everyone was chasing the American Dream. Then came the 1960s and the Vietnam War which caused an immense division among the American population. It spawned the anti-war movement that created a change in people's perception of government. In the younger generation it led to questioning authority of any kind. Music changed. Clothing

---

[17] Merriam-Webster Dictionary, http://www.merriam-webster.com/dictionary/slippery%20slope, (Accessed 08/05/2018).

[18] Ken Ham, *Already Compromised*, (Green Forest, Arkansas: Master Books, Division of New Leaf Publishing, 2011), 8.

changed. Hair styles changed. Movies and television changed. Literally, the Vietnam War changed everything.

Dr. D. James Kennedy, in the introduction to his book, *What If America Were A Christian Nation Again*, tells the story of Jeremiah Denton Jr., an American pilot captured in Vietnam in 1965. He was imprisoned in isolation and tortured until his release in 1973. For nearly eight years he heard no news from home. What would he find when he returned home? How much would America have changed? Dr. Kennedy included what Jeremiah Denton said in his own words after his return home:

> When I came home and was driven from Naval Air Station Norfolk to the hospital at Portsmouth and saw all these signs - X-rated movies, massage parlors, those dumpy-looking places – and I asked [my wife] Jane, "What are those?" And then saw the magazines on the magazine rack in the Naval Hospital, I was shocked. I couldn't believe that my country, a country which had succeeded in getting one nation under God placed back in the Pledge had gotten to this place....[19]

The story above is offered as evidence of a sudden, rapid change in social and political values that occurred during that time of national calamity; changes that are still being felt today. The young people that grew up in those chaotic times are now grandparents. Their anti-establishment beliefs, anti-war rhetoric, rebellion, and contempt for anyone or anything that represented authority affected their children and is now also affecting their grandchildren.

Jerry Rubin, a wildly popular and powerful social activist of that time, wrote, "Young kids identify short hair with authority, discipline, unhappiness, boredom, rigidity, hatred of life – and long hair with letting go, letting your hair down, being free, being

---

[19] Transcript from an interview with Jeremiah Denton, CRM-TV, on location in Mobile, Alabama, September 1991. Quoted in D. James Kennedy, *What If America Were A Christian Nation Again*, 3.

open."[20] On the following page he wrote, "Our strategy is to steal the children of the bourgeoisie right away from the parents. Dig it! Yesterday I was walking down the street. A car passed by, parents in the front seat and a young kid, about eight, in the back seat. The kid flashed me the clenched fist sign."[21] A few pages later, he again writes about long hair, the symbol of rebellion, "Long hair is the beginning of our liberation from the sexual oppression that underlies this whole military society. Through long hair we're engaged in a sexual assault that's going to destroy the political-economic structure of Amerikan [sp.] society."[22]

Author and writer Saul Alinsky, founder of modern community organizing, believed that change should be non-threatening and come from within the organization to be changed. In the prologue to his book, *Rules for Radicals*, he wrote:

There's another reason for working inside the system. Dostoevski said that taking a new step is what people fear most. Any revolutionary change must be preceded by a passive, affirmative, non-challenging attitude toward change among the mass of our people. They must feel so frustrated, so defeated, so lost, so futureless in the prevailing system that they are willing to let go of the past and change the future. This acceptance is the reformation essential to any revolution.[23]

In an article titled, "Saul Alinsky" by Jay Atkinson, on The Latter Rain Page website, the introduction to its excerpt from *Rules for Radicals*, says this regarding Mr. Alinsky:

Alinsky's field of action was the field of change and a constant stream of conflict. Alinsky knew that in today's world, people are not motivated by altruism, you need to

---

[20] Jerry Rubin, *DO IT: Scenarios of the Revolution*, (New York, New York: Simon and Schuster, 1970, 93.
[21] Ibid., 94.
[22] Ibid., 96.
[23] Saul Alinsky, *Rules for Radicals A Pragmatic Primer for Realistic Radicals*, (New York, New York: Vintage Books, 1971) preface.

somehow appeal to their self-interest. The right thing usually done for the wrong reasons. When he came into a community in order to organize it, he had to get the local churches involved. He said that he never appealed to the ministers or priests in terms of Christian principles because they did not really believe in Christianity. Therefore, Alinsky appealed to what really motivated them, their self-interests and talked more about membership and more money. It worked every time.[24]

It is particularly revealing to note that Mr. Alinsky appealed to what *"really"* motivated Christian ministers and priests – *membership and money.* Those two things are high on the list of motivators that leads to compromise. Mr. Alinsky was not a "long-haired, demonstrate in the street radical" like Jerry Rubin. No, he was recognized and respected. One writer described Alinsky thusly, "After reading the book, my personal opinion is that Alinsky was a brilliant yet cynical, habitually dishonest, utterly amoral human being with a deep understanding of large swathes of human nature."[25] *Time Magazine* once wrote, "American democracy is being altered by Alinsky's ideas,"[26]

The quotes and statements about these two men who were instrumental in fueling rebellion during the revolutionary decades of the 1960s and 1970s are extremely important because they show the basis and beginning of the rapid increase in the dismantling of American culture. And as was learned from Mr. Alinsky's statement, that dismantling effort has been taken inside Christianity. It is also necessary to understand how critically important the symbol of long hair was and is to the counter-culture movement. Since the 1960s long hair has continued to be an outward sign of radical resistance and rebellion. Many, many Christians, both young and old, chafe at that statement, but that

---

[24] Jay Atkinson, *"Saul Alinsky"*, The Latter Rain Page, http://latter-rain.com/ltrain/alinski.htm (accessed 08/05/2018).
[25] John Hawkins, http://rightwingnews.com/quotes/the-best-quotes-from-saul-alinskys-rules-for-radicals/ (accessed 08/05/2018).
[26] "Essay: Radical Saul Alinsky: Prophet of Power to the People", Time Magazine, March 2, 1970.

does not change the facts. Long hair is a sign of rebellion and that simply cannot be denied.

In earlier sections of this book detailed evidence was given regarding the Christian identity and beginnings of America. As America moved from the twentieth century into the twenty-first century, little resemblance was left of the Christian heritage many Godly men fought and died to establish. An environment conducive to the rapid change that occurred in the 1960s and 1970s was at least partly fueled by the rapid modernization and urbanization of society and all the societal problems that develop with it. Estimates are that 93 percent of Americans live in a city with a population of 50,000 or more.[27] Another factor is that America is the first major civilization to be deliberately and knowingly building itself without a religious foundation.[28] David Wells, writing about the avant-garde, artists, philosophers, and novelists, that are always seeking to break free from traditions and established morals, describes them thusly:

> In the last century, in particular, they were struggling to unhitch their vision of life from Christian and, sometimes, theistic assumptions, to develop a new way of thinking that would owe nothing to biblical revelation or Church teaching. However, those who make up the avant-garde are usually a minority, those who are seen to be different precisely because they have become unconventional. Today, the tables have been turned. Our whole society has become avant-garde as what is morally conventional has been overthrown. Those who are conventional across a wide array of issues are now a minority. Our society, then, is caught up in an orgy of experimentation that is without parallel.[29]

What are some of the signs and indicators visible in society that can be attributed to the "*unhitching from*" Christian principles

---

[27] Wells, *Losing our Virtue: Why the Church Must Recover its Moral Vision*, 23.

[28] Ibid., 26.

[29] Ibid., 27.

that Mr. Wells speaks of? The list is quite lengthy. A few random quotes should suffice.

One sign is the liberals' frequent attempts to insult Christians or to portray them as the villains. For example, one newspaper article said, "The strength of fundamentalist leaders lies in their flocks. Corporations pay public relations firms millions of dollars to contrive the kind of grass-roots response that Falwell or Pat Robertson can galvanize in a televised sermon. Their followers are largely poor, uneducated, and easy to lead."[30] Then comes a quote from media mogul, Ted Turner, "*Christians* are 'bozos' and *Christianity* is for losers."[31] An Ohio Educational Association (a division of the National Education Association) official survey asked this question, "Are any of the school board members in your school district known or suspected to be *proponents of the Radical Right*?"[32]

Another indicator is in the area of tolerance, which the liberal left is always demanding. However, the plain truth is that they do not want tolerance. What they want is unquestioned acceptance. Consider this quote from Doug Ireland of Gay City News, "Schools cannot be neutral when we're dealing with *human dignity and human rights*. I'm not talking about tolerance. I'm talking about acceptance. [The film] *It's Elementary* is a great resource for parents, teachers, and community leaders."[33]

When liberals don't get the unquestioned acceptance they are looking for from Christians, they make efforts to silence them and force them from areas of influence, especially political office. Vic Fazio, former Democratic Congressional Campaign Chairman, states, "The 'fire-breathing Christian radical right'... is about to

---

[30] Michael Weisskopf, "*Energized by Pulpit or Passion, the Public is Calling*", Washington Post, February 1, 1993, https://www.washingtonpost.com/archive/politics/1993/02/01/energized-by-pulpit-or-passion-the-public-is-calling/f747ded3-b7c5-4578-ad3b-2f500dbaeacf/, (Accessed 08/03/2018).
[31] "Ted's Latest Insults", Cincinnati Enquirer, March 2, 1999, A16. In Folger, *The Criminalization of Christianity*, 51.
[32] Ohio Human and Civil Rights Commission questionnaire, published by the Ohio Education Association, December 1994. In Folger, *The Criminalization of Christianity*, 52.
[33] Doug Ireland, "Gay Ed for Kids", The Nation 268, no. 22 (June 14, 1999), 8. In Folger, *The Criminalization of Christianity*, 52.

take over the Republican Party. They are what the American people fear the most." [34] Ralph Reed responded to Mr. Fazio's remark, "Murder is the leading cause of death for African-American males aged eighteen to thirty-four...Yet people of faith getting involved in public life is what the American people fear most."[35] The mainstream media has borrowed a major tenant from the radical's handbook, "If you scream something loud enough and long enough, the people will begin to believe it even if it is untrue." And so it has happened. Much of the secular American public actually believes that Christians are their enemies and they are to be feared.

Anti-Christian bias also exists in the state and federal court systems. Following are just a few of the anti-Christian rulings the courts have handed down:

- Verbal prayer offered in school is unconstitutional (*Engel vs. Vitale,* 1962: *Abington vs. Schempp*, 1963).
- It is unconstitutional for a student to pray out loud over his lunch (*Reed vs. Van Hoven*, 1965).
- A student may not read a Bible during his free time (*Gierke vs. Blotzer*, 1989).
- It is unconstitutional for a school library to contain books that deal with Christianity, or for a teacher to be seen with a personal copy of the Bible (*Roberts vs. Madigan*, 1990).
- It is unconstitutional for a war memorial to be erected in the shape of a cross (*Lowe vs. City of Eugene*, 1969).
- It is unconstitutional for a public cemetery to have a planter in the shape of a cross (*Warsaw vs. Tehachapi*, 1990).[36]

The cases cited above are fully documented in Janet Folger's book, *The Criminalization of Christianity*, which contains two hundred plus pages of similar material demonstrating the anti-

---

[34] John Wheeler, "Assault of Faith", Christian American, September 15, 1994, 4. In Folger, *The Criminalization of Christianity*, 54.
[35] Ralph Reed, Mainstream Values Are No Longer Politically Incorrect, (Dallas, Texas: Word, 1994), 10. In Folger, *The Criminalization of Christianity*, 54.
[36] Folger, *The Criminalization of Christianity*, 101-103.

Christian bias that literally swept across America. A complete list of rulings such as those above goes on and on and on *ad infinitum*. It is obvious that the "slippery slope" for secular America has become quite steep.

Few Christians deliberately set out to turn away from God. They do not say, "*By the end of the year I will no longer allow God to work in my life. I will no longer believe in God.*" For many the *slide* is relatively slow, perhaps nearly imperceptible at first. However, the progression is always the same. As more and more compromise is allowed into one's life, the slope becomes ever steeper and the slide into liberalism becomes ever faster.

Who would have thought that the people claiming to be Christians, even pastors and Bible college professors, would be some of the most vociferous in their attacks on Absolute Truth. There is an all out assault against truth in America. A survey conducted by The Barna Group after the horrendous events of 9/11 found a great shift in America's views on truth. At the beginning of the year 2000, nearly four out of ten adults (38%) said that there are absolute moral truths that do not change no matter what the circumstances are. When the same question was asked in November of 2001, the result was that just two out of ten adults (22%) claimed to believe in the existence of absolute moral truth.[37] But, in contrast, the two categories "consider self to be a Christian" and "absolutely committed to Christianity" only changed by two percentage points. So, it appears that those who no longer believe in moral absolutes must still consider themselves to be committed Christians. When the survey respondents were further queried as to the source of the principles or standards on which they based their moral and ethical decisions, the survey revealed that only one out of eight adults (a dismal 13%) cited the Bible. The most common source of guidance for moral decisions cited by the respondents was "feelings" with 25%.[38] Is it any wonder that churches are selling out to compromise in record numbers.

---

[37] "*How America's Faith Has Changed Since 9-11*", November 26, 2001, The Barna Group, Ltd., https://www.barna.org/component/content/article/5-barna-update/45-barna-update-sp-657/63-how-americas-faith-has-changed-since-9-11#.V6SiKPnzUx4, (Accessed 08/05/2018).

[38] Ibid.

A staggering and alarming change is taking place within Christianity. John MacArthur, in his book, *The Truth War*, says,

> Lately many unbelieving intellectuals have admitted the chain is broken and have decided the culprit is the absurdity of any quest for truth. In effect, they have given up that pursuit as something wholly futile. The world of human ideas is therefore currently in a serious state of flux. On almost every level of society, we are witnessing a profoundly radical paradigm shift – a wholesale overhaul in the way people think about truth.[39]

The great paradigm shift Mr. MacArthur describes can be considered a war. Sadly, it is certainly nothing new. However, the intensity of that war has increased greatly. Mr. MacArthur writing of the increasing conflict over truth says, "It is a savage conflict that literally spans all of human history. But the ferocity and irrationality of this present onslaught seems quite unprecedented."[40] That increased onslaught has spawned a number of articulate, self-proclaimed atheists, such as Sam Harris and Richard Dawkins. Ravi Zacharias, in his book, *The End of Reason*, describes Harris's first two books as "absolutely and unabashedly hostile to all religions – but particularly to the Christian faith".[41] Mr. Zacharias further states that Harris says it is time for Americans to outgrow their religious beliefs. Harris's vociferous hatred for all things religious is embellished with strong language and illustrations designed to convince the world that Christians in particular are either stupid buffoons or imbeciles for believing in God.[42] His ferocious and unconcealed hatred of all things religious is proven in a quote from an interview between Mr. Harris and Bethany Saltman of *The Sun Magazine*, "If I could wave a magic wand and get rid of either rape or religion, I would not hesitate to

---

[39] John MacArthur, *The Truth War*, (Nashville, Tennessee: Thomas Nelson Publishers, 2007), 7.
[40] Ibid.
[41] Ravi Zacharias, *The End of Reason*. (Grand Rapids, Michigan: Zondervan, 2008), 14.
[42] Ibid.

get rid of religion."[43] So, in Mr. Harris's mind religion is more dangerous than rape. It would seem that Mr. Harris thinks his belief in atheism is worth any price but religion is too costly.

Mr. Harris and others who blindly cling to their atheistic beliefs are far more dangerous than "true" religion. Viktor Frankl, a man who experienced the most horrific evil imaginable as an inmate at Auschwitz did not blame God. Regarding the source of the evil Mr. Frankl experienced, he said, "I am absolutely convinced that the gas chambers of Auschwitz, Treblinka, and Maidanek were ultimately prepared not in some Ministry or other in Berlin, but rather at the desks and in the lecture halls of nihilistic scientists and philosophers."[44]

Where do Christian colleges and universities stand on moral absolutes and biblical principles? Ken Ham says the idea for his book, *Already Compromised*, began as a hunch from repeated observations over thirty years. *Already Compromised* is an assessment of the 2010 survey of two hundred Christian colleges and universities all across America conducted by Britt Beemer of America's Research Group. In the introduction to the book Mr. Ham wrote:

> Our research shows that an "uncertain sound" is emanating from many of our Christian colleges. The authority of Scripture is being undermined at many levels, and the voices of naturalism, agnosticism, and even atheism are permeating the eardrums of generations of young people who become the leaders of tomorrow. And as they step into those leadership roles, most do not have the certain sound of the trumpet of truth to advance the battle as it should be fought.[45]

Even though Mr. Ham did not say so, it is likely that many of the leadership roles he spoke of were in churches, as pastors,

---

[43] Bethany Saltman, "*The Temple Of Reason*", The Sun Magazine, Issue 369, September 2006, http://www.thesunmagazine.org/issues/369/the-temple-of-reason, (accessed 08/05/2018).

[44] Zacharias, *The End of Reason*, 63.

[45] Ham, *Already Compromised*.

Christian school administrators, or perhaps even Bible college professors. A common topic Mr. Ham encountered during his extensive travels was various students' experiences in Christian colleges and universities. A common complaint came from well-meaning parents who sent their children off to college with such high hopes, only to have them return skeptical, disillusioned, and uncertain about their faith.[46]

Mr. Ham related an experience at one Christian college where he was scheduled to speak at their chapel. Before speaking, he met with the college chaplain who said, "We aren't narrow-minded like you young earth creationists at this college – we allow *all views* [emphasis added] here."[47] Mr. Ham also related an incident at another college considered to be a *conservative* Christian college, "I was ushered into the president's office, where he began to 'dress me down' in regard to our [*Answers in Genesis*] stand on six literal days and a young earth. He wanted me to know he did not approve of what I believed and was upset with my being at the college."[48]

Just a few of the shocking and disheartening results revealed from the survey will illustrate the trend that is occurring in Christian colleges and universities. The following survey results will be more than ample to get a sense of the deteriorating condition of Christian colleges and universities. Those believing in the cardinal doctrines of the New Testament, such as, the virgin birth of Christ, His death on the Cross, a literal Heaven, a literal Hell, Christ's Second Coming, and His bodily resurrection all ran in the 96% or higher range.[49] No serious problems *yet*. The next set of questions:

- Do you believe in the Flood of Noah's day? – Yes = 91%.
- Do you believe the Flood was worldwide? – Yes = 57.7%.
- Do you believe God created the Earth in 6 literal 24-hour days? – Yes = 59.6%
- Do you believe God created the Earth in 6 literal days? – Yes = 47.1%

---

[46] Ibid., 17.
[47] Ibid.
[48] Ibid., 18.
[49] Ibid., 20.

- Do you consider yourself to be a young-Earth Christian –
  Yes = 49%[50]

The responses regarding God's Holy Word shown above are *extremely* alarming especially considering they come from what are supposed to be Christian colleges.

It takes a willful and blind naiveté to deny that there is an alarming and growing crisis within Christianity. Some surveys indicate that churches will lose seventy plus percent of graduating high school seniors within two years of graduation. One survey presents that percentage as high as ninety-three percent and only eighteen months past graduation from high school. Where is the concern? Where is the outrage? Where is the alarm? It is well past time to "ring the bell", "sound the alarm", "wave the flag", or whatever else it may take to awaken the sleeping church from its stupor.

Christians are losing their children at an alarming rate. The startling truth is that it is not just to atheists, humanists, and secularists. Unbelievably, the church is losing their children to post-modern philosophies from within Christian colleges and universities all across America. But before the children can be saved, the parents must be saved. Christian parents must cry out for a return to biblical preaching. Christians must return to an unwavering belief in God and in the moral absolutes that founded this nation.

The increasing drift toward modernism and the unquestioning belief in and acceptance of worldly science is consuming not only secular society but also Christianity in the twenty-first century.

Summing Up

The truth about America's discovery, founding, and its establishment based on Christian principles has been carefully detailed in the preceding pages of this book. The evidences quoted were from the mouths of the men that lived at those times, from

---

[50] Ibid., 21,22, 24.

their recorded speeches, or from their own writings. In all but a few instances, the quotes and writings cited were taken directly from primary sources and not from modern histories that have been altered to suit the anti-Christian biases of the authors and/or the publishers. Many of the modern histories can rightly be put into the category of "Revisionist History" in that they have *deliberately* minimized or left out those portions of the *Founders'* writings that demonstrate a Christian identity or influence. Those modern historians are thereby "revising" history based upon their own biases and not upon the true facts of history. Commenting on the subject of inaccurate history in the introduction to his book, *George Washington's Sacred Fire*, Peter Lillback says:

> The erosion of accurate history is disconcerting: One scholar casts Washington in a Deistic mold. The next goes further and states – *without citing evidence* [emphasis added] – that he didn't even go to church. What will the next generation of scholars claim? This ignorance of the facts is what requires us to pursue our question concerning Washington's religion by constant interaction with his own written words and the unquestionable records of his actions.[51]

Another equally frightening malady is plaguing twenty-first century America. That malady is the alarming lack of knowledge regarding American history among the nation's younger generations. Numerous surveys given to senior high and college students reveal a disturbingly poor knowledge of American history.

In December 2009, The American Revolution Center released the results of the first national survey to assess adult knowledge of the American Revolution. The results revealed that an alarming eighty-three percent of Americans failed a basic test on knowledge of the American Revolution and the principles that have united all Americans. Dr. Bruce Cole, president and CEO of The American Revolution Center, said, "The American Revolution defined what it means to be an American. It forged those principles that unite us

---

[51] Lillback, *George Washington's Sacred Fire*, 28.

as a nation. Unfortunately, those principles are fading from memory."[52] Commenting on the survey results Dr. Cole said, "The disappointing scores clearly indicate a need that ought to be addressed. This shouldn't be taken as an indictment of those who took the survey, but rather a wake-up call for all of us."[53] Some noteworthy results from the survey are:

- Many more Americans knew that Michael Jackson sang "Beat It" than knew the Bill of Rights is part of the Constitution.
- Sixty percent of Americans correctly identified the number of children in the Gosselin reality-TV show couple's household, but more than one-third did not know the century in which the American Revolution occurred.
- Half of those surveyed believed the Civil War occurred before the American Revolution.
- More than 50 percent of those surveyed wrongly attributed the quote, "From each according to his ability, to each according to his needs" to George Washington, Thomas Paine, or Barack Obama, when it is in fact a quote from Karl Marx, author of *The Communist Manifesto*.

Examples such as these seem truly hard to believe. However, are they really that hard to believe when you consider that students are being taught a 'revised', 'warped', and 'politically correct' viewpoint about American history? A revised history which omits everything Christian. They are learning next to nothing about the Christian faith of the *Founders*, or of the *Founders'* insistence that Christianity should govern public policy in America.

Many high schools now forego teaching the American Revolution or American History classes in favor of more global studies. As was stated earlier, other sources have reported that the nation's top universities and colleges no longer include American history as a required course of study.

---

[52] Dr. Bruce Cole, *83 Percent of U.S. Adults Fail Test on Nation's Founding*, The American Revolution Center, Washington, D.C. (Dec. 1, 2009).
[53] Ibid.

The real danger lies in the subtle ways in which American society is being manipulated. Karl Marx, considered to be the father of Communism, said, "Take away the heritage of a people, and they are easily persuaded."[54] As indicated in the footnote, the preceding quote cannot be found in any of Marx's writings. A similarly worded quote attributed to V. I. Lenin says, "People separated from their history are easily persuaded." Those two quotes certainly mean the same thing. If a nation's history is changed, eradicated, or vilified, its people can easily be persuaded to believe something other than the truth. How do you separate people from their history? The straightforward and easiest method is: simply do not teach it.

You might be tempted to say that is not happening, but you would be wrong. That is precisely what is happening. In Chapter Five (See page 103) it was stated that in 2002 California's state list of recommended books for students excludes American heroes and founders. Over time the situation has only gotten worse. On August 28, 2015, Tess Hedrick of ABC television station KSFY in Sioux Falls, South Dakota, reported, "On Monday [August 24, 2015], the South Dakota Board of Education approved new guidelines that do not require high schools to teach early U.S. history beginning next year [2016]."[55] It seems that in spite of public protests, the state Board of Education agreed to overhaul the history standards after an almost yearlong public hearing process. There is no longer any requirement for teaching the first one hundred years of the nation's history, including the Revolutionary War and the drafting of the U.S. Constitution. It is impossible to deny that failing to teach the first one hundred years of America's history to America's youth will rob them of their heritage.

The biggest threat to America is not from without; it is from within. For example, consider John Adams's statement to John Taylor on April 15th, 1814, "Remember, democracy never lasts long. It soon wastes, exhausts, and murders itself. There never was

---

[54] This quote is often attributed to Karl Marx. However, no verifiable source(s) can be found for this quote. It is simply offered as quoted.

[55] Tess Hedrick, *Early American History could be a thing of the past*, http://www.ksfy.com/home/headlines/Early-American-History-could-be-a-thing-of-the-past-323022481.html (accessed 5/23/2018).

a democracy yet that did not commit suicide."[56] Is America slowly but surely committing suicide?

In late twentieth century and early twenty-first century America, an escalating decline in the following areas can be seen:

- The departure from what the *Founders* intended.
- The destruction of a cooperative relationship between Church and State.
- The usurping of state powers.
- The restricting of public religious expression.
- The crumbling of America's morals and ideals.

One of the major factors contributing to the escalating decline of each of the above areas has been a lack of accurate and factual information. For example, had the American public been truly knowledgeable of the founding documents and actually understood the philosophy behind them, the Supreme Court could not have achieved the supremacy it has enjoyed in recent decades. In a similar vein, had Americans more fully understood history and the true meaning of the *Founders'* abundant writings, they would have never accepted the false assertion that the *Founders* were irreligious and disapproved of public religious expressions nor would they have believed the ridiculous falsehood regarding the wall of separation[57] that is frequently misrepresented to deliberately stifle religious expression.

Everyone knows, or should know, that *accurate* knowledge is absolutely essential for the creation of sound public policy. That being true, what then is the solution for overcoming the threats to America's Christian heritage that have been well documented in the preceding pages of this book? The answer to overcoming those threats requires the following three steps:

1. Identifying and eliminating wrong information.
2. Obtaining correct information.

---

[56] John Adams, *The Works of John Adams, Second President of the United States*, Charles Francis Adams editor, (Boston Massachusetts; Little Brown and Company, 1854), Vol. VI, 484.
[57] David Barton, *Original Intent*, 337.

3. Acting on the correct information.

Material from many original sources, written by the individuals who lived or were eye-witnesses to the events, has been cited to satisfy step one, at least in the area of confirming the *real* truth regarding America's Christian heritage. Many quotes from Christopher Columbus, various early settlers, *Founding Fathers*, writers of the Declaration of Independence, Supreme Court Justices, and various early court opinions have been offered as evidence that America was founded as a Christian nation with the *express* intent to propagate the Christian faith. In the course of satisfying step one, correct information (the truth from the mouths of the men that were there) was presented to refute the distortions, half-truths, and in some cases lies of the 'revisionist' historians. The information presented in this book is but a tiny fraction of the information that is readily available.

The information provided in this book and the numerous footnotes cited and the articles and books listed in the bibliography will provide ample reference material for further research to anyone that feels inclined to dig deeper into this critically important subject. You *must* learn the true history of America. True history is the enemy of the liberal-progressive. The objective of liberal-progressives and historical revisionists is to minimize, or better yet eliminate, America's early history. Once the Christian principles that compelled the early settlers and the founders to risk their lives is hidden, the revisionists can easily convince you that America is not a Christian nation because it does not have a Christian heritage.

That leaves only the final step of acting on the information that was presented. That final step by its very definition must be left to the individual readers of this book. No one can be forced to act upon the information that has been provided, no matter how accurate or profound it may be. Each individual must make up his or her own mind if they will continue to accept the skewed version of America's history as stated by the 'revisionists' or if they will *hear* the words of the men who created and lived that history.

Dr. Marshall Foster, in his book *Tipping The Scales: Restoring Righteousness to a Nation in the Balance*, offered a specific strategy for how Christians can win the battle for the twenty-first century. Sadly, it seems that his strategy was not well accepted. Dr. Foster said:

> I found that the Christian community was not ready for the message. For the most part, I found that as I went to them, I could scare them. I could always get the men motivated, because men are always guilty and you could always get them to do something – at least the first week, until they fall back into the same rut they were in before. After you've done that you find that a man convinced against his will is of the same opinion still.[58]

In America, Christianity has slipped backward and now functions as a subculture rather than as the counterculture it should be. Christianity should be counter to the behavior of the world. Its purpose should be higher. Its standards should be higher. True Christianity should be lived on a higher moral level than the immoral level upon which the world lives. When Christians relinquish that higher standard, they become no different than the world and they no longer have anything to offer the world. The church has eagerly abdicated its role as a moderating influence against evil and immorality. The church's voice has become but a tiny whisper of what it once was.

Many voices, this book included, can cry out to individuals but they will remain unconvinced and unmoved unless they are willing to actually *hear* the truth of God's Word and of *true* history and then *act* upon that truth. As evidence of the apathy so sadly prevalent among Christians Dr. Foster says, "…we could browbeat them to death and tell them that only 28 percent of Christians are registered to vote (which is true) and that 95 percent of bar owners are registered to vote (which is true), but that does not change their activity. Guilt only leads you, usually, into deeper despair."[59]

---

[58] Marshall Foster, "History From God's Perspective", *In Tipping The Scales: Restoring Righteousness to a Nation in the Balance*, D. James Kennedy, Compiler, (Fort Lauderdale, Florida: Coral Ridge Ministries, 2000), 188-189.
[59] Ibid., 189.

It is long past time to lay aside the guilt and climb up out of the despair Mr. Foster describes. It is long past time to throw off the apathy that paralyzes an entire generation of adults. The most insidious mistake America is making is to expend American lives on foreign soil defending freedom while at home American youth grow up believing things which turn out to be basic Communist precepts. Materialism does not lead to Americanism. It leads to Socialism, which *always* fails, and then it leads, ultimately, to Communism.

The underlying raw government data for the six trend charts in Chapter Three ends at various years, ranging from 1992 to 2013. Do not think the situation is getting any better for the years beyond those dates. Some deeply disturbing results were recently reported as part of a national survey conducted by the Annenberg Public Policy Center (APPC) of the University of Pennsylvania. The APPC national survey was conducted on August 9-13, 2017. It revealed that many Americans are poorly informed about the basic constitutional provisions of America's government.

The survey results affirmed that only 26 percent of respondents could correctly name the three branches of government (executive, judicial, and legislative), the same percentage as from the survey in 2016. However, the percentage was down significantly from APPC's first survey in 2011, when 38 percent could name all three branches of government. Even more astonishing, 33 percent of the respondents could not name a single one of the three branches of government.[60] Those results are quite disheartening and alarming.

---

[60] Michael Rozansky, *Americans are poorly informed about basic constitutional provisions,* The Annenberg Public Policy Center, September 12, 2017, https://www.annenbergpublicpolicycenter.org/americans-are-poorly-informed-about-basic-constitutional-provisions/ (Accessed 09/06/2018).

Keith Hoar

Conclusion

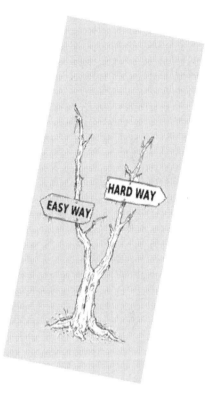

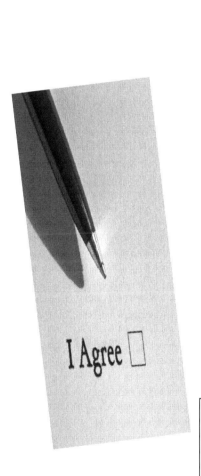

Liberty means responsibility.
That is why most men dread it.

George Bernard Shaw
Maxims for Revolutionists

Conclusion

You must realize, I suppose, 'I went on,' that there must be as many types of individual as of society? Societies aren't made of sticks and stones, but of men whose individual characters, by turning the scale one way or another, determine the direction of the whole.

Plato
'Republic'

Education Today

The public school system has become fully committed to the '*Theory of Evolution*' and its 'humanism' philosophy, which is just another form of atheism. The advocates of Humanism adhere to the belief that man is nothing more than a soulless animal; a product of billions and billions of years of undirected, random, accidental processes. Remember, this is the ideology that is the foundation for Socialism and Communism (Socialism is simply the road leading to Communism. At the end of the road, both are essentially the same). See the discussion regarding Communism's '*graduate beast*' discussed in Chapters Three and Four.

For decades the public education system has increasingly been taken over by left, and far-left, progressive-minded teachers and professors. This is strikingly true in higher education. An extensive survey published by Neil Gross of Harvard University and Solon Simmons of George Mason University reported that American professors in the Social Sciences, 93.4% were Democrat or Independent while only 6.6% were Republican; in the Humanities 89.3% were Democrat or Independent while only 10.7% were Republican; and in English an unbelievable 98.1% were Democrat or Independent while a miniscule 1.9% were Republican.[1]

The above survey was completed eleven years ago in 2007. The liberal bias on college campuses toward any form of conservative thought has certainly not improved. In fact, the liberal bias has only gotten worse. A 2016 article reported that a centrist, social psychologist at a major university cited data suggesting that the share of conservatives in academia has plunged.[2]

The attitude toward 'free speech' on college campuses has changed dramatically in the past decade and *not* for the better! In September 2017 John Villasenor of the Brookings Institute published the results of a national survey of 1,500 current undergraduate students at U.S. four-year colleges and universities.

---

[1] Neil Gross and Solon Simmons, *The Social and Political Views of American Professors*, Harvard University, 33-34.
[2] Nicholas Kristof, *On College Campuses: A Confession of Liberal Intolerance*, https://www.timesrecord.com/articles/opinion/on-college-campuses-a-confession-of-liberal-intolerance/ (Accessed 08/24/2018).

The survey underscored a growing and vocal intolerance to any speech the students considered offensive. A concern is that students now act as the only authority on what constitutes free expression on campus.

A majority of the students surveyed responded that it is acceptable to shout down a speaker they disagree with. As concerning as that fact is, the response to using violence to prevent a speaker from speaking is far more concerning. Nineteen (19) percent agreed that it would be acceptable! Mr. Villasenor said this regarding the survey results:

> These results are notable for several reasons. First, the fraction of students who view the use of violence as acceptable is extremely high. While percentages in the high teens and 20s are "low" relative to what they could be, it's important to remember that this question is asking about the acceptability of committing violence in order to silence speech. Any number significantly above zero is concerning.[3]

The survey results described above are not only concerning they are alarming to say the least. A fifth of college students now believe it is acceptable to use physical violence to silence a speaker with whom they disagree. Making the situation worse is that they, the students, make the judgment as to what is offensive or hurtful speech. That attitude creates an ever shrinking range of thought that is acceptable for discussion on campuses.

Another survey question that was asked was, *"If an on-campus organization hosts an event with a speaker whom you consider to be offensive, is the hosting organization **legally required** to ensure that the event also includes a speaker who presents an opposing view?"* The responses were shocking. Sixty-two (62) percent responded that the organization would be legally required to present an opposing viewpoint. This demonstrates an appalling

---

[3] John Villasenor, *Views among college students regarding the First Amendment: Results from a new survey*, https://www.brookings.edu/blog/fixgov/2017/09/18/views-among-college-students-regarding-the-first-amendment-results-from-a-new-survey/ (Accessed 08/24/2018).

misunderstanding of the Constitution. Nowhere does the First Amendment require the presentation of opposing viewpoints.

One final survey question. A question asked students to choose between two types of learning environments: Option 1. *A positive environment for all students by prohibiting certain speech or viewpoints*; or Option 2. *An open learning environment where students are exposed to all types of speech and viewpoints.* Sadly, but not surprisingly, the majority of students responded that they would prefer an environment in which their institution is *expected* to create an environment that shelters them from offensive views.[4]

As the acceptable subjects allowed for discussion become narrower and narrower, campuses become nothing more than echo chambers for the one dominant ideology, the ideology of those that are vocal and/or violent enough to control the platform. On college campuses there is a pronounced bias in hiring of professors who might have conservative viewpoints.

George Yancey, Professor of Sociology at the University of North Texas, conducted a survey in which up to thirty (30) percent of academics said that they would be less likely to support a job seeker if they knew that the person was a Republican. The bias becomes far worse if the applicant is an evangelical Christian. According to Yancey's study, 59 percent of anthropologists and 53 percent of English professors would be less likely to hire someone they found out was an evangelical.[5]

On college campuses, and elsewhere, those that chant and scream and demand tolerance actually turn out to be the most intolerant of all. What their actions say is, "You can *look* different than us, but you may not *think* differently than us."

Another serious obstacle affecting learning at colleges and universities is the remarkably rapid shift toward far-left, liberal ideologies among college professors. Christopher Ingraham, writing for the Washington Post, said the dramatic shift among college professors is hurting students' education. Citing survey data by the Higher Education Research Institute (HERI) at UCLA, Mr. Ingraham reported that in 1990 42 percent of professors

---

4 Ibid.
5 Nicholas Kristof, *On College Campuses: A Confession of Liberal Intolerance.*

identified as "liberal" or "far-left." But by 2014, the number identifying as "liberal" or "far-left" had jumped to 60 percent. Over the same time period, the number of professors identifying as "moderate" fell to 28 percent and "conservative" fell to 12 percent. On American college campuses in 2014, liberals outnumbered conservatives by 5 to 1.[6]

In the twenty-first century, the rampant, anti-conservative bias and elimination of *any* viewpoints that do not align with liberal, far-left ideology is causing public schools, especially colleges, in America to become little more than indoctrination centers. How can students possibly learn to research, evaluate, and form a conclusion based on the facts, *the right or wrong or the truth of any given matter*, when they are allowed to hear only one side of any issue? The simple answer is - they cannot!

Another alarming threat to the public school system is the increasing push by socialist organizations to encourage their members to become school teachers. The most disturbing issue is that they are not there to teach. They are there to foment 'class struggle'. In the introduction to a pamphlet titled '*Why Socialists Should Become Teachers'*, published by the Democratic Socialist Labor Commission and the Young Democratic Socialists of America (YDSA), they write, "This pamphlet argues that socialists should take jobs as teachers (and other school-based workers) for the political, economic, and social potential the industry holds."[7]

As the pamphlet continues presenting a basic roadmap for how to get a job in education, it says, "Rather, we as socialists need to build a "militant minority" of class-conscious teachers that can move our unions in a more militant and democratic direction."[8] On the next page the pamphlet says, "While teaching is neither easy nor especially well paid, it can be a personally fulfilling and

---

[6] Christopher Ingraham, *The dramatic shift among college professors that's hurting students' education*, January 2016, https://www.washingtonpost.com/news/wonk/wp/2016/01/11/the-dramatic-shift-among-college-professors-thats-hurting-students-education/?noredirect=on&utm_term=.837a11e47d59 (Accessed 09/01/2018)
[7] Democratic Socialist Labor Commission and Young Democratic Socialists of America, *Why Socialists Should Become Teachers*, July 2018, 4.
[8] Ibid., 10.

economically sustainable career for those *who seek to advance class struggle.* [emphasis added]"[9]

In their own words, they clearly state they are not there to teach, they are there to move teacher unions in a '*more militant*' direction and to '*advance class struggle*'. Making unions more militant and advancing class struggle does not equate to anything resembling a democratic direction. William Z. Foster, Chairman of the Communist Party USA from 1945-1957, in his book, *Towards Soviet America,* wrote that workers can only get what they have the *power to take.* Appropriated direct from the Communist playbook: militancy and class struggle is about '*power*'. It always has been and always will be about '*power*'.

By their own admission, 'Democratic Socialists' have targeted the teaching industry as a vehicle to advance their militancy and to spread class struggle. Just like the Communists they realize they cannot not win an outright, open battle. They have joined with the far-left to eliminate any dissenting freedom of thought in the public schools and replace it with socialist ideology. They have no choice because if they were to teach the '*true facts*' of history, they would lose. Properly *prepared* and *informed* children and adults are absolutely crucial if this battle is to be won. See the final section of the Conclusion, '*What Now*', for more on this issue.

This is a vital subject and it is extremely difficult to not get sidetracked by the massive number of articles available on the subject. Enough has been written here to adequately substantiate the catastrophe that is looming in public education. A quick search of the internet, the bibliography of this book, or better yet, your public library will yield more than ample sources for research on this distressing subject.

Who Defines Right and Wrong

As America approaches the end of the second decade of the twenty-first century, what is the current standard for what is right and moral? Sadly, as previously discussed, there is no distinct standard of morality. Rather, there are *countless* standards, driven

---

[9] Ibid., p 11.

only by what feels good to any particular individual at any point in time. Until the 1960s, America had a generally accepted moral code that served the country well. Beginning somewhere around the middle of that decade, a generation rose up that literally questioned everything. An aversion to enforce any standard of morality whatsoever only added fuel to the rapid decline of morality, thoroughly detailed in the trend charts of Chapter Three.

In the twenty-first century, people are searching for the meaning of life as much now as they ever did. However, that

meaning is extremely difficult to uncover today because there exists a callous skepticism regarding whether such a thing as *absolute truth* actually exists. The number one characteristic of America's present, postmodern culture is an open hostility to *truth* of any kind. Anything even remotely hinting at truth is not tolerated. The immense hypocrisy of the postmodern mind-set is that they make such an enormous uproar about tolerance, yet they are violently intolerant of anyone who *might* claim to speak a truth that may contradict what they wish to believe.

In America, technology has exploded while theology has collapsed. Scientists are learning more and more about less and less while philosophers comprehend less and less about more and more. In spite of the alleged knowledge of both these groups, they both have put on blinders to exclude any moral judgment. In America the most quoted verse from the Bible is no longer John 3:16, but rather Matthew 7:1, *"Judge not, that ye be not judged."* Nobody is willing to judge anything or anyone no matter how obviously wrong the *'thing'* may be. The *"if it feels good, do it"* mantra from the 1960s would seem to also sum up the mind-set of the twenty-first century.

What has happened to the understanding of basic right and wrong? Has it been dropped into the *'memory hole'* Orwell so succinctly described in his novel *1984?* Has the distinction between right and wrong been erased in the modern world?

Social media as it flows instantaneously across the world-wide web, can produce a widespread flood of half-truths or lies in just a few seconds. Several generations ago, news was typically obtained from books and newspapers. The newspaper and print industry has seen a massive decline in readership caused mainly by a huge shift in the way people get their news. In the case of millennials, social media is the news feed of choice. A few keystrokes entered into a web browser can return page after page of '*results*'. For example, a Google search for the phrase '*alternate facts*' produced 91,400 results in just 0.52 seconds. What percentage of those results contain unconfirmed information, inaccurate information, half-truths, or worse, outright lies? How many of those results cite a primary source or any source whatsoever? Does anybody check? Does anybody care?

So how did we reach this point? Journalists and authors used to be the caretakers of the truth in the sense that they assumed the responsibility of authenticating information by fact checking, verifying sources, and citing all sources used. Social media, along with other changes, has created a situation where the individual consumer of information is now responsible for authenticating the information they receive.

The question that is then raised is, "*How many individuals really do verify the information they consume?*" That is an extremely critical question considering such a high percentage of the younger generation get nearly all their news (information) from the Internet.

It was stated earlier that many books and articles contained not one citation identifying material they 'claimed' to reference; not even for text contained within double quotes. In addition, a surprising number of quotes were not faithful to the original source (see page 13). Validating sources and authenticating what is and is not true is absolutely crucial, especially for information related to the history of America's discovery and founding.

It has become distressingly clear that many individuals are simply unwilling to expend the time or effort required to determine if what they read is true according to the facts. Complicating matters is the natural human tendency to ignore the truth. They dismiss any facts or statements that disagree with their chosen opinion (remember the earlier discussion of '*Information Avoidance*' related to cherished beliefs or biases, see page 6).

Another noteworthy concern is how individuals define truth. A common, exasperated reply heard during a discussion where contradictory beliefs are being debated is: "*I have my truth and you have your truth.*" Suzanne Kane, Los Angeles-based writer, author, and editor, wrote an article titled *Finding Your Own Truth* for the website Addiction.com. Commenting on her and many others' philosophy that the '*truth*' is almost never simple, Ms. Kane wrote:

> That's because what is true for you may not be true for me, depending on circumstance, timing, mental mindset, age, physical well-being (or not), and a host of other conditions. I may have grown up with a different set of beliefs that inherently colors what I consider the truth, something far different from your long-held constructs about truth.[10]

The entire quote above is preposterous and unsound. The '*real, or absolute, truth*' and '*your truth*' are not the same thing. In fact, they are likely as opposite as night and day. Not only is using the term '*your truth*' wrong; it is inherently dangerous! America currently has a culture that is deeply divided ideologically. Individuals now form their own perceptions which they choose to call '*reality*' or '*truth*'. In actuality, what they form may not be reality at all, but, rather, it may merely be a set of '*beliefs*' they *choose* to label as fact. When an individual chooses to assess information using the mindset of '*your truths*', they get to choose what to believe based on their circumstances, their current mental outlook, their cultural biases, or a host of other considerations.

A thing is either true or it is not true! It simply cannot be both depending on which side of the issue you are standing. This is distinctly true concerning the topic of morality. In two national surveys, one among adults and one among teenagers, conducted by Barna Research more than fifteen years ago, the results as they related to moral absolutes was shocking. The survey results revealed nearly two-thirds of adults (64% vs. 22%) said moral

---

[10] Suzanne Kane, *Finding Your Own Truth*, Addiction.com, April 13, 2015, https://www.addiction.com/8710/finding-your-own-truth/ (Accessed 08/15/2018).

truth is always relative to the person and their situation. The responses were far more lopsided among teenagers. An astounding 83% of teens said moral truth depends on the circumstances. A dismal 6% of the respondents said moral truth is absolute.[11]

The only conclusion that can be reached is that America's youth has been conditioned to believe that '*something*' is only true for them if they *choose* to believe it to be true. The disturbing result of that thinking is a worldview that approves of pluralism, relativism, and tolerance (except for differing beliefs) without consideration of the repercussions of their opinions and actions.

The paragraph above explains exactly how America reached the point at which it now finds itself. Multiple generations have grown to adulthood believing they can define their own truth **and** without researching the underlying information that *supposedly* supports their version of truth.

What Now?

So, how does America approach this challenging issue and '*right the ship*' before it is too late? How does America return to the path set out by the Founders, a path that made the United States the greatest nation in human history? It cannot be accomplished in the public school system and it cannot be legislated by the Government. Any intended '*fix*' **MUST** begin in the home, specifically with the parents.

An individual who escaped from despair and brutality and suffered greatly under Stalin's rule understood that quite well.

Libor Brom, associate professor at the University of Denver, emigrated to the United States in 1958. Dr. Brom, a native of Czechoslovakia, and his family experienced the hideous sufferings that accompanied Communism. Their property was confiscated, their human and civil rights were abolished, and they all were jailed at one time or another. In response to people who had lost their moral perspective, Dr. Brom said this regarding the schools where he received his education:

---

[11] Barna Research, *Americans Are Most Likely to Base Truth on Feelings*, February 2002, https://www.barna.com/research/americans-are-most-likely-to-base-truth-on-feelings/ (Accessed 08/16/2018).

Introductions that enumerate the institutions of learning where I have earned my degrees amuse me. They miss the most important school and the most influential teachers I have ever had—my home and my parents. They were simple, hardworking people who had little time and very few luxuries to give. They did give me, however, their personal example and a firm springboard from which to jump into the world of confusion, terror, and war which followed. They professed one simple basic belief: Something is either good or bad, it is either decent or indecent, it serves either God or the devil, and most important, they believed that it was my duty to find out what is right and what is wrong.[12]

As the discussion shifts to focus on what must be done to correct, and avoid, if possible, the crisis that is looming for America, a quote displayed earlier, on the opening page of Chapter One, comes to mind. That quote by George Orwell says, "If liberty means anything at all, it means the right to tell people what they do not want to hear." This book, a description of and an emphatic warning regarding the results and dangers of 'revisionist history', has the liberty to make clear what must be done to '*fix*' what has happened. The 'required fix' will undoubtedly be what many '*do not want to hear*'.

Thinking about those individuals that '*will hear*' the warning, another quote referencing liberty, from the opening page of this conclusion, comes to mind. That quote by George Bernard Shaw says, "Liberty means responsibility. That is why most men dread it."

For those that '*will listen*', there comes a great responsibility. That responsibility lies directly at their feet. It can be accepted or rejected, but it cannot be passed off to someone else. Those that hear will be required to either reject their responsibility and suffer guilt for their inaction or they will be required to stand up against

---

[12] Libor Brom, *Where is Your America*, Imprimis, Hillsdale College, (Hillsdale Michigan: Vol. 11, No. 8, August 1982), 5.

the '*untruths*'. They will be required to do some research, get informed, and then actually do something!

Mr. Brom unquestionably understood the evils of Socialism and Communism. Why is it America's younger generations spout the slogans and propaganda of Socialism and Communism and yet seemingly have no knowledge of the misery, brutality, and evil meted out by socialist and communist dictators, both past and present? Reread the above quote by Mr. Brom. Remember, he was an individual that suffered much at the hands of the Socialists and Communists. In his quote, he clearly called attention to the critical importance of home and parents and their role in teaching him that something was either good or bad. Even more important, they taught him it was *his* duty to find out which. Once again, a responsibility that can be accepted or rejected, but cannot be passed off to someone else.

The one absolute, most crucial responsibility entrusted to parents is to teach their children the difference between right and wrong. But sadly, far too many parents are abdicating their moral responsibility, being too busy with the pressures of work, social life, sports, the demands of keeping up with the 'Joneses', or a hundred other things. An alarming number of parents have relinquished their role and have allowed the public school system to teach their children the difference between right and wrong, what is acceptable behavior, and what is moral and what is not.

As Mr. Brom said, the most effective, and lasting, way to teach children right from wrong is by personal example. So then, the obvious questions become:

- *Mr. and Mrs. Parent do you teach your children right from wrong by the <u>personal example</u> of your life?*
- *Do you expect your children to spontaneously develop a moral compass?*
- *Do you really want your children to develop their moral compass from school or their peers?*

Uh-oh; meddling alert! Many parents will not be willing to answer those uncomfortable questions. Without a doubt, **ALL** schools, public or private, should support and enforce the morals that parents teach at home. But many parents would complain, *"That is not **our** right and wrong, or those are not **our** morals, or that is not **our** truth."*

Some parents may have attempted to take an amoral position and, thereby, assume a middle-of-the-road approach toward morality and right and wrong. Some may hold the opinion that amorality is a razor-thin delineation between morality and immorality. However, as Mr. Brom stated a *thing* is either good or it is bad, it is either decent or it is indecent. Therefore, it is either moral or immoral. There is no amoral middle ground. So then, maintaining an amoral viewpoint would be impossible because it does not exist.

A majority of Americans are living in total ignorance and deception – unaware of the dangers facing their children who will be called upon to lead this nation in a few short years. The American people have become victims of their own educational system, as well as their own apathy.

Well then, what is the solution?

It would be wonderful if America's public schools would turn off the flood of politically correct garbage and far-left ideology and would return to focusing on reading, writing, and math again. But, sadly, everyone knows that is not going to happen.

As Mr. Brom said, responsibility rests upon individual parents. It is their responsibility to instill in their children the ability and desire to determine what is right and wrong. America's children are not going to receive a high quality education in the public schools, but they are not going to be successful in life without one.

The public school's objective is rapidly shifting away from education to one of political indoctrination. Rather than focusing on the curriculum necessary to produce valuable and productive members of society, their desire is to *'shape young minds'* to accept the far-left agenda of the Democratic Socialists and the progressives. If necessary, reread the first section of this Conclusion regarding the YDSA using the teaching industry as a vehicle to advance their militancy and spread class struggle.

If parents knew what was going on in the classrooms they would be absolutely shocked and horrified. Wait, you mean parents do not know what is going on? Yes, in far too many homes that is absolutely true. Parents need to become informed, not just regarding what is occurring in the school system but also regarding their duty as parents to teach their children what is right and what is wrong. As stated earlier, with that knowledge comes great responsibility.

Exercising that responsibility is especially difficult when confronted by educators and administrators with numerous degrees in their title. They are highly-educated. They know far more than you do. You should just be quiet and let them tell you what is right. How many parents can or will debate them or stand up to them? Far too few. Too many will acquiesce and tell themselves they cannot 'fight' with the school.

The situation is many, many times worse when young people graduate high school and head off to college. Remember the discussion earlier regarding the absurd college courses that are now being offered at colleges and universities, even at those that are called 'ivy league' schools. You can view a long list of the ridiculous college courses in the Appendix.

Trying to undo the damage done *after* a student has spent sixteen years or more in the public school system being molded by well-trained socialists using their ideology of militancy and class struggle will likely be a hopeless task. The best alternative would be for parents to educate their children outside the public system. For those parents who cannot or will not consider a private, or home school, the only remaining choice is to adequately prepare their children to know right from wrong and to resist error with truth. Parents, it will be a tremendously difficult battle. You will be in the minority. You will need to be constantly vigilant for the anti-American rants that so often accompany the far-left and socialist ideologies.

It is paramount that children be taught civics, 'true' history, philosophy (the correct kind), an old-fashioned sense of right and wrong, and the ideas and principles of the Founders. Failing that, true Americanism will fade away and die out. If that happens, the grand experiment the Founders called the United States of America will be lost. The 'grand' experiment will have failed.

It seems America has nearly lost the knowledge and understanding of its Christian discovery and founding. Children are being taught history and government from textbooks that have been written to satisfy the biases of *revisionist historians* who depict a history as they *'wish it were'* or a history *'they can live with'*. Historians who openly admit they dismiss the meditation of those they write about as irrelevant. Historians who express *'opinions'* as fact and provide no citation for their source(s). Worst of all, historians who misquote the original works they cite.

Understanding of and belief in America's Christian heritage has slipped to such a low point that the Governor of one of the most populous states in the Union, talking about America, made the unbelievable statement, "It was never that great."[13] Equally troubling is the fact that so many in the younger generations seem to readily agree with that statement.

If those that wish to destroy America's Christian heritage are allowed to succeed, the far-left radicals and Democratic Socialists will succeed in implementing the preposterous agenda they believe will usher in their vision of a Socialist Utopia. If they do succeed, their platform of *'free stuff for everyone; paid for by someone else'* will turn the American Dream into a nightmare!

It is appropriate that the closing words of Chapter Three be 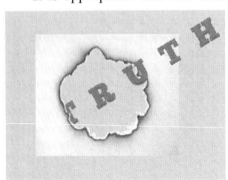 repeated here. Now that you have been confronted with clear, irrefutable evidence of how *'historical revisionists'* are rewriting history and now that you know what the *actual* history says in regard to America's Christian discovery and founding, can you remain unconvinced and

[13] Joseph Spector, *New York Gov. Andrew Cuomo: America 'was never that great'*, https://www.usatoday.com/story/news/politics/2018/08/15/andrew-cuomo-new-york-governor-trump-america-never-great/1004708002/ (Accessed 08/27/2018).

unmoved? Will you continue to allow the '*historical revisionists*' to toss the truth regarding America's precious Christian heritage into the *memory hole*? Will you remain silent? Will you say and do nothing? Will you fall back into the same old rut, paralyzed by apathy? America's future hangs in the balance. Will you not join the battle and sound the alarm?

Unless Americans wake up and get involved and take back their responsibility, the grand experiment the Founders created called the United States of America will most assuredly be over. It will have failed!

Appendices

Communism's Stated Goals

The forty-five goals of the Communist Party listed below were derived from W. Cleon Skousen's book *The Naked Communist*.[1] These goals were read into the Congressional Record on Thursday, January 10, 1963, by Congressman Albert S. Herlong Jr. of Florida. The list of the then "Current Communist Goals" is contained in the appendix to the official Congressional Record for 1963 at pages 34-35.[2]

1. U.S. acceptance of coexistence as the only alternative to atomic war.
2. U.S. acceptance to capitulate in preference to engaging in atomic war.
3. Develop the illusion that total disarmament by the U.S. would be a demonstration of moral strength.
4. Permit free trade between all nations regardless of Communist affiliation and regardless of whether or not items could be used for war.
5. Extension of long-term loans to Russia and Soviet satellites.
6. Provide American aid to all nations regardless of Communist domination.
7. Grant recognition of Red China. Admission of Red China to the U.N.
8. Set up East and West Germany as separate states in spite of Khrushchev's promise in 1955 to settle the Germany question by free elections under supervision of the U.N.

---

[1] Skousen, The Naked Communist, 259-262.
[2] U. S. Congress, Congressional Record 1963, Appendix, A34-35.

9. Prolong the conferences to ban atomic tests because the U.S. has agreed to suspend tests as long as negotiations are in progress.
10. Allow all Soviet satellites individual representation in the U.N.
11. Promote the U.N. as the only hope for mankind. If its charter is rewritten, demand that it be set up as a one-world government with its own independent armed forces. (Some communist leaders believe the world can be taken over as easily by the UN as by Moscow. Sometimes these two centers compete with each other as they are now doing in the Congo.)
12. Resist any attempt to outlaw the Communist Party.
13. Do away with loyalty oaths.
14. Continue giving Russia access to the U.S. Patent Office.
15. Capture one or both of the political parties in the United States.
16. Use technical decisions of the courts to weaken basic American institutions, by claiming their activities violate civil rights.
17. Get control of the schools. Use them as transmission belts for Socialism and current Communist propaganda. Soften the curriculum. Get control of teachers associations. Put the party line in textbooks.
18. Gain control of all student newspapers.
19. Use student riots to foment public protests against programs or organizations which are under Communist attack.
20. Infiltrate the press. Get control of book review assignments, editorial writing, policy-making positions.
21. Gain control of key positions in radio, TV & motion pictures.
22. Continue discrediting American culture by degrading all form of artistic expression. An American Communist cell was told to "eliminate all good sculpture from parks and buildings," substituting shapeless, awkward and meaningless forms.
23. Control art critics and directors of art museums. " Our plan is to promote ugliness, repulsive, meaningless art."

24. Eliminate all laws governing obscenity by calling them "censorship" and a violation of free speech and free press.

25. Break down cultural standards of morality by promoting pornography and obscenity in books, magazines, motion pictures, radio and TV.

26. Present homosexuality, degeneracy and promiscuity as "normal, natural and healthy."

27. Infiltrate the churches and replace revealed religion with "social" religion. Discredit the Bible and emphasize the need for intellectual maturity, which does not need a "religious crutch."

28. Eliminate prayer or any phase of religious expression in the schools on the grounds that it violates the principle of "separation of church and state."

29. Discredit the American Constitution by calling it inadequate, old fashioned, out of step with modern needs, a hindrance to cooperation between nations on a world-wide basis.

30. Discredit the American founding fathers. Present them as selfish aristocrats who had no concern for the "common man."

31. Belittle all forms of American culture and discourage the teaching of American history on the ground that it was only a minor part of "the big picture." Give more emphasis to Russian history since the Communists took over.

32. Support any socialist movement to give centralized control over any part of the culture - education, social agencies, welfare programs, mental health clinics, etc.

33. Eliminate all laws or procedures which interfere with the operation of the Communist apparatus.

34. Eliminate the House Committee on Un-American Activities.

35. Discredit and eventually dismantle the FBI.

36. Infiltrate and gain control of more unions.

37. Infiltrate and gain control of big business.

38. Transfer some of the powers of arrest from the police to social agencies. Treat all behavioral problems as

psychiatric disorders which no one but psychiatrists can understand or treat.

39. Dominate the psychiatric profession and use mental health laws as a means of gaining coercive control over those who oppose communist goals.
40. Discredit the family as an institution. Encourage promiscuity and easy divorce.
41. Emphasize the need to raise children away from the negative influence of parents. Attribute prejudices, mental blocks and retarding of children to suppressive influence of parents.
42. Create the impression that violence and insurrection are legitimate aspects of the American tradition; that students and special interest groups should rise up and make a "united force" to solve economic, political or social problems.
43. Overthrow all colonial governments before native populations are ready for self-government.
44. Internationalize the Panama Canal.
45. Repeal the Connally Reservation so the U.S. cannot prevent the World Court from seizing jurisdiction over domestic problems. Give the World Court jurisdiction over domestic problems. Give the World Court jurisdiction over nations and individuals alike.

Raw Data Tables for Chapter Four Trend Charts

Table 4.1 Family Stability

Year	Total Population	Pop. Growth	Unmarried Households	Pop. Growth in MM	Unmarried Hshlds in MM
1947	144,126,071	2,737,505	4,352,000	2.74	4.35
1948	146,631,302	2,505,231	4,729,000	2.51	4.73
1949	149,188,130	2,556,828	4,823,000	2.56	4.82
1950	152,271,417	3,083,287	4,763,000	3.08	4.76
1951	154,877,889	2,606,472	5,111,000	2.61	5.11
1952	157,552,740	2,674,851	5,071,000	2.67	5.07
1953	160,184,192	2,631,452	4,963,000	2.63	4.96
1954	163,025,854	2,841,662	5,072,000	2.84	5.07
1955	165,931,202	2,905,348	5,481,000	2.91	5.48
1956	168,903,031	2,971,829	5,546,000	2.97	5.55
1957	171,984,130	3,081,099	5,545,000	3.08	5.55
1958	174,881,904	2,897,774	5,515,000	2.90	5.52
1959	177,829,628	2,947,724	5,561,000	2.95	5.56
1960	180,671,158	2,841,530	5,650,000	2.84	5.65
1961	183,691,481	3,020,323	5,763,000	3.02	5.76
1962	186,537,737	2,846,256	5,858,000	2.85	5.86
1963	189,241,798	2,704,061	5,984,000	2.70	5.98
1964	191,888,791	2,646,993	6,040,000	2.65	6.04
1965	194,302,963	2,414,172	6,149,000	2.41	6.15
1966	196,560,338	2,257,375	6,136,000	2.26	6.14
1967	198,712,056	2,151,718	6,343,000	2.15	6.34
1968	200,706,052	1,993,996	6,505,000	1.99	6.51
1969	202,676,946	1,970,894	6,643,000	1.97	6.64
1970	205,052,174	2,375,228	6,728,000	2.38	6.73
1971	207,660,677	2,608,503	7,174,000	2.61	7.17
1972	209,896,021	2,235,344	7,439,000	2.24	7.44
1973	211,908,788	2,012,767	7,967,000	2.01	7.97
1974	213,853,928	1,945,140	8,130,000	1.95	8.13
1975	215,973,199	2,119,271	8,612,000	2.12	8.61
1976	218,035,164	2,061,965	8,759,000	2.06	8.76
1977	220,239,425	2,204,261	9,001,000	2.20	9.00
1978	222,584,545	2,345,120	9,601,000	2.35	9.60
1979	225,055,487	2,470,942	9,836,000	2.47	9.84
1980	227,224,681	2,169,194	10,438,000	2.17	10.44
1981	229,465,714	2,241,033	11,015,000	2.24	11.02
1982	231,664,458	2,198,744	11,389,000	2.20	11.39
1983	233,791,994	2,127,536	11,485,000	2.13	11.49
1984	235,824,902	2,032,908	11,934,000	2.03	11.93
1985	237,923,795	2,098,893	12,357,000	2.10	12.36
1986	240,132,887	2,209,092	12,625,000	2.21	12.63
1987	242,288,918	2,156,031	12,955,000	2.16	12.96
1988	244,498,982	2,210,064	13,530,000	2.21	13.53
1989	246,819,230	2,320,248	13,737,000	2.32	13.74
1990	249,464,396	2,645,166	13,774,000	2.65	13.77

Year	Total Population	Pop. Growth	Unmarried Households	Pop. Growth in MM	Unmarried Hshlds in MM
1991	252,153,092	2,688,696	14,175,000	2.69	14.18
1992	255,029,699	2,876,607	14,717,000	2.88	14.72
1993	257,782,608	2,752,909	15,126,000	2.75	15.13
1994	260,327,021	2,544,413	15,319,000	2.54	15.32
1995	262,803,276	2,476,255	15,446,000	2.48	15.45
1996	265,228,572	2,425,296	16,027,000	2.43	16.03
1997	267,783,607	2,555,035	16,637,000	2.56	16.64
1998	270,248,003	2,464,396	16,563,000	2.46	16.56
1999	272,690,813	2,442,810	16,765,000	2.44	16.77

Source: a U.S. Census Bureau, Population Division, "Historical National Population Estimates: 1900-1999", Released June 2000. b U.S. Census Bureau, "Table HH-1. Households, by Type: 1940 to Present", Released Nov. 2013.

Table 4.2 Married vs. Unmarried Households

Year	Total Population	Population Growth	Married % of Total Hshlds	Unmarried % of Total Hshlds
1947	144,126,071	2,737,505	78.3	21.7
1948	146,631,302	2,505,231	78.7	21.3
1949	149,188,130	2,556,828	78.8	21.2
1950	152,271,417	3,083,287	78.2	21.8
1951	154,877,889	2,606,472	77.0	23.0
1952	157,552,740	2,674,851	77.2	22.8
1953	160,184,192	2,631,452	76.7	23.3
1954	163,025,854	2,841,662	76.5	23.5
1955	165,931,202	2,905,348	75.7	24.3
1956	168,903,031	2,971,829	75.8	24.2
1957	171,984,130	3,081,099	75.9	24.1
1958	174,881,904	2,897,774	75.1	24.9
1959	177,829,628	2,947,724	74.7	25.3
1960	180,671,158	2,841,530	74.3	25.7
1961	183,691,481	3,020,323	74.0	26.0
1962	186,537,737	2,846,256	73.8	26.2
1963	189,241,798	2,704,061	74.0	26.0
1964	191,888,791	2,646,993	73.6	26.4
1965	194,302,963	2,414,172	72.6	27.4
1966	196,560,338	2,257,375	72.4	27.6
1967	198,712,056	2,151,718	72.2	27.8
1968	200,706,052	1,993,996	71.5	28.5
1969	202,676,946	1,970,894	70.9	29.1
1970	205,052,174	2,375,228	70.5	29.5
1971	207,660,677	2,608,503	69.4	30.6
1972	209,896,021	2,235,344	68.6	31.4
1973	211,908,788	2,012,767	67.8	32.2
1974	213,853,928	1,945,140	67.0	33.0
1975	215,973,199	2,119,271	66.0	34.0

Table A2 Continued

Year	Total Population	Population Growth	Married % of Total Hshlds	Unmarried % of Total Hshlds
1976	218,035,164	2,061,965	64.9	35.1
1977	220,239,425	2,204,261	64.0	36.0
1978	222,584,545	2,345,120	62.3	37.7
1979	225,055,487	2,470,942	61.6	38.4
1980	227,224,681	2,169,194	60.8	39.2
1981	229,465,714	2,241,033	59.8	40.2
1982	231,664,458	2,198,744	59.4	40.6
1983	233,791,994	2,127,536	59.5	40.5
1984	235,824,902	2,032,908	58.7	41.3
1985	237,923,795	2,098,893	58.0	42.0
1986	240,132,887	2,209,092	57.6	42.4
1987	242,288,918	2,156,031	57.6	42.4
1988	244,498,982	2,210,064	56.7	43.3
1989	246,819,230	2,320,248	56.1	43.9
1990	249,464,396	2,645,166	56.0	44.0
1991	252,153,092	2,688,696	55.3	44.7
1992	255,029,699	2,876,607	54.8	45.2
1993	257,782,608	2,752,909	55.1	44.9
1994	260,327,021	2,544,413	54.8	45.2
1995	262,803,276	2,476,255	54.4	45.6
1996	265,228,572	2,425,296	53.8	46.2
1997	267,783,607	2,555,035	53.1	46.9
1998	270,248,003	2,464,396	53.0	47.0
1999	272,690,813	2,442,810	52.7	47.3
2000	282,160,000	9,469,187	52.8	47.2
2001	284,970,000	2,810,000	52.3	47.7
2002	287,630,000	2,660,000	51.9	48.1
2003	290,110,000	2,480,000	51.5	48.5
2004	292,810,000	2,700,000	51.5	48.5
2005	295,520,000	2,710,000	51.2	48.8
2006	298,380,000	2,860,000	50.9	49.1
2007	301,230,000	2,850,000	50.8	49.2
2008	304,090,000	2,860,000	50.0	50.0
2009	306,770,000	2,680,000	50.5	49.5
2010			49.7	50.3
2011			48.9	51.1
2012			48.7	51.3
2013			48.3	51.7

Source: a U.S. Census Bureau, Population Division, "Historical National Population Estimates: 1900-1999", Released June 2000. b U.S. Census Bureau, "Table HH-1. Households, by Type: 1940 to Present", Released Nov. 2013.

Table 4.3 Percentage of Births to UnWed Girls

Year	< 15	Age 15	Age 16	Age 17	Age 18	Age 19	Age 15-19
1955	0.66	0.43	0.27	0.18	0.12	0.09	0.14
1956	0.66	0.42	0.27	0.17	0.12	0.08	0.14
1957	0.66	0.43	0.27	0.17	0.12	0.08	0.14
1958	0.66	0.43	0.27	0.18	0.12	0.09	0.14
1959	0.68	0.44	0.28	0.19	0.13	0.09	0.15
1960	0.68	0.44	0.28	0.18	0.13	0.09	0.15
1961	0.70	0.47	0.29	0.19	0.14	0.10	0.16
1962	0.70	0.47	0.31	0.21	0.14	0.10	0.16
1963	0.71	0.50	0.32	0.22	0.15	0.11	0.17
1964	0.74	0.53	0.35	0.23	0.16	0.12	0.19
1965	0.79	0.56	0.37	0.26	0.18	0.13	0.21
1966	0.76	0.58	0.41	0.28	0.19	0.14	0.22
1967	0.80	0.60	0.43	0.30	0.21	0.16	0.24
1968	0.81	0.63	0.45	0.33	0.24	0.18	0.27
1969	0.79	0.63	0.46	0.34	0.25	0.19	0.28
1970	0.81	0.65	0.48	0.35	0.26	0.20	0.30
1971	0.82	0.66	0.49	0.37	0.27	0.20	0.31
1972	0.82	0.67	0.50	0.38	0.29	0.22	0.33
1973	0.85	0.66	0.51	0.39	0.29	0.22	0.34
1974	0.85	0.69	0.53	0.40	0.31	0.24	0.35
1975	0.87	0.71	0.56	0.43	0.34	0.26	0.38
1976	0.86	0.72	0.59	0.46	0.36	0.28	0.40
1977	0.88	0.74	0.61	0.49	0.40	0.30	0.43
1978	0.87	0.74	0.62	0.50	0.41	0.32	0.44
1979	0.89	0.77	0.65	0.53	0.43	0.34	0.46
1980	0.89	0.78	0.66	0.55	0.45	0.36	0.48
1981	0.89	0.79	0.67	0.57	0.47	0.37	0.49
1982	0.89	0.80	0.69	0.59	0.49	0.39	0.51
1983	0.90	0.81	0.72	0.62	0.52	0.41	0.53
1984	0.91	0.83	0.73	0.63	0.54	0.44	0.56
1985	0.92	0.84	0.74	0.65	0.56	0.47	0.58
1986	0.93	0.86	0.77	0.67	0.59	0.49	0.61
1987	0.93	0.87	0.79	0.71	0.62	0.52	0.63
1988	0.94	0.88	0.80	0.73	0.64	0.54	0.65
1989	0.92	0.87	0.81	0.73	0.66	0.56	0.67
1990	0.92	0.87	0.80	0.74	0.66	0.58	0.67
1991	0.91	0.87	0.81	0.75	0.68	0.59	0.69
1992	0.91	0.87	0.82	0.76	0.69	0.61	0.70
1993	0.91	0.87	0.82	0.77	0.71	0.63	0.71
1994	0.95	0.91	0.86	0.81	0.75	0.66	0.76
1995	0.94	0.90	0.86	0.81	0.75	0.66	0.75
1996	0.94	0.90	0.86	0.82	0.75	0.67	0.76
1997	0.96	0.93	0.89	0.84	0.78	0.69	0.78
1998	0.97	0.94	0.89	0.85	0.78	0.70	0.79
1999	0.97	0.94	0.89	0.85	0.79	0.71	0.79
2000	0.97	0.94	0.90	0.85	0.79	0.71	0.79
2001	0.96	0.94	0.90	0.85	0.79	0.71	0.79
2002	0.97	0.94	0.90	0.86	0.80	0.73	0.80
2003	0.97	0.95	0.91	0.88	0.82	0.74	0.81
2004	0.97	0.95	0.92	0.88	0.83	0.76	0.82
2005	0.98	0.96	0.92	0.89	0.84	0.77	0.83
2006	0.98	0.97	0.93	0.90	0.84	0.78	0.84
2007	0.99	0.98	0.94	0.91	0.86	0.80	0.86

Table A3 Continued

Year	< 15	Age 15	Age 16	Age 17	Age 18	Age 19	Age 15-19
2008	0.99	0.98	0.95	0.92	0.87	0.81	0.87
2009	0.99	0.98	0.96	0.93	0.88	0.82	0.87
2010	0.99	0.99	0.96	0.94	0.89	0.83	0.88

Rate per 1,000 females

Source: U.S. Department of Justice, OJJDP Statistical Briefing Book, Released Dec. 2012 National Center for Health Statistics, Annual, "Births: Final Data", years 1999-2010 National Center for Health Statistics, "Non-marital childbearing in the United States, 1940-1999"

Table 4.4 Morality – Sexually Transmitted Disease Cases of Gonorrhea

Year	Total Population	Pop. in 10MM	Pop. Growth	Total Cases	Yearly Growth	Cases Per 10K
1952	157,552,740	15.76	2,674,851	244,957	-9,513	15.548
1953	160,184,192	16.02	2,631,452	238,340	-6,617	14.879
1954	163,025,854	16.30	2,841,662	242,050	3,710	14.847
1955	165,931,202	16.59	2,905,348	236,197	-5,853	14.235
1956	168,903,031	16.89	2,971,829	224,346	-11,851	13.283
1957	171,984,130	17.20	3,081,099	214,496	-9,850	12.472
1958	174,881,904	17.49	2,897,774	232,386	17,890	13.288
1959	177,829,628	17.78	2,947,724	240,254	7,868	13.510
1960	180,671,158	18.07	2,841,530	258,933	18,679	14.332
1961	183,691,481	18.37	3,020,323	264,158	5,225	14.381
1962	186,537,737	18.65	2,846,256	263,714	-444	14.137
1963	189,241,798	18.92	2,704,061	278,289	14,575	14.705
1964	191,888,791	19.19	2,646,993	300,666	22,377	15.669
1965	194,302,963	19.43	2,414,172	324,925	24,259	16.723
1966	196,560,338	19.66	2,257,375	351,738	26,813	17.895
1967	198,712,056	19.87	2,151,718	404,836	53,098	20.373
1968	200,706,052	20.07	1,993,996	464,543	59,707	23.145
1969	202,676,946	20.27	1,970,894	534,872	70,329	26.390
1970	205,052,174	20.51	2,375,228	600,072	65,200	29.264
1971	207,660,677	20.77	2,608,503	670,268	70,196	32.277
1972	209,896,021	20.99	2,235,344	767,215	96,947	36.552
1973	211,908,788	21.19	2,012,767	842,621	75,406	39.763
1974	213,853,928	21.39	1,945,140	906,121	63,500	42.371
1975	215,973,199	21.60	2,119,271	999,937	93,816	46.299
1976	218,035,164	21.80	2,061,965	1,001,994	2,057	45.956
1977	220,239,425	22.02	2,204,261	1,002,219	225	45.506
1978	222,584,545	22.26	2,345,120	1,013,436	11,217	45.530
1979	225,055,487	22.51	2,470,942	1,004,058	-9,378	44.614
1980	227,224,681	22.72	2,169,194	1,004,029	-29	44.187
1981	229,465,714	22.95	2,241,033	990,864	-13,165	43.181
1982	231,664,458	23.17	2,198,744	960,633	-30,231	41.467
1983	233,791,994	23.38	2,127,536	900,435	-60,198	38.514
1984	235,824,902	23.58	2,032,908	878,556	-21,879	37.255
1985	237,923,795	23.79	2,098,893	911,419	32,863	38.307

217

Table A4 Continued

Year	Total Population	Pop. in 10MM	Pop. Growth	Total Cases	Yearly Growth	Cases Per 10K
1988	244,498,982	24.45	2,210,064	738,160	-49,372	30.191
1989	246,819,230	24.68	2,320,248	733,294	-4,866	29.710
1990	249,464,396	24.95	2,645,166	690,042	-43,252	27.661
1991	252,153,092	25.22	2,688,696	621,918	-68,124	24.664
1992	255,029,699	25.50	2,876,607	502,858	-119,060	19.718
1993	257,782,608	25.78	2,752,909	444,649	-58,209	17.249
1994	260,327,021	26.03	2,544,413	419,602	-25,047	16.118
1995	262,803,276	26.28	2,476,255	392,651	-26,951	14.941
1996	265,228,572	26.52	2,425,296	328,169	-64,482	12.373
1997	267,783,607	26.78	2,555,035	327,665	-504	12.236
1998	270,248,003	27.02	2,464,396	356,492	28,827	13.191
1999	272,690,813	27.27	2,442,810	360,813	4,321	13.232
2000	282,160,000	28.22	9,469,187	363,136	2,323	12.870

Source: U.S. Dept. of Health and Human Services, Centers for Disease Control and Prevention, Sexually Transmitted Disease Surveillance 2012, Table 1, pgs. 79,80.

Table 4.5 Educational Achievement

Year	Total Population	Population Growth	SAT Scores
1952	157,552,740	2,674,851	970
1953	160,184,192	2,631,452	971
1954	163,025,854	2,841,662	962
1955	165,931,202	2,905,348	971
1956	168,903,031	2,971,829	980
1957	171,984,130	3,081,099	969
1958	174,881,904	2,897,774	968
1959	177,829,628	2,947,724	973
1960	180,671,158	2,841,530	975
1961	183,691,481	3,020,323	969
1962	186,537,737	2,846,256	971
1963	189,241,798	2,704,061	980
1964	191,888,791	2,646,993	973
1965	194,302,963	2,414,172	969
1966	196,560,338	2,257,375	967
1967	198,712,056	2,151,718	958
1968	200,706,052	1,993,996	958
1969	202,676,946	1,970,894	956
1970	205,052,174	2,375,228	948
1971	207,660,677	2,608,503	943
1972	209,896,021	2,235,344	937
1973	211,908,788	2,012,767	926
1974	213,853,928	1,945,140	924
1975	215,973,199	2,119,271	906
1976	218,035,164	2,061,965	903
1977	220,239,425	2,204,261	899
1978	222,584,545	2,345,120	897

Table A5 Continued

Total Year	Population Population	SAT Growth	Scores
1979	225,055,487	2,470,942	894
1980	227,224,681	2,169,194	890
1981	229,465,714	2,241,033	890
1982	231,664,458	2,198,744	893
1983	233,791,994	2,127,536	893
1984	235,824,902	2,032,908	897
1985	237,923,795	2,098,893	906
1986	240,132,887	2,209,092	906
1987	242,288,918	2,156,031	906
1988	244,498,982	2,210,064	904
1989	246,819,230	2,320,248	903
1990	249,464,396	2,645,166	900
1991	252,153,092	2,688,696	896
1992	255,029,699	2,876,607	899
1993	257,782,608	2,752,909	902
1994	260,327,021	2,544,413	902
1995	262,803,276	2,476,255	910
1996	265,228,572	2,425,296	911
1997	267,783,607	2,555,035	914
1998	270,248,003	2,464,396	915
1999	272,690,813	2,442,810	914
2000	282,160,000	9,469,187	917
2001	284,970,000	2,810,000	918
2002	287,630,000	2,660,000	918
2003	290,110,000	2,480,000	923
2004	292,810,000	2,700,000	923
2005	295,520,000	2,710,000	925
2006	298,380,000	2,860,000	919
2007	301,230,000	2,850,000	913
2008	304,090,000	2,860,000	913
2009	306,770,000	2,680,000	912

Source: College Entrance Examination Board, College-Bound Seniors: Total Group Profile [National] Report; College Board, Report on Declining SAT Scores; National Center for Education Statistics (www.nces.ed.gov)

Table 4.6 Violent Behavior

Year	Total Population	Population Growth	Total Violent Crime	Population Growth Per MM	Violent Crime Per MM
1957	171,984,130	3,081,099	198,760	0.31	0.2
1958	174,881,904	2,897,774	211,970	0.29	0.2
1959	177,829,628	2,947,724	214,560	0.29	0.2
1960	180,671,158	2,841,530	288,460	0.28	0.3
1961	183,691,481	3,020,323	289,390	0.30	0.3
1962	186,537,737	2,846,256	301,510	0.28	0.3
1963	189,241,798	2,704,061	316,970	0.27	0.3
1964	191,888,791	2,646,993	364,220	0.26	0.4

Table A6 Continued

Year	Total Population	Population Growth	Total Violent Crime	Population Growth Per MM	Violent Crime Per MM
1965	194,302,963	2,414,172	387,390	0.24	0.4
1966	196,560,338	2,257,375	430,180	0.23	0.4
1967	198,712,056	2,151,718	499,930	0.22	0.5
1968	200,706,052	1,993,996	595,010	0.20	0.6
1969	202,676,946	1,970,894	661,870	0.20	0.7
1970	205,052,174	2,375,228	738,820	0.24	0.7
1971	207,660,677	2,608,503	816,500	0.26	0.8
1972	209,896,021	2,235,344	834,900	0.22	0.8
1973	211,908,788	2,012,767	875,910	0.20	0.9
1974	213,853,928	1,945,140	974,720	0.19	1.0
1975	215,973,199	2,119,271	1,039,710	0.21	1.0
1976	218,035,164	2,061,965	1,004,210	0.21	1.0
1977	220,239,425	2,204,261	1,029,580	0.22	1.0
1978	222,584,545	2,345,120	1,085,550	0.23	1.1
1979	225,055,487	2,470,942	1,208,030	0.25	1.2
1980	227,224,681	2,169,194	1,344,520	0.22	1.3
1981	229,465,714	2,241,033	1,361,820	0.22	1.4
1982	231,664,458	2,198,744	1,322,390	0.22	1.3
1983	233,791,994	2,127,536	1,258,090	0.21	1.3
1984	235,824,902	2,032,908	1,273,280	0.20	1.3
1985	237,923,795	2,098,893	1,329,000	0.21	1.3
1986	240,132,887	2,209,092	1,489,170	0.22	1.5
1987	242,288,918	2,156,031	1,484,000	0.22	1.5
1988	244,498,982	2,210,064	1,566,220	0.22	1.6
1989	246,819,230	2,320,248	1,646,040	0.23	1.6
1990	249,464,396	2,645,166	1,820,130	0.26	1.8
1991	252,153,092	2,688,696	1,911,770	0.27	1.9
1992	255,029,699	2,876,607	1,932,270	0.29	1.9

Source: U.S. Federal Bureau of Investigation, Crime in the United States 1960-2002, as of 8/26/2017 access to the Uniform Crime Reporting Statistics for years earlier that 1990 has changed. Crime in the United States 1990-2009, http://www2.fbi.gov/ucr/cius2009/data/table_01.html (Accessed 8/26/2017)

Progressive Agenda vs. SPUSA and CPUSA

Progressive Agenda: "Raise the federal minimum wage, so that it reaches $15/hour, while indexing it to inflation."

> SPUSA: "We call for a minimum wage of $15 per hour, indexed to the cost of living."
>
> CPUSA: Calls for "struggles for peace, equality for the racially and nationally oppressed, equality for women job creation programs, increased minimum wage. ... Even with ultra-right control of the Federal government, peoples legislative victories, such as increasing the minimum wage, can be won on an issue-by-issue basis locally, statewide, and even nationally."

Progressive Agenda: "Reform the National Labor Relations Act, to enhance workers' right to organize and rebuild the middle class."

> SPUSA: "The Socialist Party stands for the right of all workers to organize, for worker control of industry through the democratic organization of the workplace."
>
> CPUSA: "One of the most crucial ways of increasing the strength and unity of the working class as a whole is organizing the unorganized. Working-class unity depends on uniting all the diverse sectors of the multiracial, multinational working class in the U.S. ... Speeding up the organization of unorganized workers is one of the most important challenges to labor and all progressive forces."

Progressive Agenda: "Pass comprehensive immigration reform to grow the economy and protect against exploitation of low-wage workers."

> SPUSA: "We defend the rights of all immigrants to education, health care, and full civil and legal rights and call for an unconditional amnesty program for all undocumented people. We oppose the imposition of any fees on those receiving

amnesty. We call for full citizenship rights upon demonstrating residency for six months."
CPUSA: Declares the "struggle for immigrant rights is a key component of the struggle for working class unity in our country today."

Progressive Agenda: Pass national paid sick leave. Pass national paid family leave.

CPUSA: In October 2014, hails that "women are fighting back to defend their jobs and their families against candidates who want to destroy women's reproductive rights, health care, family leave and paid sick days. Women's voices and votes can make the difference in this election in the U.S. Senate and House, for Governors and State Legislatures, and in the movement going forward for full equality."

Progressive Agenda: "Make Pre-K, after-school programs and childcare universal."

SPUSA: "We support public child care starting from infancy, and public education starting at age three, with caregivers and teachers of young children receiving training, wages, and benefits comparable to that of teachers at every other level of the educational system."

Progressive Agenda: "Earned Income Tax Credit." "Implement the 'Buffett Rule' so millionaires pay their fair share."

SPUSA: "We call for a steeply graduated income tax and a steeply graduated estate tax. ..."
CPUSA: "No taxes for workers and low and middle income people; progressive taxation of the wealthy and private corporations. ..."

Ridiculous College Course - Majoring in Stupid

The table below contains a compilation of just a few of the more unbelievable college courses offered by universities and colleges. The list of courses below does not come from just schools that would be considered far-out or left-wing. No, these courses are offered at major, and highly respected colleges and universities, at least in some eyes. Some of the courses are even from what would be considered premier, top-tier schools.

1	What If Harry Potter Is Real	Appalachian State University
2	God, Sex, Chocolate: Desire and the Spiritual Path	UC, San Diego
3	GaGa for Gaga: Sex, Gender, and Identity	University of Virginia
4	Lady Gaga and the Sociology of Fame	University of South Carolina
5	Philosophy And Star Trek	Georgetown
6	Invented Languages: Klingon and Beyond	University of Texas
7	The Science Of Superheroes	UC, Irvine
8	Learning From YouTube	Pitzer College
9	Arguing with Judge Judy	UC, Berkeley
10	Elvis As Anthology	University of Iowa
11	The Feminist Critique Of Christianity	Univ of Pennsylvania
12	Zombies In Popular Media	Columbia College
13	Far Side Entomology	Oregon State
14	Interrogating Gender: Centuries of Dramatic Cross-Dressing	Swarthmore College
15	Oh, Look, a Chicken!	Belmont University
16	The Textual Appeal of Tupac Shakur	Univ. of Washington
17	Cyberporn And Society	State Univ. of New York
18	Sport For The Spectator	Ohio State Univ.
19	Getting Dressed	Princeton
20	How To Watch Television	Montclair
21	On Being Bored	Brown University
22	Wasting Time On The Internet	Univ of Pennsylvania
23	How to Win a Beauty Pageant: Race, Gender, Culture	Oberlin College
24	Tree Climbing	Cornell University
25	Stupidity	Occidental College
26	Tattoos, Piercing, and Body Adornment	Pitzer College
27	Kanye Versus Everybody!	Georgia State Univ.
28	The American Vacation	University of Iowa
29	The Sociology of Miley Cyrus	Skidmore College
30	Demystifying the Hipster	Tufts University
31	Breaking Down 'Breaking Bad'	State Univ. of New York
32	Politicizing Beyonce	Rutgers University

33	Game of Thrones	Univ. of Virginia
34	Surviving the Coming Zombie Apocalypse	Michigan State Univ.
35	The Art of Walking	Centre College
36	Queer Musicology	UC, Los Angeles
37	The Unbearable Whiteness of Barbie	Occidental College
38	Nip, Tuck, Perm, Pierce, and Tattoo: Adventures with Embodied Culture	Alfred University
39	Geology and Cinema	Univ. of Minnesota
40	UFOs in American Society	Temple University
41	Theatrical Fencing	Univ. of Wisconsin
42	Disc Jockey: History, Culture, and Technique	New York University
43	Queer Theory	Univ. of Florida
44	Queering the Bible	Swarthmore College
45	Rednecks, Queers, and Country Music:	Univ. of Michigan
46	Saints and Sexuality	Univ. of Mississippi
47	The Power of Whiteness	Providence College
48	Transgender Latina Immigration:	Bowdoin College
49	Hand to Mouth: Writing, Eating, and the Construction of Gender	Dartmouth College
50	Rainbow Republic: American Queer Culture from Walt Whitman to Lady Gaga	Wellesley College

The list of college courses above was compiled from the following sources:

1 thru 20 - http://theeconomiccollapseblog.com/archives/20-completely-ridiculous-college-courses-being-offered-at-u-s-universities (Accessed 07/27/2018)
21 thru 30 - http://dailycaller.com/2015/08/21/the-daily-caller-proudly-presents-the-dumbest-college-courses-for-2015/ (Accessed 07/27/2018)
31 thru 35 - http://www.seethruedu.com/updates13-most-ridiculous-college-courses/ (Accessed 07/27/2018)
36 thru 42 - http://jimfishertruecrime.blogspot.com/2012/03/majoring-in-stupid-ridiculous-college.html (Accessed 07/27/2018)
43 thru 50 - https://www.academia.org/far-left-courses-at-american-colleges/ (Accessed 08/09/2018)

BIBLIOGRAPHY

Adams, John. *The Works of John Adams, Second President of the United States*, Charles Francis Adams editor, Boston Massachusetts; Little Brown and Company, 1854, Vol. VI.

Adams, Samuel. Old South Leaflets, No. 173. *The Rights of the Colonists. Report Of The Committee Of Correspondence To The Boston Town Meeting*, Directors Of The Old South Work, Old South Meeting-house, Boston, Mass. Nov. 20, 1772.

Alinsky, Saul. *Rules for Radicals* A Pragmatic Primer for Realistic Radicals, New York, New York: Vintage Books, 1971.

"America's Christian Identity Myth", Lloyd Thomas Web Pages, http://www.lloydthomas.org/5 SpecialStudies/USA.html (Accessed 07/22/2016).

Ames, Fisher. *The Works of Fisher Ames*, Boston, Massachusetts: T. B. Wait & Co., 1809.

Ariarajah, S. Wesley, *"A Turning Point in Interfaith Relations"*, Global Ministries The United Methodist Church, http://www.umcmission.org/Find-Resources/New- World-Outlook-Magazine/New-World-Outlook-Archives/2013/November- December-2013/1106-A-Turning-Point-in-Interfaith-Relations (Accessed 09/06/2018).

Arum, Richard and Roksa, Josipa. *Academically Adrift: Limited Learning on College Campuses,* Chicago and London: University of Chicago Press, 2011.

Bachtell, John. *A radical third party? I agree!,* http://www. peoplesworld.org/article/a-radical-third-party-i-agree/ (Accessed 06/25/2018).

Barham, Francis, Esq. *The Political Works of Marcus Tullius Cicero* Vol. I, London: Edmund Spettigue, 1841.

Barna, George, "*Six Megathemes Emerge from Barna Group Research in 2010*", The Barna Group Ltd., December 13, 2010, pgs. 1-2; http://www.barna.org/culture-articles/462-six-megathemes-emerge-from-2010 (Accessed July 20, 2016).

_____, *Americans Are Most Likely to Base Truth on Feelings*, February 2002, https://www.barna.com/research/americans-are-most-likely-to-base-truth-on-feelings/ (Accessed 08/16/2018).

_____, "*How America's Faith Has Changed Since 9/11*", https://www.barna.org/component/content/article/5-barna-update/45-barna-update-sp-657/63-how-americas-faith-has-changed-since-9-11#.V446m_nzUx4 (accessed 09/02/2017).

_____, "*Marketing the Church*", Colorado Springs, Colorado, Navpress, 1988.

_____, *State of the Church Series, 2011*, The Barna Group (July 26, 2011) as found at https://www.barna.com/research/barna-examines-trends-in-14-religious-factors-over-20-years-1991-to-2011/, (Accessed 09/06/2018)..

_____, *The End of Absolutes: America's New Moral Code*, May 25, 2016, https://www.barna.com/research/the-end-of-absolutes-americas-new-moral-code/ (accessed 12/9/2017).

_____, *Year in Review: Barna's 10 Most-Read Articles of 2016*, December 22, 2016, https://www.barna.com/research/year-review-barnas-10-read-articles-2016/ (accessed 12/9/2017).

Barton, David , *Original Intent: The Courts, the Constitution, & Religion*, Aledo, Texas: Wallbuilder Press, 1996.

_____, *The Myth of Separation*, Aledo, Texas: Wallbuilder Press, 1992.

_____, *"Treaty of Tripoli"*, Wallbuilders.com, http://www.wallbuilders.com/LIBissuesArticles.asp?id=125 (accessed 07/22/2016).

Begg, Alistair. *Pathway To Freedom*, Chicago, Illinois: Moody Publishers, 2003.

Bowers, Curtis. *AGENDA: Grinding America Down*, DVD, Black Hat Films in association with Copybook Heading Productions LLC, 2010.

Bradford, William, *Of Plymouth Plantation*, Harvey Wish, ed., New York, New York: Capricorn Books, 1952.

_____, *Bradford's History of the Plymouth Settlement 1608-1650*, Rendered into Modern English by Harold Paget, New York, New York, E. P. Dutton & Company, 1920).

Brom, Libor. *Where is Your America*, Imprimis, Hillsdale College, Hillsdale Michigan: Vol. 11, No. 8, August 1982.

Buber, Martin. *Eclipse Of God*, Westport CT: Greenwood Press Publishers, 1977.

Buzzard, Lynn R., Ericsson, Samuel, *The Battle For Religious Liberty*, Elgin, Illinois: David C. Cook Publishing Company, 1982.

Caffery, Kate, *The Mayflower*, New York, New York: Stein and Day Publishers, 1974.

Carlyle, Thomas. *The Works of Thomas Carlyle And Miscellaneous Essays,* Vol. XXVIII, London: Chapman And Hal, 1899.

Carr, William Guy. *Pawns in the Game*, Ontario, Canada: Gadsby-Leek Company, 1956.

Cicero, Marcus Tullius. *Orations of Marcus Tullius Cicero*, Charles Duke Yonge A.B. Translator, New York: Colonial Press, Revised Edition, 1900.

Cloud, David. *A SURVEY OF "YOUNG FUNDAMENTALISTS"*, Port Huron, Michigan: Fundamental Baptist Information Service, September 26, 2006.

Cole, Dr. Bruce. *83 Percent of U.S. Adults Fail Test on Nation's Founding*, The American Revolution Center, Washington, D.C. (Dec. 1, 2009).

Cole, Edwin Louis. *Absolute Answers To Prodigal Questions*, Nashville, Tennessee: Thomas Nelson Publishers, 1998.

Colson, Charles. *Can We Be Good Without God?*, Imprimis, Vol. 22, No.4, Hillsdale College, April 1993, p 2.

Columbus, Christopher, *Book of Prophesies*, Edited by Roberto Rusconi, Translated by Blair Sullivan, Berkeley, California: University of California Press, 1997.

De Blasio, Bill. City of New York, Transcript: *Mayor de Blasio and National Progressive Leaders Unveil the Progressive Agenda*, https://www1.nyc.gov/ office-of-the-mayor/news/ 307-15/transcript-mayor-de-blasio-national-progressive-leaders-the-progressive-agenda-to#/0 (Accessed 07/06/2018).

"Declaration of Independence", http://www.archives.gov/exhibits/charters/declaration_transcript.html (accessed 07/22/2016).

Democratic Socialist Labor Commission and Young Democratic
Socialists of America, *Why Socialists Should Become
Teachers*, July 25, 2018.

DeRose, Laurie, Lyons-Amos, Mark, et. al., *THE
COHABITATION-GO-ROUND: COHABITATION AND
FAMILY INSTABILITY ACROSS THE GLOBE*, New York,
New York, Social Trends Institute, 2017.

Devlin, Sir Patrick. *The Enforcement of Morals*, London ; New
York, New York: Oxford University Press, 1965.

Dollar, George W. *The Fight For Fundamentalism*, Orlando,
Florida: Daniels Publishing 1983.

D'ooge, Benjamin L., Ph.D. *Cicero Select Orations*, Chicago &
New York: Benjamin H. Sanborn & Co., 1922

Dorsey, David. *A Crisis in Student Achievement*, Topeka Capital-
Journal, Jan. 19, 2017.

Dunphy, John J. *The Book that Started It All*, Council for Secular
Humanism, Secular Humanist Bulletin, vol 21 issue 4,
https://www. secularhumanism.org/index.php/articles/3452
(accessed 12/11/217).

Education Reporter, *"Education Briefs"*, Washington, D.C.: Eagle
Forum, November 2002, http://www.eagleforum.org/educate/
2002/nov02/er_nov02.sh ml (accessed 07/21/2016).

Farand, Max. *The records of the Federal Convention of 1787* Vol.
III, New Haven: Yale University Press, 1911.

Federer, William J., *America's God and Country, Encyclopedia of
Quotations*, Coppell, Texas: FAME Publishing Inc., 1996.

Fink, Roger and Stark, Roger, *The Churching of America: Winners and Losers in Our Religious Economy*, New Brunswick, New Jersey: Rutgers University Press, 1992.

Folger, Janet L., *The Criminalization Of Christianity*, Sisters, Oregon: Multnomah Publishers, Inc., 2005.

Foster, Marshall. *"History From God's Perspective"*, In *Tipping The Scales: Restoring Righteousness to a Nation in the Balance*, Complied by D. James Kennedy, 188-189. Fort Lauderdale, Florida: Coral Ridge Ministries, 2000.

Foster, Stephen. *Their Solitary Way, the Puritan social ethic in the first century of settlement in New England*, New Haven, Connecticut: Yale University Press, 1971.

Foster, William Z. *Toward Soviet America*, New York, New York: International Publishers by Coward – McCann, Inc., 1932.

Fox, Maggie. *CDC Sees 'Alarming' Increase in Sexually Transmitted Diseases*, https://www.nbcnews.com/health/sexual-health/cdc-sees-alarming-increase-sexually-transmitted-diseases-n465071 (Accessed 08/08/2018).

Gales, Joseph, *The Debates and Proceedings in the Congress of the United States, First Congress, First Session, Volume 1*. Washington, D.C.: Gales & Seaton, 1843, Washington D.C. UNT Digital Library, http://digital.library.unt.edu/ark:/67531/metadc29465/. (accessed July 26, 2016).

Geller, J. D., ed., *They Knew They Were Pilgrims: Essays in Plymouth History*, New York: Poseidon Books, Inc., 1971.

Gingrich, Newt. *Rediscovering God in America*, Nashville, Tennessee: Integrity Publishers, 2006.

Golman, Russell, Hagmann, David and Loewenstein, George. *Information Avoidance*, Journal of Economic Literature, Vol. 55, No., 2017.

Gross, Neil and Simmons, Solon. *The Social and Political Views of American Professors,* Harvard University, 33-34.

Hagmen, David and Golman, Russel. Carnegie Mellon University, *Information Avoidance: How People Select Their Own Reality*, https://www.cmu.edu/news/stories/archives/2017/march/information-avoidance.html (Accessed 6/12/2018)

Hall, Timothy L. *Religion in America*, New York, New York: Infobase Publishing, 2007.

Ham, Ken *Already Compromised*, Green Forest, Arkansas: Master Books, Division of New Leaf Publishing, 2011.

Hazard, Ebenezer, Editor. *Historical Collections: Consisting of State Papers and other Authentic Documents: Intended as Material for an History of the United States of America*, Ebenezer Hazard, editor Philadelphia, Pennsylvania: T. Dobson, 1792, Vol. I.

Heck, Peter *Revisionism about Columbus misleads students*, http://www.indystar.com/story/opinion/2015/09/24/heck-revisionism-columbus-misleads-students/72735766/ (accessed July 20, 2016).

Heckscher August ed., *The Politics of Woodrow Wilson*, New York, New York: Harper & Brothers, 1956.

Hedrick, Tess. Early *American History could be a thing of the past*, http://www.ksfy.com/home/headlines/Early-American-History-could-be-a-thing-of-the-past-323022481.html (accessed 9/23/2017).

Heffron, Paul, *"The Religious Right's Revision of American History"*, American Humanist Association, http://www.americanhumanist.org/HNN/details/2011-06-the-religious-rights-revision-of-american-history (accessed 07/22/2016).

Henderson, John, M.A. *Second Oration of Cicero Against Catiline*, Toronto: The Copp, Clark Company, 1889.

Hordern, William, *A Layman's Guide to Protestant Theology*, New York, New York: Macmillan, 1955.

Hume, Britt, "*The Political Grapevine*", February 22, 2005, Fox News, Quoted in Peter Lillback, *George Washington's Sacred Fire*, (Bryn Mawr, PA, 2006).

Huxley, Aldous. *Proper Studies*, (London, Chatto and Windus, 1927), p 195.

Idaho, State of, Executive Proclamation, signed by Governor C. L. "Butch" Otter and Secretary of State Ben Ysura, October 16, 2011, https://gov.idaho.gov/mediacenter/ proc/2011/procOct11/10-16-2011 %20Christian%20 Heritage%20Week.html (accessed 07/27/2016).

Ingraham, Christopher. *The dramatic shift among college professors that's hurting students' education*, January 2016, https://www.washingtonpost. com/news/wonk/wp/2016/ 01/11/the-dramatic-shift-among-college-professors-thats-hurting-students-education/?noredirect=on&utm_term =.837a11e47d59 (Accessed 09/01/2018)

Jay, John. Letter to John Murray dated October 12, 1816 in *The correspondence and Public Papers of John Jay*, Henry P. Johnston, editor, (New York, New York: Burt Franklin, 1970), Vol. IV, 393.

Johnson, Philip. *Darwin On Trial*, Downers Grove, Illinois: Intervarsity Press: 1993.

Jones, Jeffery. *On Social Ideology, the Left Catches Up to the Right*, Gallup: 2015, http://www.gallup.com/poll/183386/ social-ideology-left-catches-right.aspx?utm_source=Politics& utm_medium =newsfeed&utm_campaign=tiles, (accessed 8/24/2017).

Kane, Suzanne. *Finding Your Own Truth*, Addiction.com, April 2015, https://www.addiction.com/8710/finding-your-own-truth/ (Accessed 08/15/2018).

Kass, John. *Eating the zoo creatures in Venezuela*, Chicago Tribune, http://www.chicagotribune.com/news/columnists/kass/ct-venezuela-zoo-animals-kass-0818-20170817-column.html (Accessed 08/23/2018).

Kelsey, Francis W. *Select Orations and Letters of Cicero*, Sixth Edition, Boston: University of Michigan, 1898

Kennedy, D. James. *What If America Were A Christian Nation Again?*, Nashville, Tennessee: Thomas Nelson, Inc., 2003.

King, Rev. John Richard, M.A. *The Philippci Orations of M. Tullius Cicero*, Oxford: Clarendon Press, 1868.

Kirk, Russell. *The Roots of American Order*, First Edition, La Salle, Illinois: Pepperdine University, 1974.

Kling, August J. *"Columbus – A Layman 'Christ-Bearer' to Uncharted Isles"*, The Presbyterian Layman, October 1971.

Kristof, Nicholas. *On College Campuses: A Confession of Liberal Intolerance,* https://www.timesrecord.com/articles/opinion/on-college-campuses -a-confession-of-liberal-intolerance/ (Accessed 08/24/2018).

Langbert, Mitchell. *Homogeneous: The Political Affiliations of Elite Liberal Arts College Faculty*, National Association of Scholars, https://www.nas.org/articles/homogenous_political_affiliations_of_elite_liberal (Accessed 09/04/2018)

Lasswell, Harold D. and Dorothy Blumenstock. *World Revolutionary Propaganda: Chicago Study*. New York, New York: Alfred A. Knopf, 1939.

Lenin, V. I. *Religion*, New York, New York: International
 Publishers, 1933.

_____, *"Left-Wing" Communism: an Infantile Disorder*, Detroit,
 Michigan: The Marxian Education Society, 1921.

Library of Congress, *"1492: An Ongoing Voyage"*,
 http://www.loc.gov/exhibits/1492/columbus.html (accessed
 07/20/2016).

_____, *Jefferson's Letter to the Danbury Baptist*, The Final Letter
 as Sent, http://www.loc.gov/loc/lcib/9806/ danpre.html,
 (accessed 07/27/2016).

Lillback, Peter A. *George Washington's Sacred Fire*, Bryn Mawr,
 Pennsylvania: Providence Forum Press, 2006.

Long, George. *The Decline of The Roman Republic,* Vol. III,
 Cambridge: Bell & Daldy, 1869.

MacArthur, John. *The Truth War: Fighting for Certainty in an Age
 of Deception*, Nashville, Tennessee: Thomas Nelson
 Publishers, 2007.

Marsden, George M. *Fundamentalism and American Culture,* New
 York, New York: Oxford University Press, Inc., 2006.

Marshall, Peter J. and Manuel, David B. *The Light And The Glory*,
 Grand Rapids, Michigan: Baker Book House, 1977.

Marx, Karl. *Das Kapital*, http://www.petermarshallministries.com/
 about/heritage.cfm (Accessed 12/26/2011).

Marx, Karl, and Engels, Friedrich, Samuel Moore translator,
 Manifesto of the Communist Party, Moscow, USSR: Progress
 Publishers, 1971.

Metaxas, Eric. *BONHOEFFER: Pastor, Martyr, Prophet, Spy*, Nashville: Thomas Nelson Inc., 2010.

Middleton, Conyers D.D. *The Life of Marcus Tullius Cicero*, London: W. Green, 1816.

Morris, Benjamin Franklin. *The Life of Gouverner Morris, with Selections from His Correspondence and Miscellaneous Papers*, "Notes on the Form for the King of France", Vol. III, 1792. Jared Sparks, editor, Boston, Massachusetts: Gray and Bowen, 1832.

National Center for Education Statistics (www.nces.ed.gov), *College Board, Report on Declining SAT Scores*.

National Center for Health Statistics, Annual "*Births: Final Data*" *for years 1999-2010.*

_____, "*Non-marital childbearing in the United States, 1940-1999*".

Newport, Frank. *Americans Continue to Shift Left on Key Moral Issues,* Gallup: 2015, http://www.gallup.com/poll/183413/americans-continue-shift-left-key-moral-issues.aspx, (accessed 8/24/2017).

Nichols, James H. *History of Christianity 1650-1950*, New York, New York: The Ronald Press Company, 1956.

Nin, Anais. *The Diary of Anais Nin*: Vol. 1 (1931-34), New York & London: Harcourt, Brace, Jovanovich, 1966.

Northrop, Stephen Abbott. *A Cloud Of Witnesses*, Fort Wayne, Indiana: The Mason Long Publishing Company, 1894.

Olford, Stephen F. *Anointed Expository Preaching*, Nashville, Tennessee: B&H Publishing Group, 1998.

Olson, David T. *The American Church in Crisis*, Grand Rapids, MI: Zondervan, 2008.

Ortberg, John. *The Me I Want To Be*, Grand Rapids, Michigan: Zondervan, 2010.

Orwell, George. https://www.orwellfoundation.com/the-orwell-foundation/orwell/essays-and-other-works/the-freedom-of-the-press/ (Accessed 6/11/2018).

Oxford Dictionary. *Das Kapital*, http://http://www.oxforddictionaries.com/us/definition/american_english/heritage (accessed 07/21/2016).

Parton, James. *The Life of Thomas Jefferson*, Boston: James R. Osgood and Company, 1874.

Patterson, James, and Kim, Peter. *The Day America Told The Truth*, New York, New York: Prentice Hall Press, 1991.

Peabody, Andrew P. *Ethical Writings of Cicero*, Boston: Little, Brown, and Company, 1887.

Pearcy, Nancy R. *Love Thy Body*, Grand Rapids MI: Baker Books, 2018.

Penny, Timothy J. *Facts Are Facts*, National Review, September 4, 2003.

Piketty, Thomas. *CAPITAL In The Twenty-First Century*, Arthur Goldhammer translator, Cambridge, MA, Belknap Press of Harvard University, 2014.

Plato, *The Republic of Plato*, 380 B.C., 373

Pollock, John. *George Whitefield and the Great Awakening*, Garden City, New York, New York: Doubleday & Company, Inc., 1972.

Powell, Neil. *"Money Has a Power Over Us"*, http://www. afaithtoliveby.com/2011/02/24/money-has-a-power-over-us/ (accessed 07/24/2018).

Regan, Ronald. Gubernatorial Inaugural Address, January 5, 1967, https://reaganlibrary.archives.gov/archives/speeches/govspeec h/01051967a.htm (accessed 12/11/217).

Roan, Shari. *U.S. teen pregnancy rate remains highest in developed world*, Los Angeles Times, January 19, 2012, http://articles.latimes.com/2012/jan/19/news/la-heb-teen-pregnancy-20120119, (accessed 8/24/2017).

Rozansky, Michael. *Americans are poorly informed about basic constitutional provisions*, The Annenberg Public Policy Center, September 12, 2017.

Rubin, Jerry. *Do It: Scenarios of the Revolution*, New York, New York: Simon and Schuster, 1970.

Rudolph , Frederick., editor, *Essays on Education in the Early Republic*, Cambridge, Massachusetts: Harvard University Press, 1965.

Rush, Benjamin. *Letters of Benjamin Rush*, L. H. Butterfield, editor, Princeton, New Jersey: American Philosophical Society Princeton University Press, 1951, Volumes I & II.

Sammartino, Frank J. *"Options for Changing the Tax Treatment of Charitable Giving"*, Congressional Budget Office, http:// permanent. ccess.gpo.gov/gpo14068/10-18-charitableTestimony.pdf (Accessed 06/07/2018).

Senior, Antonia. *"Yes, abortion is killing. But it's the lesser evil*, London Times, June 2010, https://www.thetimes.co.uk/article/ yes-abortion-is-killing-but-its-the-lesser-evil-f7v2k2ngvf8 (Accessed 08/13/2018).

Skousen, W. Cleon. *The Naked Communist*, Salt Lake City, Utah, Ensign Publishing Company: 1962, 11th Edition.

Simanek, Donald E. *The Decline of Education 1*, Lock Haven University, https://www.lhup.edu/~dsimanek/decline1.htm, (accessed 8/25/2017).

_____, *The Decline of Education 2*, Lock Haven University, https://www.lhup.edu/ ~dsimanek/decline2.htm, (accessed 8/25/2017).

Singleton, James E., compiler. *The Fundamentalist Phenomenon or Fundamentalist Betrayal*. Tempe, Arizona: Tri-City Baptist Church, undated.

Smietana, Bob. *"Statistical Illusion: New study confirms that we go to church much less than we say",* Christianity Today, April 2006.

Smith, Chad Powers. *Yankees and God*, New York, New York: Hermitage House, 1954.

Smith, Marion. *Millennials think socialism would create a great safe space, study finds*, Fox News, November 3, 2017, http://www.foxnews. com/us/2017/11/03/millennials-think-socialism-would-create-great-safe-space-study-finds.html (accessed 12/11/2017).

_____, *Thomas Piketty And The Coming Marxist Moment*, https://thefederalist.com/2014/05/29/thomas-piketty-and-the-coming-marxist-moment/, (Accessed 06/21/2018).

Sorokin, Ellen. *"No Founding Fathers? That's our new history",* Washington Times, January 28, 2002, http://www.washingtontimes.com/news/2002/jan/28/20020128-035145-4351r/, (accessed 07/22/2016).

Sparks, Jared. *The Life of George Washington*, Boston: Ferdinand Andrews, 1839.

Spector, Joseph. *New York Gov. Andrew Cuomo: America 'was never that great'*, https://www.usatoday.com/story/news/politics/2018/08/15/andrew-cuomo-new-york-governor-trump-america-never-great/1004708002/ (Accessed 08/27/2018).

Stout, Harry S., *"In Search of Christian America"*, Yale Divinity School's Reflections, Fall 2007 edition, http://reflections.yale.edu/article/faith-and-citizenship-turbulent-times/search-christian-america (accessed 08/02/2016).

Taschereau, Honorable Robert, Kellock, Honorable R. L. et.al. *The Report of the Royal Commission* Appointed Under in Council P.C. 411, Ottawa: Edmond Cloutier, June 27, 1946.

Taylor, Hannis. Cicero, *A Sketch of His Life and Works*, Chicago: A. C. McClurg & Co., 1916

Thacker, Jerry. "Young Fundamentalists' Beliefs and Personal Life Survey Findings", Fleetwood, Pennsylvania: Right Ideas, Inc., 2005.

Thomas, Cal. *Moral relativism one problem politicians will not solve*, Topeka Capital-Journal, April 9, 2016.

Tocqueville, Alexis de. *Democracy in America*, Third Edition, Henry Reeve Esq. Translator, New York: George Adlard, 1839.

Tuveson, Ernest Lee. *Redeemer Nation*, Chicago & London, University of Chicago Press, 1974.

United States Census Bureau, Population Division. *Historical National Population Estimates*: 1900-1999, Released June 2000.

_____, *Table HH-1. Households, by Type: 1940 to Present*, Released Nov. 2013.

United States Department of Commerce, Bureau of the Census, *Statistical Abstract of the United States*, 81St Annual Edition, 1960.

_____, *Statistical Abstract of the United States*, 82nd Annual Edition, 1961.

_____, *Statistical Abstract of the United States*, 83rd Annual Edition, 1962.

_____, *Statistical Abstract of the United States*, 97th Annual Edition, 1976.

_____, *Statistical Abstract of the United States*, 111th Annual Edition, 1991.

United States Department of Health and Human Services, Centers for Disease Control and Prevention, *Sexually Transmitted Disease Surveillance 2012*, Table 1, 79,80.

United States Department of Justice, *OJJDP Statistical Briefing Book*, Released December 17, 2012.

United States Federal Bureau of Investigation, *Crime in the United States 1960-1990*, http://WWW.fbi.GOV/ucr/cius_01/ 01crime.pdf, as of 8/26/2017 link is broken.

_____, *Crime in the United States 1990-2009*,http://www2.fbi.gov/ ucr/cius2009/data/table_01.html (accessed 8/26/2017)

United States Supreme Court, *Church Of The Holy Trinity V. United States, 143 U. S. 457 (1892),* http://supreme. justia.com/us/143/457/case.html (accessed 08/01/2016).

_____, *Engle v. Vitale, 370 U.S. 421 (1962)*, 370, https://supreme.justia.com/cases/federal/us/370/421/case.html, (accessed 8/16/2017).

_____, *Everson v. Board of Education, 330 U.S. 1 (1947)*, https://supreme.justia.com/cases/federal/us/330/1/case.html#3, (accessed 8/16/2017).

_____, *School Dist. of Abington Tp. v. Schempp, 374 U.S. 203 (1963)*, https://Supreme.justia.com/cases/federal/us/374/203/case.html, (accessed 8/18/2017).

_____, *Stone v. Graham, 1980, 449, U.S. 39 (1980)*, 45-46, https://supreme.justia.com/cases/federal/us/449/39/case.html, (accessed 08-01-2016).

_____, *Zorach v. Clauson, 343, U.S. 306 (1952)*, 312-315, https://supreme.justia.com/cases/federal/us/343/306/case.html, (accessed 08/01/2016).

Victims of Communism Memorial Foundation, *Annual Report on US Attitudes Toward Socialism*, October 2017.

Villasenor, John. *Views among college students regarding the First Amendment: Results from a new survey*, https://www.brookings.edu/blog/ fixgov/2017/09/18/views-among-college-students-regarding-the-first-amendment-results-from-a-new-survey/ (Accessed 08/24/2018).

Wacker, Grant. *Religion in Nineteenth Century America*, John Butler & Harry S. Stout General Editors, New York, New York: Oxford University Press, 2000.

Walls, Andrew F. *The Missionary Movement in Christian History*, Maryknoll, New York: Orbis Books, 1996.

Walters, Jonah. *A Guide to the French Revolution*, https://www.
jacobinmag.com/2015/07/french-revolution-bastille-day-
guide-jacobins-terror-bonaparte/ (Accessed 08/21/2018).

Watkinson, W. L., D.D., LL.D. *The Supreme Conquest and other
Sermons Preached in America*, New York & Chicago,
Fleming H. Revell Company, 1907.

Weisskopf, Michael. *"Energized by Pulpit or Passion, the Public
is Calling"*, Washington Post, February 1, 1993, https://
www.washingtonpost.com/archive/ politics/1993/ 02/01/
energized-by-pulpit-or-passion-the-public-is-calling /f747
ded3-b7c5-578-ad3b-2f500dbaeacf/, (accessed 08/03/2016).

Wells, David F. *God in the Wasteland*. Grand Rapids, Michigan:
William B. Erdman Publishing Company, 1994.

_____, *Losing our Virtue: Why the Church Must Recover Its Moral
Vision*, Grand Rapids, Michigan: William B. Erdman
Publishing Company, 1998.

Whitefield, George. *A Continuation of Reverend Mr. Whitefield's
Journal,* Seventh Journal Second Edition, London, England:
W. Strahan, March 11, 1741,

Williamson, G. I. *Historical Revisionism*, http://www.reformed.
org/misc/HistoricalRevisionism.pdf (accessed 07/20/2016).

Willison, George F, *Behold Virginia*, New York, New York:
Harcourt, Brace and Company, 1951.

Wilson, Woodrow. *The Papers of Woodrow Wilson*, Volume 18:
1908-1909, Arthur S. Link editor, Princeton, New Jersey:
Princeton University Press, 1974.

Yancey, Phillip. *What's So Amazing About Grace*, Grand Rapids,
Michigan: Zondervan Publishing House, 1997.

Young America Foundation, *Comedy & Tragedy: College Course Descriptions and What They Tell Us About Higher Education Today,* http://www.yaf.org/wp-content/uploads/2016/12/ComedyTragedy.pdf

Yonge, C. D., B.A. *Treatises of M. T. Cicero*, London: Henry G. Bohn, 1853.

Zacharias, Ravi. *The End of Reason.* Grand Rapids, Michigan: Zondervan, 2008.

INDEX

Jay, John, 54, 124
Jefferson, Thomas, 48, 107, 121, 122
Jesus Christ, 113, 117, 118, 134
Gospel of, 138
Kane, Suzanne, 200
Kennedy, D. James, 161, 172
Khrushchev, Nikita, 43
Kinnaman, David, 87, 88
Kling, August J., 109, 110
Langbert, Mitchell, 76
Lasswell, Harold, 57
Laws, Curtis Lee, 148
Lenin, V. I., 58, 79, 90, 185
Leninism, 58
Liberal progressives, 187
Liberalism, 163
Library of Congress, 103
Lillback, Peter, 104, 107, 183
Lincoln, Abraham, 126
Lock Haven University, 69
Long hair, 172, 173, 174
Los Angeles Times, 66
Louden, Trevor, 23
Lowenstein, George, 6
Lumina Foundation, 73
Lux, Mike, 41
MacArthur, John, 179
Madison, James, 123, 129
Magnalia Christi Americana, 118
Maidanek, 180
Marshall, Peter, 114
Marx, Karl, 19, 57, 60, 63, 90, 185
Marxism, 58
Massachusetts, 113

Materialism, 63, 81, 167, 189
dialectical, 58, 59, 78
scientific, 60
Mather, Cotton, 118
Maximus, Quintus Fabius, 30
Mayflower, 107, 113
Mayflower Compact, 105, 113
McGavran, Donald, 146
McGill University, 35
Medicare-for-all, 45
Memory hole, 91, 96, 198, 207
Millennials, 89, 90
Missionary Conference
Ecumenical, 137
Edinburgh, 137
New York, 137
Modernism, 29, 134, 143, 159, 182
Modernity, 159
Morality, 127
absolute vs relative, 201
declining, 22, 30, 96
definiton of, 24
rapid decline, 198
statistical trends, 53
Morris, Benjamin Franklin, 126
Morris, Gouverneur, 123
Mott, John R., 138
Moynihan, Daniel Patrick, 13
Murray, John, 124
Murray, William, 55
National Council of Teachers of English
annual convention, 77

National Department of
  Education, 59
National Education
  Association, 176
National Gonorrhea Control
  Program, 68
Naturalism, 180
NBC News, 68
New Age dogma, 88
New World Order, 33, 35
Newport, Frank, 65
Nichols, James, 143, 144,
  145
Nietzsche,Friedrich, 159
Nin, Anais, 14
Nineteen Eighty-Four, 96
O'Hair, Madalyn Murray, 55
Old Testament, 94, 117
Olson, David, 150, 153, 154
Original Intent, 54, 122
Orwell, George, 6, 96, 202
Parton, James, 48
Penny, Timothy J., 14
Piketty, Thomas, 20
Pilgrim Fathers, 105
Pilgrims, 107, 111
Plato, 98
Pluralism, 201
Plymouth Colony, 114, 118
Plymouth Harbor, 111
Postmodernism
  hypocrisy, 198
Presumption
  definition of, 160
  spiritual, 164
Princeton University, 69
Progressive agenda, 42
Promiscuity, 66
Protestantism, 133

Provine, William, 26
Public school
  decline of, 144
Public school system, 53
Puritan, 117, 120
Putin, Vladimr, 90
Reagan, Ronald, 91
Reed, Ralph, 177
Reformation, 116
Religion
  Christian, 112
  expected demise, 143
*Report of the Royal
  Commission*, 36
Reproductive rights, 26
Revisionist History, 5, 183,
  202
Revivalism, 136, 141
Revolution, World, 173
Revolutionary War, 139, 185
Riverside Church, 142
Robertson, Pat, 176
Rockefeller Foundation, 142
Roksa, Josipa, 74
Rome, 31
Rubin, Jerry, 172, 174
Rules for Radicals, 173
Rush, Benjamin, 121, 124
Saltman, Bethany, 179
Sartre, Jean-Paul, 159
SAT Scores, 70, 71
Satan, 92
Saxe, David, 107
Scientific intellectualism,
  158, 160
Secular humanism, 26
Secular liberalism, 171
Secularism, 134
Self-fulfillment

About the Author

Keith Hoar is a writer and former IBM Certified Business Intelligence and Solutions Expert who consulted for numerous Fortune 100 companies. He designed executive suite business intelligence reporting systems and software sub-systems for companies such as: Motorola C&E, Cigna Insurance, Hyundai Motors NA, Continental Airlines, Wells Fargo, and others.

Keith also owned his own consulting company that designed custom software systems and sophisticated reporting systems.

Keith proudly served his country in the United States Navy for ten years. His duties included: setup of training scenarios, input of attack center maneuvering orders, monitoring of firing point procedures, and tracking outcome of weapons launch.

Keith is a PADI certified SCUBA diver with 100+ dives all over the Caribbean. Keith has also published his first novel, *Edge of Madness*, an edge-of-your-seat, hold-your-breath thriller.

Keith lives with his wife in Northeast Kansas.

Keith Hoar

37104205R00149

Made in the USA
Lexington, KY
21 April 2019